25 Real Life Math Investigations that will ASTOUND Teachers and Students

Edward Zaccaro

Luke Zaccaro

Ed lives outside of Dubuque, Iowa, with his wife and three children. He has been involved in education in various forms since graduating from Oberlin College in 1974. Ed has taught students of all ages and abilities, but his focus for the past ten years has been working with mathematically gifted students at the elementary and middle school level. When unable to find sufficient curriculum and materials for his students, he began to develop his own, resulting in the following collection of books.

- Primary Grade Challenge Math
- Challenge Math for the Elementary and Middle School Student
- Real World Algebra
- The Ten Things All Future Mathematicians and Scientists Must Know (But are Rarely Taught)
- Becoming a Problem Solving Genius
- 25 Real Life Math Investigations That Will Astound Teachers and Students

Ed holds a Masters degree in gifted education from the University of Northern Iowa and has presented at state and national conferences in the areas of mathematics and gifted education.

Layout and design by Blue Room Productions (memories2movies@aol.com)

Phone: 563-583-4767
E-mail: challengemath@aol.com
http://www.challengemath.com

Library of Congress Control Number: 2007940034
ISBN 10: 0-9679915-8-7
ISBN 13: 978-0-9679915-8-0

This book is dedicated to my students,
whose passion for math and science
is the reason that I teach.

Table of Contents

Chapter 1

The Nightmare of Payday Loans

Step 1:
You write a check for $115.

Step 2:
You receive $100 in cash from the payday loan store.

Step 3:
The payday loan store will hold your check for two weeks before they cash it. This gives you time to get $115 into your checking account.

Step 4:
You better have the $115 in your checking account when the payday loan store deposits your check for $115 or you pay fees and penalties.

The math investigation we will do will show how quickly consumers get into trouble when they use this type of loan.

Man Goes
BANKRUPT
Blames
Check-Cashing Store

Houston Herald

Woman
LOSES CAR
to
Check-Cashing Store

Galesburg Gazette

"MY DEBT DOUBLES IN 2 MONTHS"
Complains Victim of Payday Loan Industry

Eric borrowed $100 and was charged 15% interest every two weeks. If Eric never pays on the loan, what will his debt grow to in six years?

We won't even count late fees and penalties. We will only count interest.

Look at this problem. What do you think Eric's debt will grow to in six years? I will show you the growth for the first six weeks.

Start: **$100**

Two weeks: 1.15 x $100 = **$115**

Four weeks: 1.15 x $115 = **$132.25**

Six weeks: 1.15 x $132.25 = **$152.09**

I see how you found the amount owed every two weeks. Instead of doing two steps, you combined the two steps into one.
Two steps:
15% of $100 = .15 x $100 = $15
$100 + $15 = $115
One step: 1.15 x $100 = $115
Before we find what $100 grows to in six years, I want to show you how normal loans work.
Before you start, can I rant and rave about "payday" loans for a minute?
Oh sure. Go ahead and vent for a little while.
Thank You ...

Payday loans are a very dangerous trap and are not used just once like the industry claims they are!!
You are absolutely right. People who use these loans are usually very desperate and have a lot of trouble repaying the loan because of the high interest rates.
The interest rates are way, way, way too high!!
They used to call this type of lender a loan shark. These interest rates used to be illegal until the law was changed.

These stores open in poor neighborhoods and around military bases and take advantage of the people who can least afford to pay this kind of interest!

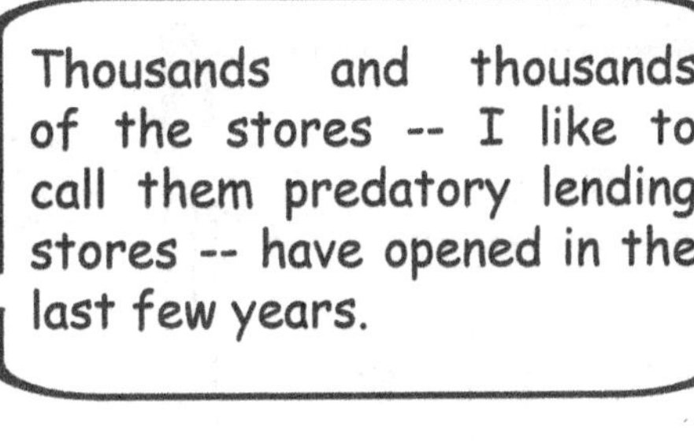

Thousands and thousands of the stores -- I like to call them predatory lending stores -- have opened in the last few years.

Actually Congress is now talking about regulating interest rates charged to men and women in the military.

Sorry for my ranting. Please explain the differences between car loans, credit card loans and payday loans.

No problem. I hope you feel better now. Look at how the debt on a $100 car loan with a 5% interest rate will grow in six years if no payments are made.

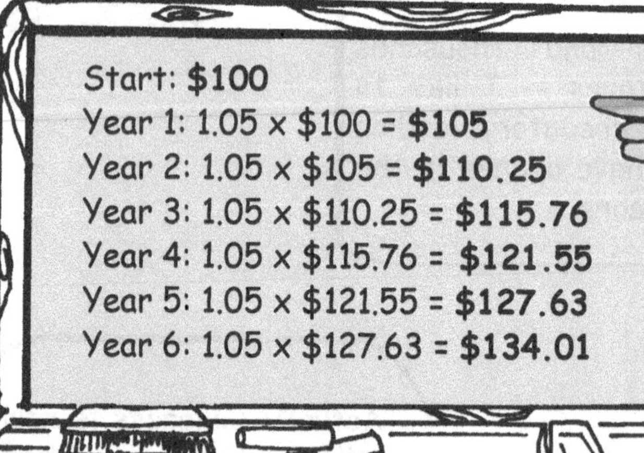

Start: **$100**
Year 1: 1.05 x $100 = **$105**
Year 2: 1.05 x $105 = **$110.25**
Year 3: 1.05 x $110.25 = **$115.76**
Year 4: 1.05 x $115.76 = **$121.55**
Year 5: 1.05 x $121.55 = **$127.63**
Year 6: 1.05 x $127.63 = **$134.01**

Again, we will not count penalties. In reality, the car will be taken back by the bank if payments are not made on the loan.

$100 borrowed turning into a $134 debt in six years seems very reasonable.

How quickly will a credit card debt grow if no payments are made?

A credit card with an interest rate of 22.9% is fairly typical so we will see what happens when $100 is charged and left unpaid for 6 years. We will again not count any penalties and fees.

Start: **$100**
Year 1: 1.229 x $100 = **$122.90**
Year 2: 1.229 x $122.90 = **$151.04**
Year 3: 1.229 x $151.04= **$185.63**
Year 4: 1.229 x $185.63= **$228.14**
Year 5: 1.229 x $228.14= **$280.38**
Year 6: 1.229 x $280.38= **$344.59**

Wow! The credit card debt more than tripled in six years. It looks like you really have to be careful when you use credit cards.

Now let's see what happens when $100 is borrowed at an interest rate of 15% every two weeks.

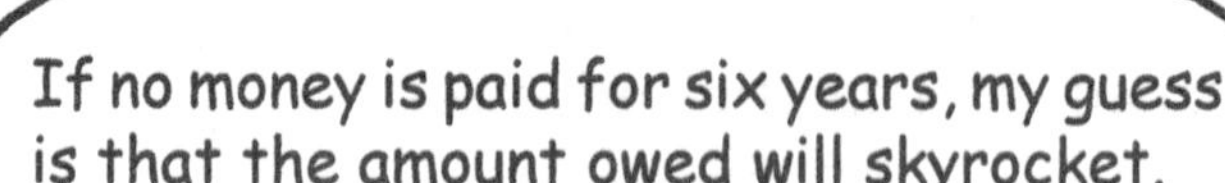

If no money is paid for six years, my guess is that the amount owed will skyrocket.

We are going to take a shortcut because there are 156 two-week segments in six years. We are going to find how many weeks it will take for the debt to double.

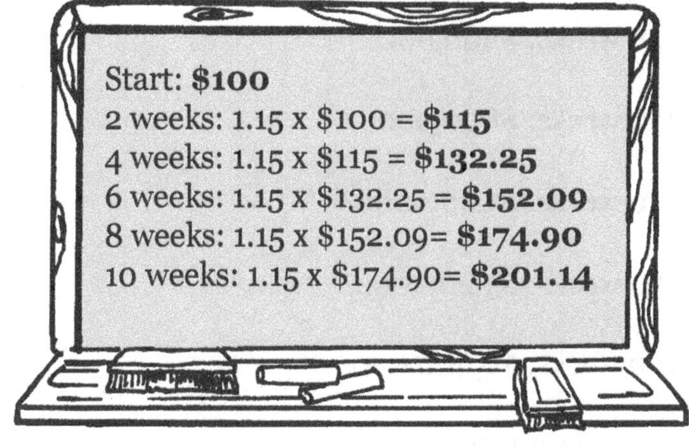

Start: **$100**
2 weeks: 1.15 x $100 = **$115**
4 weeks: 1.15 x $115 = **$132.25**
6 weeks: 1.15 x $132.25 = **$152.09**
8 weeks: 1.15 x $152.09= **$174.90**
10 weeks: 1.15 x $174.90= **$201.14**

10 weeks: About $200

20 weeks: $400

30 weeks: $800

40 weeks: $1600

50 weeks: $3200

60 weeks: $6400

70 weeks: $12,800

80 weeks: $25,600

90 weeks: $51,200

100 weeks: $102,400 *(We will round to $100,000)*

110 weeks: $200,000

Now we know the debt doubles every 10 weeks. Let's see how much debt our $100 loan turns into in 312 weeks.

120 weeks: $400,000

130 weeks: $800,000

140 weeks: $1,600,000

150 weeks: $3,200,000

160 weeks: $6,400,000

170 weeks: $12,800,000

180 weeks: $25,600,000

190 weeks: $51,200,000 *(We will round to $50,000,000)*

200 weeks: $100,000,000

210 weeks: $200,000,000

220 weeks: $400,000,000

230 weeks: $800,000,000

Wow! I can see why people get in over their heads so quickly. The debt grows so fast that it is hard to ever pay it off.

240 weeks: $1,600,000,000

250 weeks: $3,200,000,000

260 weeks: $6,400,000,000

270 weeks: $12,800,000,000

280 weeks: $25,600,000,000

290 weeks: $51,200,000,000

300 weeks: $102,400,000,000 *(We will round to $100,000,000,000)*

310 weeks: $200,000,000,000

312 weeks: 1.15 x $200,000,000,000 = $230,000,000,000

An easier way to calculate the debt after six years is to use exponents.

$$100 \times (1.15)^{156} = \$294{,}349{,}359{,}502$$

I see. Because you are multiplying the 100 by 1.15 → 156 times, we can make the problem $100 \times (1.15)^{156}$.

Our two answers are a little different because we rounded when we doubled our debt every 10 weeks.

The purpose of this math exercise isn't to say that if you borrow $100, you may end up owing 250 billion dollars. You will not. The reason we did this exercise is to show you how quickly your debt will grow when interest rates are so high.
Another dangerous type of loan is called an "Auto Title Loan". It is similar to payday loans except that you will lose your car if you cannot repay the loan.
Remember, borrowing money at these high interest rates is never, NEVER the right solution when you are in debt and need money.

Level 1

1) If you borrow $1000 for a year with a credit card that charges 27.9% annual interest, how much interest will you pay for the year?

2) If you borrow $1000 to buy a car at an annual interest rate of 6%, how much interest will you pay for the year?

3) If you borrowed $300 from a "payday loan" company with an interest rate of 20% every two weeks, how much interest will you pay for the two weeks?

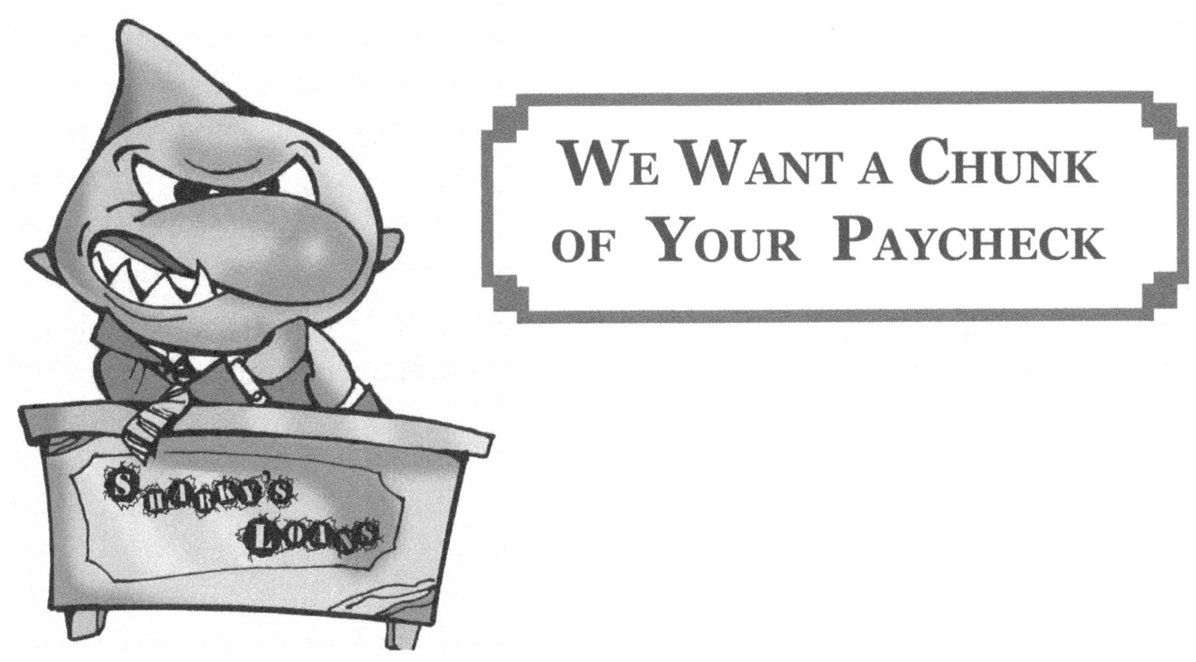

Level 2

1) If you borrow $300 from a "payday loan" company that charges 20% interest every two weeks, how long until your debt doubles if no payments are made?

2) If you borrow money for a car at 6% interest, how long until your debt doubles if no payments are made?

3) Many credit card companies give a daily interest rate along with the annual interest rate. If the annual interest rate is 18.240%, what is the daily interest rate?

Level 3

1) There are many heartbreaking stories of people who unwisely took out "payday loans". (Google: payday loan nightmare.) In one case a man struggled to pay $1400 each month in interest to keep his loan debt from increasing. If this man had an interest rate of 35% each month, what was his loan amount?

Questions 2 and 3 are based on the following information.

Another lending practice that has hurt thousands of consumers is the "Auto Title Loan". This loan is very similar to payday loans, except that a car title is used to secure the loan. If the loan is not repaid, the lender has the option of taking your car and selling it to pay off the loan. Auto title loans often lead to the loss of something that is essential to the financial well-being of working families----their car!

2) Allison took out an auto title loan for $2000 on June 1, 2007. She was told that if the amount she owed ever reaches $4500, the car will be taken. (The value of Allison's car was $4500.)

If the interest rate is 18% every two weeks, in what month will Allison's car be taken if she is unable to make any payments on the loan?

3) James took out an auto title loan of $1000 with the title to his $2000 car. The interest rate for his loan is 35% per month.

James was able to pay $150 each month on his loan. How many months until James loses his car?

Einstein

We saw that when you borrow $100 at an interest rate of 15% every two weeks, your debt will grow to more than 200 billion dollars in six years if no payments are made.

If the $100 was borrowed at an interest rate of 20% every two weeks, how much will your debt be in six years if no payments are made?

Chapter 2

Corn-Based Ethanol is the Answer to our Dependence on Foreign Oil! ----Or Is It?

(Mathematics will answer the question)

Many people believe that increased ethanol production would be a major step towards energy independence for the United States. The production of corn-based ethanol is increasing dramatically, but is ethanol really the answer to our dependence on foreign oil?

Math will answer this question. The questions you will be answering will be based on the information listed on the next page.
After you have answered the questions, we will have a discussion about ethanol and its place in developing renewable sources of energy for the United States.

A gallon of ethanol contains approximately 80,000 Btu of energy.

A gallon of gasoline contains approximately 120,000 Btu of energy.

In 2006, the United States used 5 billion gallons of ethanol.

In 2006, the United States used 140 billion gallons of gasoline and diesel fuel.

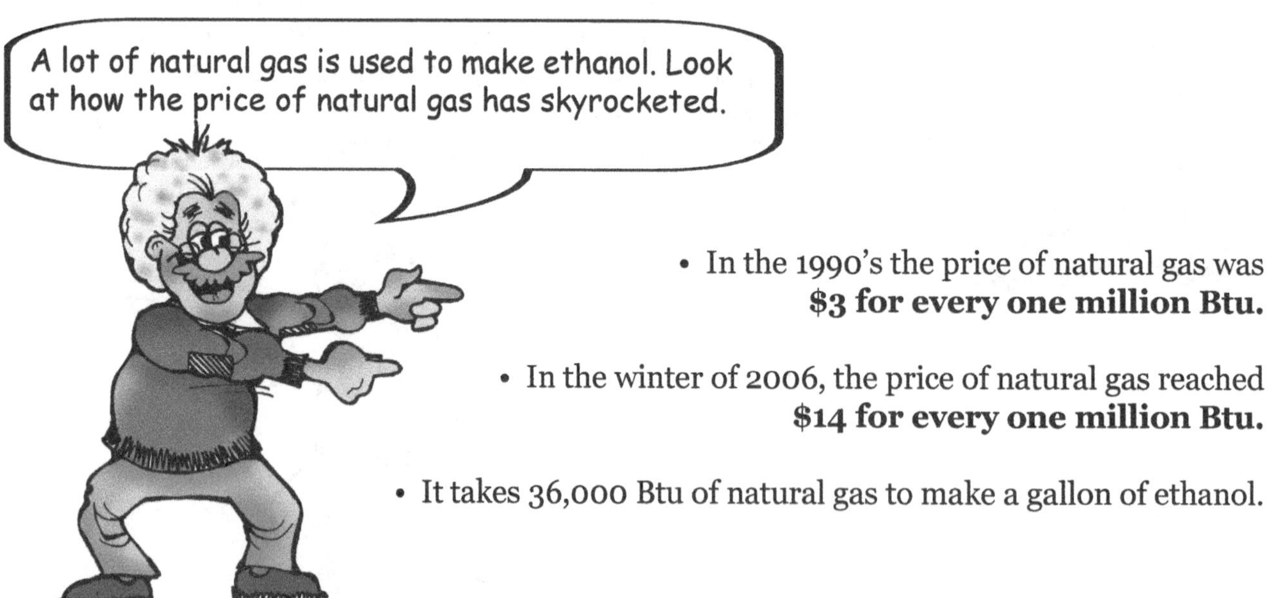

- In the 1990's the price of natural gas was **$3 for every one million Btu.**
- In the winter of 2006, the price of natural gas reached **$14 for every one million Btu.**
- It takes 36,000 Btu of natural gas to make a gallon of ethanol.

- The production of corn uses approximately 7,500,000 Btu per acre. *(U.S. Department of Agriculture)*

- An acre produces approximately 120 bushels of corn.

- A bushel of corn yields approximately 2.5 gallons of ethanol.

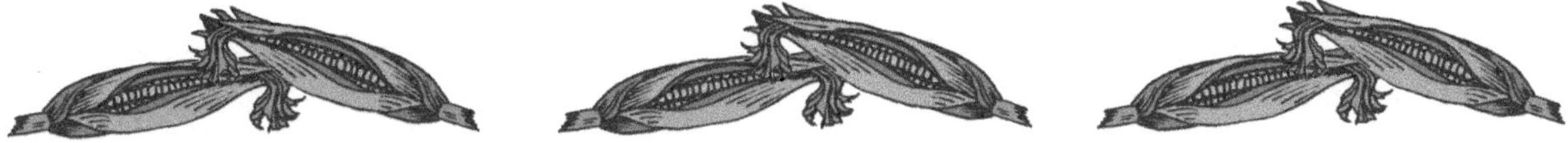

In the year 2005, 14% of the corn crop in the United States went towards the production of ethanol.

3.4 billion gallons of ethanol were produced in the year 2005.

- The American Institute of Biological Sciences concluded that ethanol from corn yielded only about 10 percent more energy than the energy required to produce it.

- Ethanol from sugarcane yields 370% more energy than the energy to produce it.

(All information is from Scientific American January 2007)

Level 1

1) How many Btu of energy does it take to grow a bushel of corn?

2) How many Btu of energy does it take to produce enough corn for a gallon of ethanol?

3) According to the American Institute of Biological Sciences, if you use 100,000 Btu of energy to make corn ethanol, how many Btu will be in the energy you made?

Level 2

1) Ethanol was what percent of gasoline and diesel fuel usage in 2006?

2) Al has a vehicle that can run on ethanol or gasoline. Gasoline costs $3 per gallon and ethanol costs $2.75 per gallon, so Al always fills his car with ethanol. Is this a wise financial decision?

3) In the year 2005, 14% of the corn crop in the United States was used to make ethanol. If 100% of the corn crop was used to make ethanol, how many gallons of ethanol could be made?

Level 3

1) A car that is equipped to run on ethanol or gasoline has a 20 gallon tank. If the tank is filled with unleaded regular gasoline it can travel 360 miles. How far will it travel using ethanol fuel?

2) If gasoline is $3.50 per gallon and ethanol fuel is $2.50 per gallon, which fuel is a better buy?

3) What was the cost of the natural gas to produce a gallon of ethanol in the winter of 2006?

Einstein

Explain what these political cartoons are trying to say.

There is a difference of opinion concerning the wisdom of our current move towards corn-based ethanol as a means of lowering our dependence on foreign sources of energy. There are dramatic differences in the calculations that are made to determine whether making corn-based ethanol provides a sufficient amount of energy over and above the energy it takes to produce the ethanol.

David Pinentel, a leading Cornell University agricultural expert, has determined that it takes more energy to make ethanol than the amount of energy that is produced when the ethanol is burned.

An extensive study by the American Institute of Biological Sciences concludes that corn-based ethanol yields only 10% more energy than the energy it takes to produce it.

It is clear from the mathematics that corn-based ethanol is at best a very marginal help in developing more renewable sources of energy.

Ethanol fuel does pollute less where it is burned, but some ethanol producers are burning coal to make ethanol - which of course is not clean or renewable.

Downsides to corn-based ethanol

- Food prices have increased
- Growing corn is hard on soil
- Taxpayers are paying billions per year in subsidies
- The United States will have to import natural gas to make ethanol
- Ethanol production pushes the price of natural gas higher

Chapter 3
Media Math Mistakes
Part 1

Part of a guest editorial from USA Today June 1, 2005

USA TODAY

"Sure, it may take several years to recoup the initial costs of hybrid technology. But what should be examined is its impact on reducing our dependency on fossil fuels and, more importantly, foreign oil. Using a conservative savings of 10 miles per gallon over a similar vehicle, one such car traveling 15,000 miles a year can save 1500 gallons of fuel."

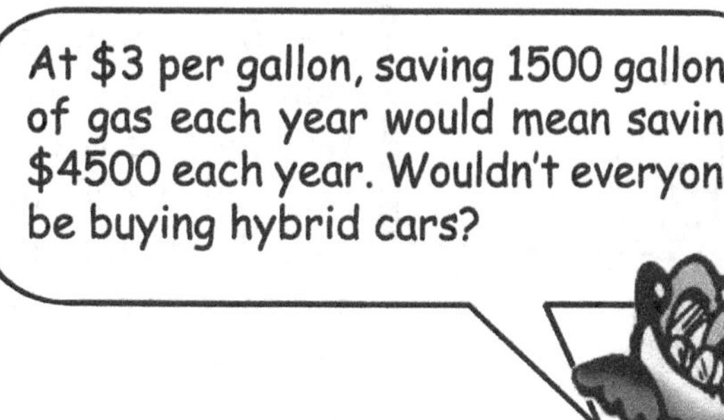

The writer of this editorial was trying to make the point that driving a hybrid car will save a lot of gas. I am not sure if his math is correct.
At $3 per gallon, saving 1500 gallons of gas each year would mean saving $4500 each year. Wouldn't everyone be buying hybrid cars?
M

Good point! Let's see if a savings of 1500 gallons per year is correct.

"Sure, it may take several years to recoup the initial costs of hybrid technology. But what should be examined is its impact on reducing our dependency on fossil fuels and, more importantly, foreign oil. Using a conservative savings of 10 miles per gallon over a similar vehicle, one such car traveling 15,000 miles a year can save 1500 gallons of fuel."

The first obvious mistake that the writer makes is that he does not mention what two cars he is comparing. Is it a 50 miles per gallon car and a 40 miles per gallon car? Is it an 11 miles per gallon car and a one mile per gallon car?

I own a Toyota Prius Hybrid that gets 50 miles per gallon of gas. A normal Toyota about the same size, but not a hybrid, gets 40 miles to a gallon of gas. Let's compare these two cars.

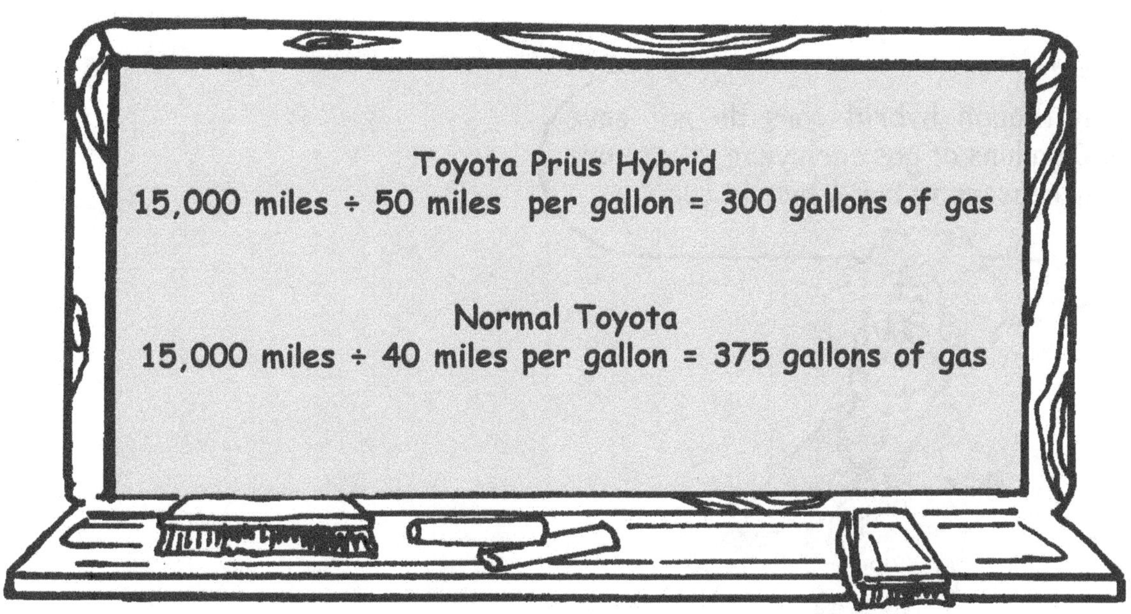
Toyota Prius Hybrid
15,000 miles ÷ 50 miles per gallon = 300 gallons of gas
Normal Toyota
15,000 miles ÷ 40 miles per gallon = 375 gallons of gas

Wow! The gas savings are only 75 gallons each year and not 1500 gallons.
That was a bad math mistake because it may have led readers to think they will save $4500 per year, when in reality a hybrid car will only save them $225 each year.

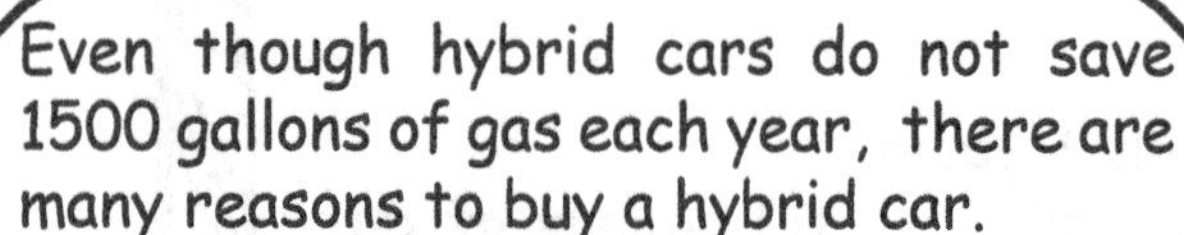

Even though hybrid cars do not save 1500 gallons of gas each year, there are many reasons to buy a hybrid car.

1) They do not pollute as much as other cars.

2) Buying a hybrid car helps lower our dependence on foreign oil.

Some states have tax credits that help make buying a hybrid car a wise financial decision.

Level 1

1) If a car that gets 12 miles to a gallon of gas is driven 15,000 miles each year, how many gallons of gas will the car use in 5 years?

2) If a car that gets 40 miles to a gallon of gas is driven 15,000 miles each year, how many gallons of gas will the car use in 5 years?

3) If the cost of gas is $3.50 per gallon, how much money will the driver of the 40 mpg car save each year compared to the driver of the 12 mpg car?
(See questions #1 and #2)

Level 2

1) Melinda bought a car that gets 40 miles to a gallon of gas. Blake bought a car that gets 15 miles per gallon of gas. If the price of gas is $3 per gallon and they both drive 15,000 miles per year, how much more will Blake spend for gas than Melinda in one year?

2) If the price of gas increases to $7 per gallon, how much more will Blake spend on gas than Melinda each year?

3) Jordan bought a hybrid Honda Civic that travels 45 miles per gallon of gas. LaKisha bought a Honda Civic that is not a hybrid. Her car gets 34 miles per gallon of gas. If they both drive 10,000 miles each year, how many more gallons of gas will LaKisha use in 5 years?

Level 3

Use the following information to answer questions 1-2:

	Gas tank	Distance on one tank	Number of passengers vehicle will hold
Automobile	20 gallons	500 miles	5
Motorcycle	3 gallons	180 gallons	1
Jet (Boeing 747)	57,285 gallons	8350 miles	525

1) Determine the "miles per gallon" for each vehicle.

2) If 525 people must travel from New York City to Los Angeles, what method of travel would use the least gas? (Distance is 3000 miles.)

Option 1: Use automobiles with 5 people in each car.

Option 2: Travel by motorcycle with one person on each motorcycle.

Option 3: Fly a Boeing 747 from New York to Los Angeles.

3) There is a plan for every Yellow Cab in New York City to be a hybrid car by the year 2012. The standard Yellow Cab in the year 2007 traveled 14 miles on a gallon of gas. The Ford Escape Hybrid, one of the hybrids being considered to replace current taxis, goes 36 miles on a gallon of gas.

Taxi drivers in New York City currently drive an average of 180 miles per day and work approximately 300 days per year. If gas cost $4 per gallon, how much money will each cab driver save each year by switching to a Ford Escape Hybrid?

Einstein

Use the information given below and determine how many years it will take to pay off the extra cost of a hybrid car with the savings from using less gas.

- Hybrid car: \$21,960 plus sales tax of 7%
  Non-hybrid car: \$18,390 plus sales tax of 7%

- The hybrid car qualifies for a \$2100 tax credit.
  (This reduces the cost of the car by \$2100.)

- Hybrid car: 50 miles per gallon of gas
  Non-hybrid car: 40 miles per gallon of gas

Price of gas: \$4.00 per gallon

Miles driven per year: 12,000 miles

Chapter 4
Media Math Mistakes
Part 2

In the April 2004 issue of the AARP Bulletin, there was an article about the possible medical and social consequences of snoring. See if you agree with the math.

> AARP Bulletin
>
> **"Doctors now know that snoring can take an extraordinary toll on those who snore – and on those who lie awake listening to them. A study of a cross-section of Americans ages 30 to 60 found that 45 percent of the men and 25 percent of the women snore."**
>
> **"When the doors are closed, the lights are out and a man and a woman are in bed together, then there is a 70 percent chance someone is snoring."**

This last statement was made by a doctor, so we know that he must be really smart, but is the math correct?

Well it seems right, but can you simply add the percents?

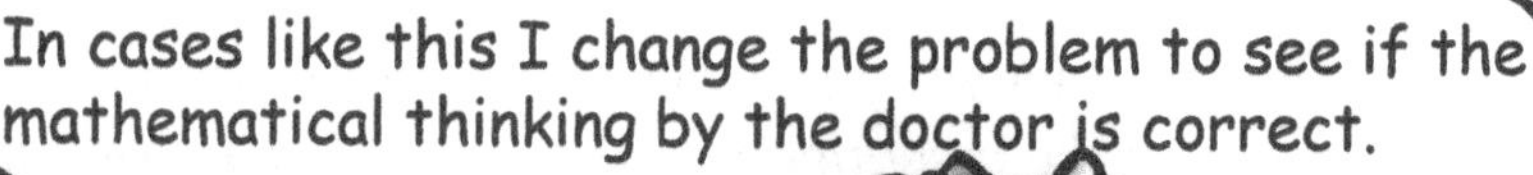

In cases like this I change the problem to see if the mathematical thinking by the doctor is correct.

I'll change the numbers to 50 percent instead of 45 percent and 25 percent.

A study of a cross-section of Americans ages 30 to 60 found that **50** percent of the men and **50** percent of the women snore.

Using the same mathematical thinking as the doctor used, the answer would be that there is a 100% chance that someone is snoring.
A study of a cross-section of Americans ages 30 to 60 found that 50 percent of the men and 50 percent of the women snore.
That is obviously the wrong answer. I guess we now know that the math is incorrect.
We can even change the problem to one that makes it even more obvious that the math was done incorrectly.
A study of a cross-section of Americans ages 30 to 60 found that 60 percent of the men and 60 percent of the women snore.

Wow!! Now it is really obvious that the math is wrong. There certainly cannot be a 120% probability that someone is snoring!

Now that we know that the math is wrong, what is the right way to solve the problem?

This is a type of problem where it is much easier to ask what the probability is of someone not snoring.

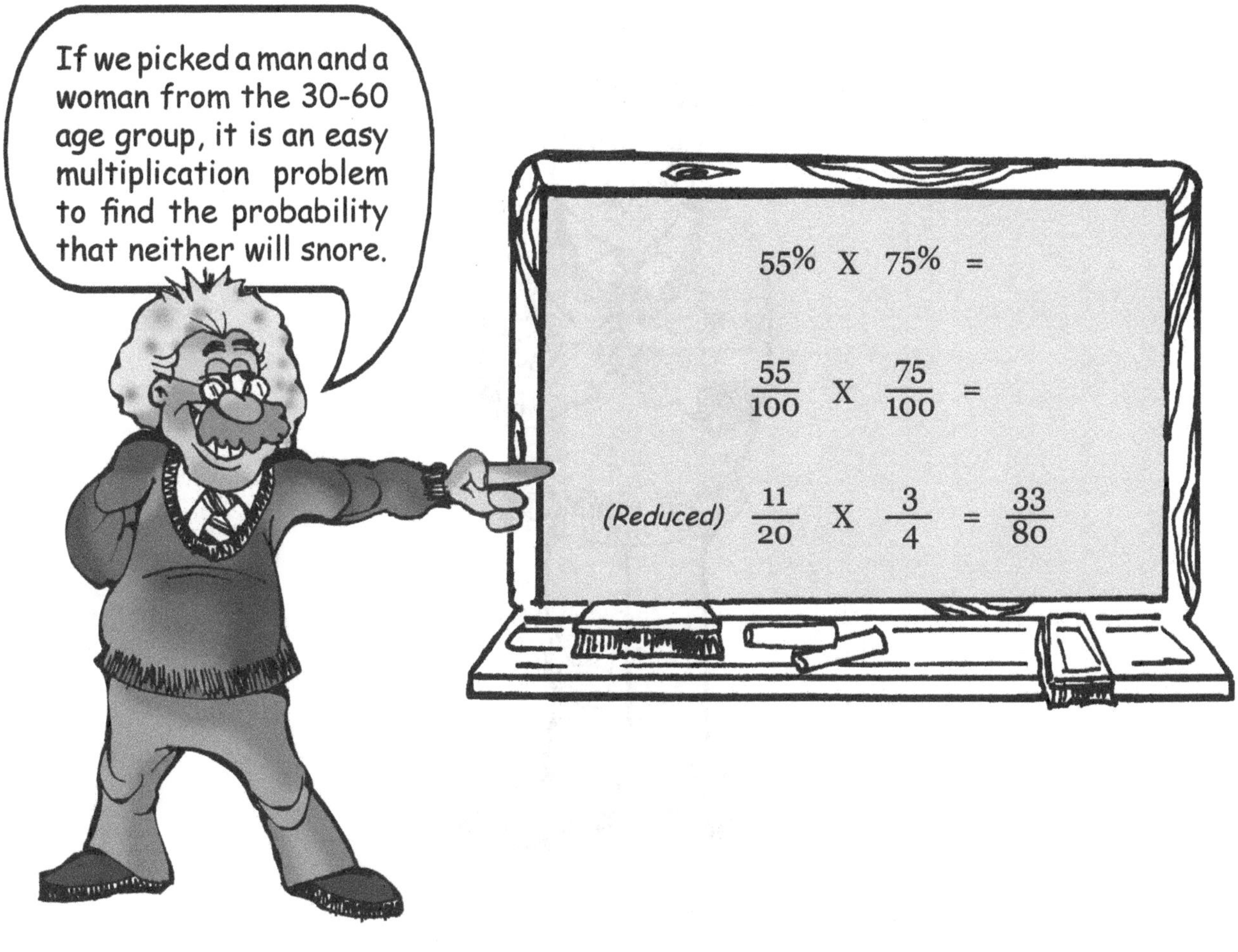

If we picked a man and a woman from the 30-60 age group, it is an easy multiplication problem to find the probability that neither will snore.

$$55\% \times 75\% =$$

$$\frac{55}{100} \times \frac{75}{100} =$$

(Reduced) $\frac{11}{20} \times \frac{3}{4} = \frac{33}{80}$

If the probability is 33/80 that neither is snoring, then the probability that someone is snoring is all the other possibilities:

$$1 - \frac{33}{80} = \frac{47}{80} \quad \text{or} \quad 58\tfrac{3}{4}\%$$

When you are solving difficult problems, it is often easier to first solve the opposite of what is asked.

Level 1

1) If you pick two people at random, what is the probability that you would pick at least one girl?

2) If you picked three people at random, what is the probability that you would pick at least one girl?

3) If you picked ten people at random, what is the probability that you would pick at least one girl?

Level 2

1) The population of the United States is approximately 15% left-handed. If two people were picked at random, what is the probability they would both be left-handed?

2) If three people were picked at random in the United States, what is the probability that all three would be left-handed?

3) If two people were picked at random in the United States, what is the probability that neither would be left-handed?

Level 3

1) If three people were picked at random in the United States, what is the probability that there would be at least one left-handed person picked?
(Remember that 15% of the population is left-handed.)

2) If two people were picked at random, what is the probability that there would be at least one left-handed girl?

3) Although blue eyes are very common in the United States, they are relatively rare throughout the rest of the world. Approximately 8% of the world's population has blue eyes.

The United States has a higher rate of people who are left-handed than the rest of the world. Approximately 10% of the world's population is thought to be left-handed.

If a person was picked at random from the world's population, what is the probability the person would NOT be a left-handed, blue-eyed male?

Einstein

An eccentric mathematician decided that she would give you one million dollars if you roll two dice and get double ones. She wants to give you a better chance of winning, so she will let you roll the dice six times. If any of the six rolls are double ones, you will win the million dollars. What is the probability that you will win?

Chapter 5
Media Math Mistakes
Part 3

From the novel "Thank You For Smoking"

By the way, the book is an anti-smoking book. Also, OSAP refers to the Office of Substance Abuse Prevention.

Page 30:

Though it had been calculated that the tobacco industry spends $2.5 billion a year, or $4000 per second promoting smoking, Nick nonetheless railed against OSAP's "runaway budget".

Although 2.5 billion dollars is a lot of money, does the math work out to $4000 each second?

This seems like a very easy calculation. First I will need to know how many seconds there are in a year.

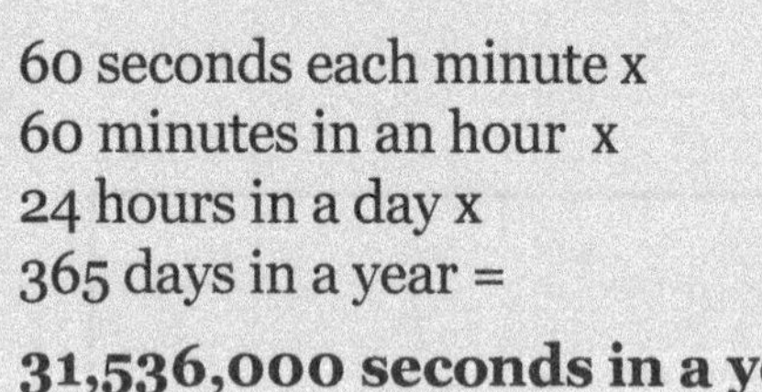

60 seconds each minute x
60 minutes in an hour x
24 hours in a day x
365 days in a year =
31,536,000 seconds in a year

If there are 31,536,000 seconds in a year, we need to divide 2.5 billion dollars by 31,536,000 seconds to find the amount of money spent each second to promote smoking.

$2,500,000,000 ÷ 31,536,000 seconds in a year = $79.27 per second

It is very surprising how many math mistakes there are in books, magazines and newspapers!

Level 1

1) Smoking related diseases kill approximately 5 million people every year (Worldwide). How many fully loaded jumbo jets would have to crash each day to equal this number of deaths? (A jumbo jet can hold 500 people.)

2) Smoking related diseases cost the United States more than 150 billion dollars each year. If this cost was equally divided among the entire population of the United States, what would it cost each person per year? (The population of the United States is 300,000,000.)

3) Approximately 100,000 children worldwide start smoking every day. How many children start smoking every year?

Level 2

1) Approximately 15 billion cigarettes are sold each day. How many is this every second?

2) One survey found that 96% of Chinese adults did not know that smoking can cause heart disease. If there are 500,000,000 adults in China, how many would not be aware of the connection between heart disease and smoking?

3) In 2004, 44.5 million or 20.9% of adults in the United States were smokers. From this information, determine how many adults there were in the United States in 2004. (Round to the nearest million.)

Level 3

1) Statistically, every cigarette smoked causes the smoker to lose 5 minutes off his/her life span. How many years of his/her life would a 2-pack a day smoker who smoked for 30 years expect to lose? (There are 20 cigarettes in one pack of cigarettes.)

2) The average number of cigarettes smoked in the United States in 1976 was 2900 per person. By 2003, this number dropped to 1545 cigarettes per person. What was the percentage drop for cigarettes smoked per person from 1976 to 2003?

3) In the year 2004, 23.4% of males and 18.5% of females in the United States smoked. If there were 44.5 million smokers, how many male smokers were there? (Assume the population is evenly divided between males and females.)

Einstein

How much tax must be placed on each pack of cigarettes to pay for the 150 billion dollar cost of smoking related diseases in the United States?

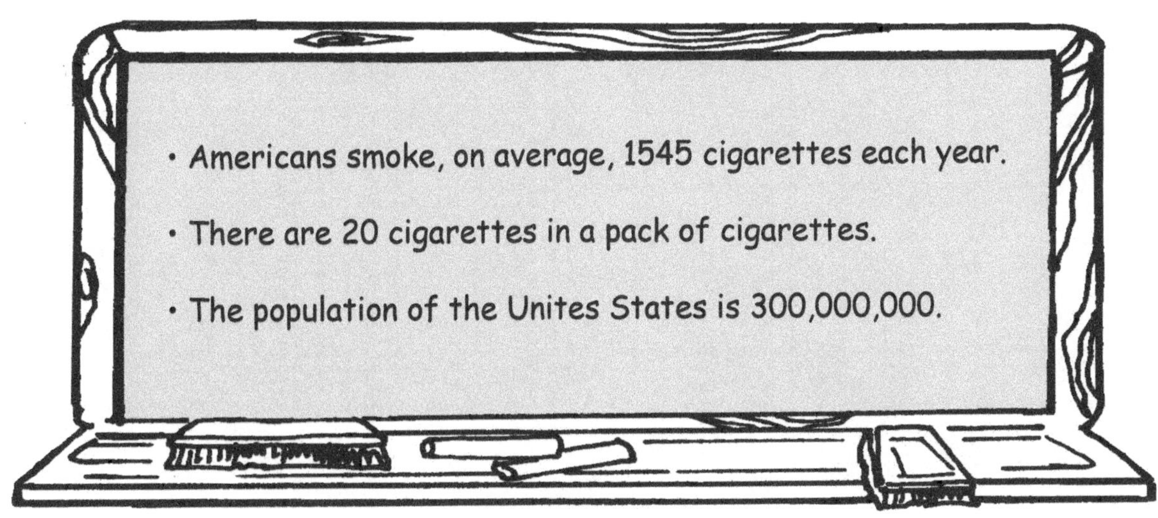

• Americans smoke, on average, 1545 cigarettes each year.
• There are 20 cigarettes in a pack of cigarettes.
• The population of the Unites States is 300,000,000.

Chapter 6
The Perplexing Birthday Paradox

Many teachers are astonished to find that they often have matching birthdays in their classroom. This fact seems to defy the laws of probability and is very perplexing to many people.

We will answer four very interesting questions that concern matching birthdays in a classroom.

1) If there are 23 children in a classroom, how likely is it that there will be at least one matching pair of birthdays?

2) If we have 80 people in a room, would we expect to have a large number of matching birthdays?

3) If we have 80 people in a room, how likely is it that there will be three people with the same birthday?

4) We have 122 people in a room. We slowly go around the room and ask each person to announce the month and day of their birthday. Predict how many birthday matches we will have when we have only gone through the first 25 people.

By the way, when we talk about matching birthdays, we mean month and day, not the year.
Sorry, I meant to mention that. April 5, 1952 and April 5, 1978 are considered matching birthdays.

These questions are not as complex as they appear.
Be honest Einstein!
Okay, they are a little complex, so we will start with a fairly simple concept and move up to the birthday questions.
?
E=M
E²=MC
E=M²C
We will start with six people who each have one die. They all roll their die and compare numbers.
M

Is it likely that we will have any matching numbers? How many?

To answer this question, we will need to know how many possible pairs of two people there are who will be comparing the numbers they rolled.

Six People

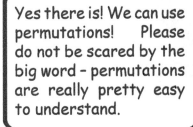

A	**B**	**C**	**D**	**E**	**F**
AB	BC	CD	DE	EF	
AC	BD	CE	DF		
AD	BE	CF			
AE	BF				
AF					

15 possible groups of 2 people

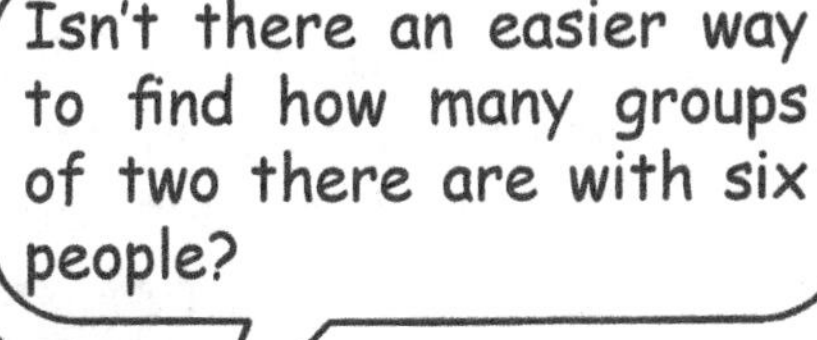

Isn't there an easier way to find how many groups of two there are with six people?

Yes there is! We can use permutations! Please do not be scared by the big word - permutations are really pretty easy to understand.

This means there are six people and we are taking two at a time..
P
6 2
There are 30 permutations when we have six people and take two at a time.
6 x 5 = 30
By the way, permutations are when things are arranged in different orders, such as: AB, BA, CD, DC, etc.
I noticed you multiplied by the next lowest number, which is 5. I guess that must be a rule.

We can even do this with different numbers of people.

If we had 10 people, we would do it this way. There are 90 permutations when we have 10 people taken 2 at a time.
P
10 2
10 x 9 = 90

If we had 100 people and we took two at a time, we would do it this way.
P
100 2
100 x 99 = 9900

There is one more very, very important step we need to learn. When we found the permutations for six people taken two at a time, we came up with 30.

With permutations, AB and BA are counted as two separate pairings. For our problem, these should not be counted twice, so we divide by two.

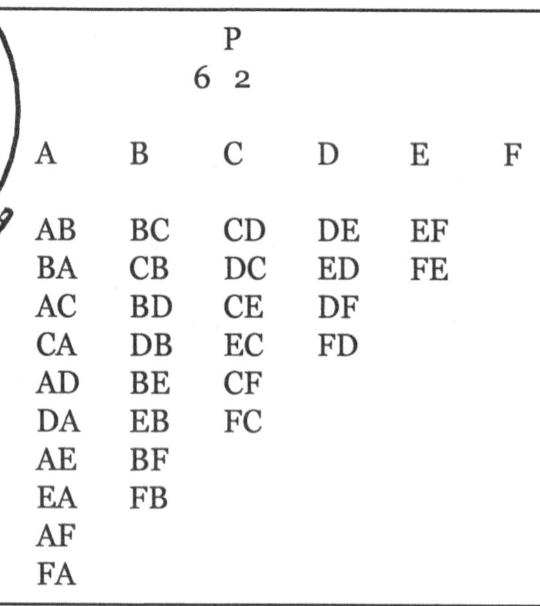

P
6 2

A	B	C	D	E	F
AB	BC	CD	DE	EF	
BA	CB	DC	ED	FE	
AC	BD	CE	DF		
CA	DB	EC	FD		
AD	BE	CF			
DA	EB	FC			
AE	BF				
EA	FB				
AF					
FA					

That makes sense. When Bob and Mary compare birthdays, it is the same as when Mary and Bob compare birthdays.

When we divide by two, we come up with our 15 pairs.

$_6P_2$ *No duplicates*

A	B	C	D	E	F
AB	BC	CD	DE	EF	
AC	BD	CE	DF		
AD	BE	CF			
AE	BF				
AF					

So what we found was that there were 15 combinations when we have a group of six people and take two at a time.
That's correct. When we do our problems, we will find permutations and then divide to find combinations.

Let's get back to our six people rolling dice. After all six people each roll his/her die, they are instructed to shake hands with everyone else and at the same time compare the numbers they have each rolled.

As the six people wander around the room and meet everyone else and see if their dice match each other, we will have 15 meetings.

Because we have 15 meetings, we know that it is very likely that we will have at least one match.
A B
E F

Is there a way we can predict how many matches we will have?

YES! Because each handshake meeting has close to a 1/6 chance of each of the two people having rolled the same number on their dice, we can predict that approximately every 6 meetings will have a matching pair of dice.

I found six friends to do this experiment. They each rolled a die and then compared what they rolled with each other's roll.

When they did their 15 handshakes, they compared what they rolled with each other. The first time they did this there were 4 matches. They decided to roll again and found 2 matches the second time. They were having so much fun that they rolled 100 times. I'll show you the results for the first 25 times they did the experiment.

Number of matches out of a possible 15

1st Experiment: 4 matches
2nd Experiment: 2 matches
3rd Experiment: 2 matches
4: 2 matches
5: 2 matches
6: 2 matches
7: 2 matches
8: 1 match
9: 2 matches
10: 3 matches
11: 2 matches
12: 1 match
13: 3 matches
14: 2 matches
15: 4 matches
16: 3 matches
17: 3 matches
18: 1 match
19: 2 matches
20: 1 match
21: 2 matches
22: 1 match
23: 4 matches
24: 3 matches
25: 2 matches

When I average all 100 experiments, I found that there were 2.43 matches each time we did the experiment. I have a confession to make. I wasn't totally honest when I said that my friends rolled dice. I did the experiment with my computer to simulate the rolls.

Here is the website if you would like to try it.

http://betterexplained.com/articles/understanding-the-birthday-paradox/

A very interesting situation occurs when 6 people roll one die each and then compare results. Look at the results for 12 experiments: (We'll call each experiment a trial.)

Person	1	2	3	4	5	6
Trial #1	5	3	3	2	6	6
Trial #2	1	1	4	2	4	4
Trial #3	3	3	5	1	6	6
Trial #4	2	2	1	1	2	2
Trial #5	5	4	5	1	1	2
Trial #6	4	5	2	5	3	4
Trial #7	5	6	3	2	1	6
Trial #8	1	6	2	4	5	1
Trial #9	1	5	3	1	1	1
Trial #10	6	4	4	1	3	4
Trial #11	4	3	4	3	5	5
Trial #12	4	4	5	1	1	1

Wow! Not only did the same number show up twice, but there were several times three people rolled the same number. In two of the trials, four people rolled the same number!

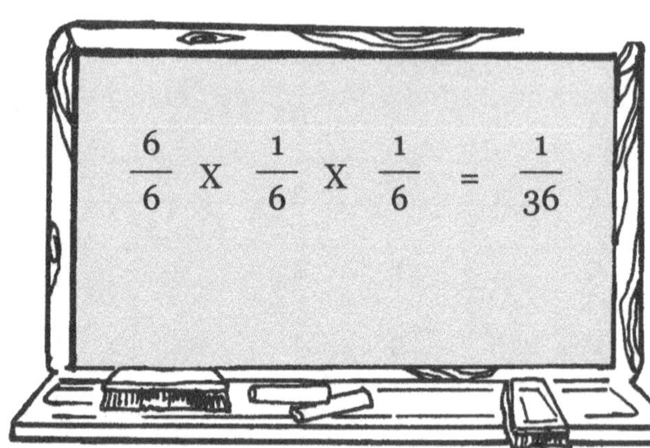
$\frac{6}{6}$ X $\frac{1}{6}$ X $\frac{1}{6}$ = $\frac{1}{36}$

To predict how many times three people will roll the same number, we first have to predict the probability of rolling three of a kind when three dice are rolled.

Remember that the first roll can be anything (6/6) and then rolls two and three each have a 1/6 probability of matching the first roll.

When we had six people taken two at a time, we did this.
P
6 2
6 x 5 = 30 permutations
30 ÷ 2 = 15 groups of 2 with no duplicates
Now we have to find how many different groups of three we have with six people.
P
6 3
6 x 5 x 4 = 120 permutations

To eliminate the permutations that are the same except for order we must divide by 6.

Look at why we divide by 6: When 3 people meet, it can be in six different ways, but they are still the same three people meeting.

ABC
ACB
BAC
BCA
CAB
CBA

Combinations

120 ÷ 6 = 20 groups of 3

These are really only one combination, so we need to divide by 6.

We found earlier that the probability of rolling "3 of a kind" is 1/36 and we have 20 different groups of three. (Remember that we found that 6 people taken 3 at a time had 120 permutations and we divided that by six.)

Each time the group of six people does the experiment, this consists of 20 separate groups of three people meeting to see if they have a triple match. Because there are so many groups of three, there is a fairly good probability that triple matches will show up now and then.

Let's try 12 more experiments (trials) on the computer. We can predict that there will be several "triple matches".

Person	1	2	3	4	5	6
Trial #1	5	4	2	3	6	1
Trial #2	4	4	3	6	2	5
Trial #3	1	1	6	4	3	3
Trial #4	**3**	**3**	**3**	5	1	4
Trial #5	2	3	4	4	3	5
Trial #6	1	**4**	**4**	**4**	6	**4**
Trial #7	**2**	1	**2**	6	6	**2**
Trial #8	4	6	5	6	1	4
Trial #9	**1**	6	**1**	**1**	**1**	5
Trial #10	2	4	3	4	6	6
Trial #11	**3**	4	6	**3**	1	**3**
Trial #12	1	6	3	6	5	1

WOW! That was amazing. There were not only "triple matches", but there were also matches where there were four dice that matched!

Let's try another experiment that is a little more fun. Take a group of 10 people and give each person a deck of cards (52 cards). Have each person pick a card at random from his/her deck of cards.

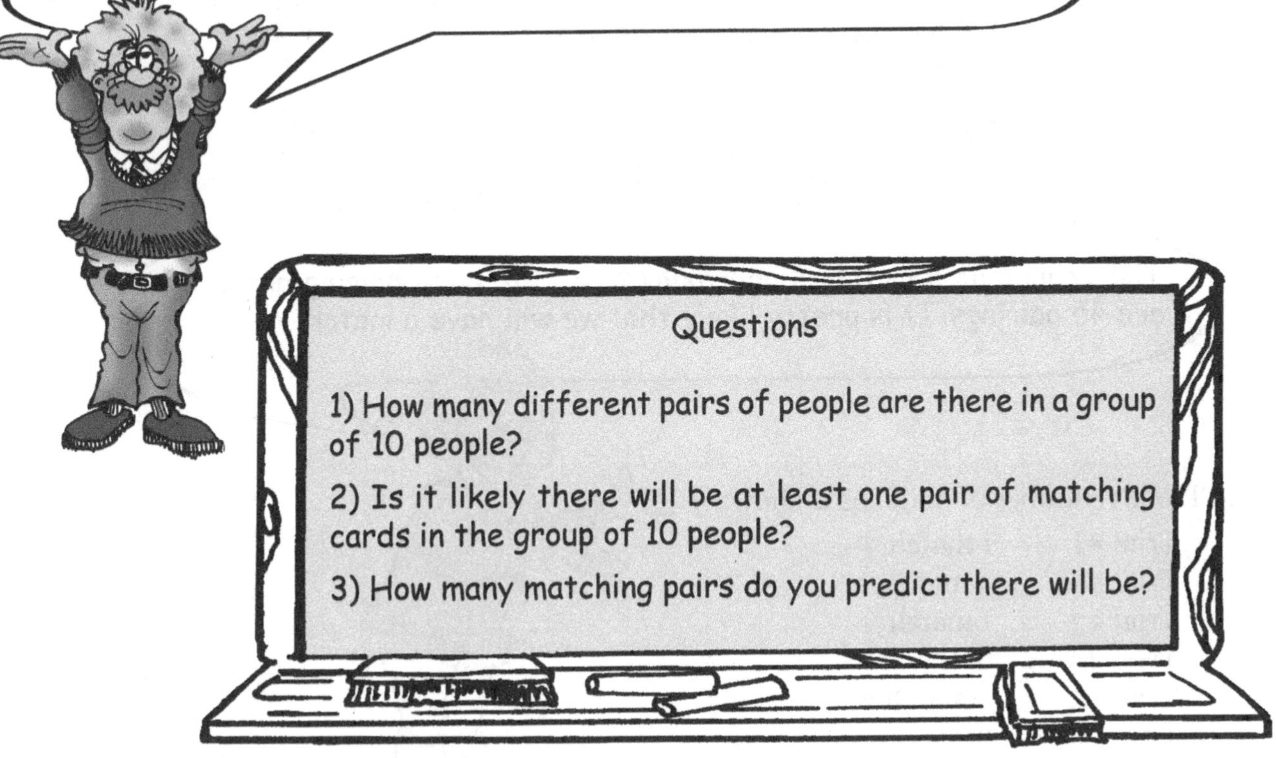

Questions
1) How many different pairs of people are there in a group of 10 people?
2) Is it likely there will be at least one pair of matching cards in the group of 10 people?
3) How many matching pairs do you predict there will be?

We will need to know the number of permutations of 10 people taken two at a time. 10 x 9 = 90 permutations. Remember that we need to eliminate copies such as AB and BA so we will divide by two.

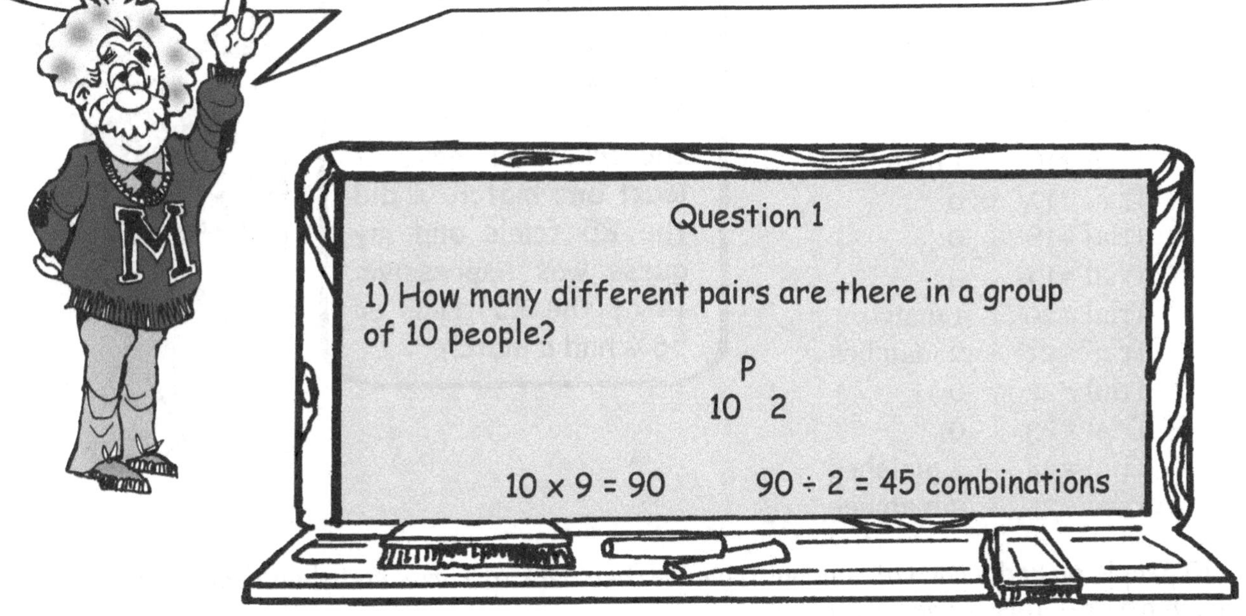

Question 2
2) Is it likely there will be at least one pair of matching cards in the group of 10 people?

The chance of a match is approximately 1/52 each pairing and there are 45 pairings. It is pretty likely that we will have a match.

25 Trials (Number of matches is shown.)

Trial #1	1 match
Trial #2	3 matches
Trial #3	1 match
Trial #4	0
Trial #5	2 matches
Trial #6	0
Trial #7	0
Trial #8	2 matches
Trial #9	0
Trial #10	0
Trial #11	2 matches
Trial #12	1 match
Trial #13	1 match
Trial #14	1 match
Trial #15	0
Trial #16	1 match
Trial #17	0
Trial #18	0
Trial #19	0
Trial #20	1 match
Trial #21	2 matches
Trial #22	0
Trial #23	0
Trial #24	2 matches
Trial #25	3 matches

I will do 25 trials (or experiments) on my computer at the web-site mentioned earlier. I predict that 58% of the trials will have at least one match. I did the 25 trials and my guess was impressive. 14 of the 25 trials or 56% had a match.

(10 people picked a card at random from his/her deck of cards and then compared with each other---this is one trial.)

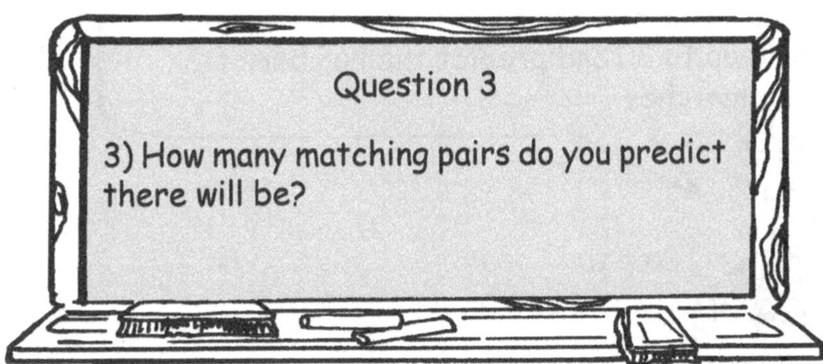

Question 3
3) How many matching pairs do you predict there will be?

Because you have 45 different groups of two and there should be a match approximately 1/52 of the time (52 different cards), the number of matches should average slightly less than one per experiment. (Remember that each experiment has 45 different pairs of people meeting and comparing the card each person picked.)

When you look at the 25 trials that were done on the computer, you find that there were a total of 23 matches. This is 92%, or slightly less than one per trial. Math is a great predictor!!!!

Just for the fun of it, let's jump the number of people up to 20 and predict the number of matches.

Step 1: P
20 2

20 x 19 = 380 ÷ 2 = 190 different pairs

Step 2: The probability of matching for each pair is approximately 1/52. 190 pairs ÷ 52 = 3.6

I predict that there will be an average of 3 or 4 matches each time we do the experiment. Back to the computer for 25 trials.

25 Trials (Number of matches is shown.)

Trial #1	2 matches	Trial #14	6 matches
Trial #2	9 matches	Trial #15	3 matches
Trial #3	3 matches	Trial #16	4 matches
Trial #4	2 matches	Trial #17	3 matches
Trial #5	3 matches	Trial #18	2 matches
Trial #6	6 matches	Trial #19	3 matches
Trial #7	3 matches	Trial #20	3 matches
Trial #8	2 matches	Trial #21	0
Trial #9	7 matches	Trial #22	4 matches
Trial #10	3 matches	Trial #23	3 matches
Trial #11	3 matches	Trial #24	2 matches
Trial #12	4 matches	Trial #25	3 matches
Trial #13	2 matches		

The average for the 25 trials was 3.4 matches per trial. Pretty close to the prediction!

I noticed that one of the trials had no matches. This is a rare event, but of course it is possible.

Even though there was only a very small probability of no matches for the 190 pairings, you had a zero show up. An unlikely outcome, but possible.

Now we are ready to answer the questions at the beginning of the chapter.
Question 1
• If there are 23 children in a classroom, how likely is it that there will be at least one matching pair of birthdays?

Step 1: Number of pairs with 23 children *(Number of handshakes if everyone must meet every other person.)*

$$_{23}P_{2}$$

Permutations of 23 people taken 2 at a time:
23 x 22 = 506

Step 2: Eliminate matching pairs by dividing by 2 (AB and BA are really only one pair.)

506 ÷ 2 = 253

Step 3: The probability of a match for each pairing is approximately 1/365. (365 days in the year - one matches your birthday.)

Step 4: The probability of a match after 253 pairings is pretty good.

I'll run 25 trials on my computer. This means I will simulate 25 classrooms of 23 children each. Because there are 253 pairs and 365 days in a year, there should be a match fairly often.

Matching Birthdays in a Classroom of 23

25 Trials	***(Number of Matches)***
Trial #1	3 matches
Trial #2	1 match
Trial #3	1 match
Trial #4	1 match
Trial #5	0
Trial #6	1 match
Trial #7	2 matches
Trial #8	1 match
Trial #9	0
Trial #10	1 match
Trial #11	0
Trial #12	0
Trial #13	1 match
Trial #14	0
Trial #15	3 matches
Trial #16	0
Trial #17	0
Trial #18	2 matches
Trial #19	2 matches
Trial #20	0
Trial #21	1 match
Trial #22	0
Trial #23	0
Trial #24	0
Trial #25	1 match

14 of the trials had a match and 11 did not. That is pretty close to half. Again, math is a great predictor!

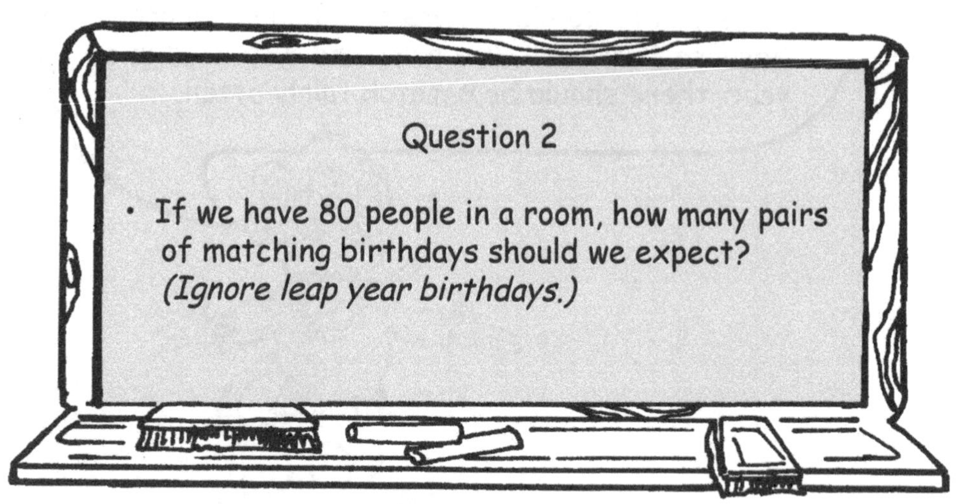

Step 1: Number of pairs with 80 people

$_{80}P_{2}$

Permutations 80 people taken 2 at a time: 80 x 79 = 6320

Step 2: Eliminate matching pairs (AB and BA are really one pair.)

6320 ÷ 2 = 3160

Step 3: The probability of a match for each of the 3160 pairs is approximately 1/365. 3160 ÷ 365 = 8.7

We can predict that we will have approximately 8 or 9 matches each trial.

Matching Birthdays in a Classroom of 80 Children

Trial #1	9 matches
Trial #2	6 matches
Trial #3	10 matches
Trial #4	8 matches
Trial #5	8 matches
Trial #6	8 matches
Trial #7	8 matches
Trial #8	10 matches
Trial #9	9 matches
Trial #10	6 matches
Trial #11	9 matches
Trial #12	16 matches
Trial #13	10 matches
Trial #14	9 matches
Trial #15	13 matches
Trial #16	8 matches
Trial #17	6 matches
Trial #18	11 matches
Trial #19	11 matches
Trial #20	15 matches
Trial #21	3 matches
Trial #22	13 matches
Trial #23	13 matches
Trial #24	6 matches
Trial #25	7 matches

I'll run 25 trials on my computer. (Simulate 25 classrooms with 80 students in each classroom.) My prediction is that there will be an average of 8 or 9 matches each trial.

Your 25 trials averaged 9.28 matches per trial. Again your prediction was really close.

When I ran this simulation, there were several triple matches. I recorded each triple match as three pair matches. This is why.

http://betterexplained.com/articles/understanding-the-birthday-paradox/

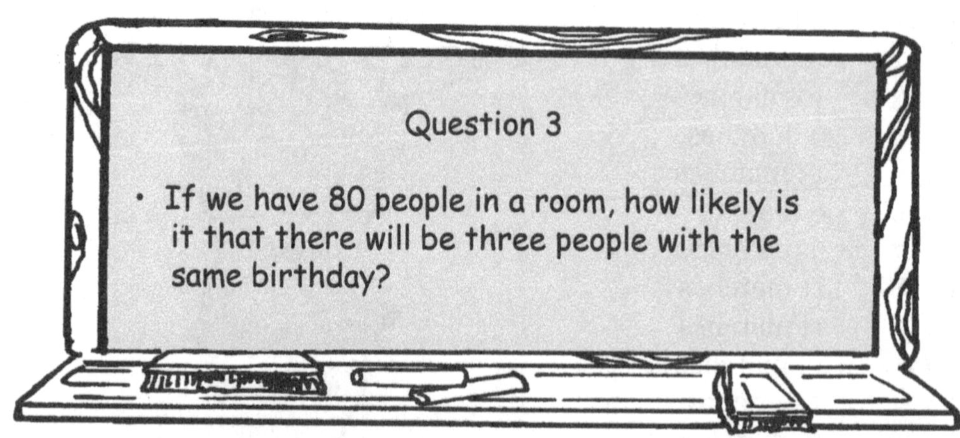

Question 3
• If we have 80 people in a room, how likely is it that there will be three people with the same birthday?

Step 1: We first must find how many groups of three we have in a room with 80 people.

$_{80}P_{3}$

Permutations 80 taken 3 at a time: 80 x 79 x 78 = 492,960

Step 2: Eliminate matching triples by dividing by 6.
(ABC, ACB, BAC, BCA, CAB, CBA are really only one unique group of three people.)

492,960 ÷ 6 = 82,160

Step 3: Probability of 3 people sharing the same birthday:

$$\frac{365}{365} \times \frac{1}{365} \times \frac{1}{365} = \frac{1}{133{,}225}$$

Even though it is very unlikely that three people picked at random will share the same birthday (1/133,225), we have 82,160 separate groups of three people in this situation.

I get it! There is a $\frac{1}{7776}$ probability of rolling five sixes, when five dice are rolled. Even though it is unlikely that we will roll five sixes, if we rolled the dice thousands of times, there is a reasonable chance that we will eventually roll five sixes.

Let's run the computer simulation again. This time I will write if there is a triple match or not.

Triple Matches in a Group of 80 People

Trial	Result	Trial	Result
Trial #1	0	Trial #13	0
Trial #2	0	Trial #14	4 matches
Trial #3	0	Trial #15	2 matches
Trial #4	0	Trial #16	1 match
Trial #5	1 match	Trial #17	0
Trial #6	0	Trial #18	0
Trial #7	1 match	Trial #19	1 match
Trial #8	0	Trial #20	0
Trial #9	0	Trial #21	0
Trial #10	1 match	Trial #22	2 matches
Trial #11	0	Trial #23	1 match
Trial #12	0	Trial #24	2 matches
		Trial #25	1 match

In 25 trials we had 17 times where there was a triple match, even though three randomly selected people have only a 1/133,225 probability of having the same birthday! *(approximately)*

I noticed that there was one trial with four triple matches. I know that is very unlikely, but those kinds of things happen.

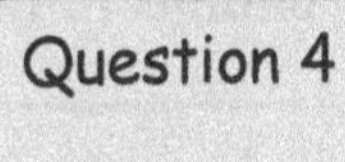

• We have 122 people in a room. We slowly go around the room and ask each person to announce the month and day of their birthday. Predict how many birthday matches we will have when we have only gone through the first 25 people.

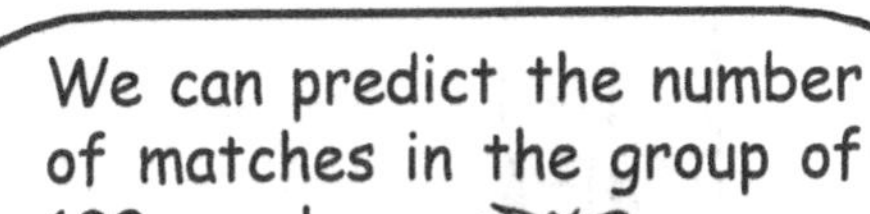

We can predict the number of matches in the group of 122 people.

Step 1: Number of pairs with 122 people

$$_{122}P_2$$

122 people taken 2 at a time: 122 x 121 = 14,762

Step 2: Eliminate matching pairs (AB and BA are really one pair.)

14,762 ÷ 2 = 7,381 pairs

Step 3: The probability of a match for each of the 7381 pairs is approximately 1/365. 7381 ÷ 365 = 20

We know 20 matches is a good estimate for the total, but as people announce their birthday, the people in the beginning are much more likely to get "hits". The last person to announce his birthday has no chance of a "hit" because everyone has already announced his/her birthday. If the last person matched any other birthdays, it would have already happened before it is his turn to say his birthday.

The first person has 121 other people to match.

The second person has 120 other people to match. The third person has 119 other people to match. The fourth 118 and so forth.

Because there are 365 possible birthdays and about 120 people, each person at the beginning has about a 1 in 3 chance of getting a "hit".
Because we can predict that approximately every three people at the beginning will get a "hit", the answer to the question is 8!

Level 1

1) A classroom with 20 students is having a chess tournament. Every student must play one chess game with every other student. How many chess games will there be?

2) In a classroom with 5 students, it is easy to find how many pairs can be made to check for matching birthdays:

AB AC AD AE BC BD BE CD CE DE

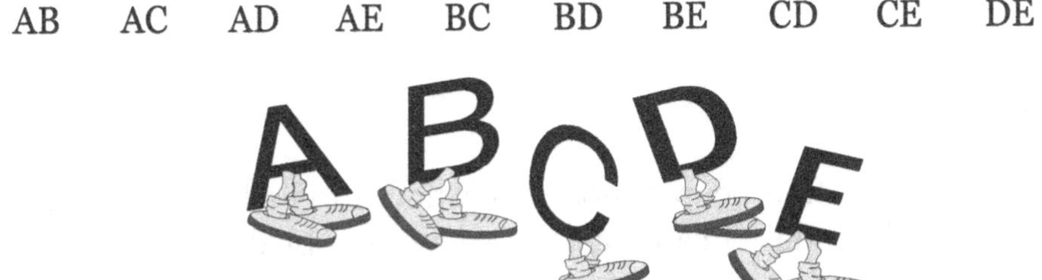

With 5 students it is possible, though unlikely, that there will be any matching birthdays because there are only 10 pairs of students.

In a classroom with 31 students, how many pairs can be made to check for matching birthdays?

3) A classroom with 40 students is having a tennis tournament. Each student must play every other student. How many tennis games will there be in the tournament?

Level 2

1) Predict how many matching birthdays there will be in a classroom of 50 students.

2) 30 students in a classroom were each given a deck of cards (52 in each deck). They were then instructed to randomly pick one card. How many pairs of matching cards would you predict there will be in the classroom?

3) What is the probability that four people chosen at random will all have the same birthday? (We will assume 365 birthdays in a year; ignore leap year birthdays.)

Level 3

1) How many different groups of three are there in a room with 100 people?

2) In a group of 100 people, how many matching pairs of birthdays would you predict there will be?

3) In a group of 100 people, how many matching groups of three birthdays would you predict will occur?

a) 0

b) 1

c) 10

Einstein

A list of all citizens of the United States who were born in January is placed into a computer and sixteen of the names are drawn randomly.

There is a high probability that there will be several matching birthdays. How many matching birthdays would you expect will be two females?

Chapter 7
Pilots Make Math Mistakes

It was July 23rd, 1983 and Air Canada 143 was being prepared for departure from Montreal when the crew discovered that the fuel gauge did not work.

Instead of canceling the flight, the crew and mechanics decided to check the amount of fuel in the tank by hand. They used a procedure that is call a "drip". This procedure, which has been used since the beginning of flight, is similar to the dipstick in a car.

When the mechanics measured each wing tank, they found that the plane had a total of 7682 liters of jet fuel.

The crew knew that their flight that day called for 22,300 kilograms of fuel. Your job is to determine how many liters of jet fuel need to be added to the fuel tanks.

Fuel Calculation

____
____
____
____
____
____
____

Liters needed ____________________________________

Signature of pilot ________________________________
Signature of mechanic _____________________________

Before we go through the correct way to calculate the amount of fuel needed, I am going to tell you what happened to Flight 143.

The mechanics and pilot went through these steps.

1) A maintenance worker discovered that the fuel gauge did not work.

2) The fuel level was measured manually and found to contain 7682 liters of jet fuel.

3) The flight crew and pilot knew the flight required 22,300 kilograms of fuel. They needed to know how many more liters of jet fuel to add to make the total amount of fuel 22,300 kilograms.

4) They used a conversion of 1.77 and determined that there were 7682 x 1.77 = 13,597 kilograms of jet fuel already in the tanks.

5) 22,300 – 13,597 = 8703 kilograms of jet fuel were needed.

6) 8703 kilograms divided by the conversion factor of 1.77 = 4917 liters of jet fuel needed.

So 4917 liters of jet fuel were added and flight 143 took off for its destination of Edmonton. (With a short stop in Ottawa.)
They did recheck their calculations several times because the pilot and the ground crew were a little nervous about the results.

As flight 143 cruised at 41,000 feet, the pilots received a warning that a fuel pump in the left wing had probably failed. Shortly after that, a second fuel pressure warning light alerted the crew that another fuel pump was failing.

The pilot now became very concerned and decided to divert to Winnipeg. Shortly after making this decision, another left wing fuel pressure gauge lit up and the left engine stopped completely.

As the pilots prepared for a single engine landing, the remaining engine on the right side of the plane also stopped. Now the pilots were trying to control and land a 132 ton glider because the jet had run out of fuel!

To further complicate the problem the pilots were facing was the fact that they soon discovered that the huge jet was sinking too fast to make it to the Winnipeg Airport. Their only chance was a pair of abandoned Royal Canadian Air Force runways.

What the pilot and the air traffic controllers who began to guide flight 143 to the abandoned runways did not know was that parts of both runways were being used by the Winnipeg Sports Car Club for a "Family Day" celebration. The runway that Flight 143 was heading for was filled with spectators, racers, and children who all fled when they saw the jet approaching.

The plane did manage to land, but the front landing gear collapsed. The passengers quickly evacuated the plane and all survived. (Several were injured sliding down the emergency chute.)

Pilots in Canada for years had determined their fuel load in pounds, not kilograms. Because Canada was in the process of converting to the metric system, mistakes were bound to be made. The mistake made during the refueling of Flight 143 was everyone's worst nightmare.

Because jet fuel is added by weight and the manual "dipstick" method gives an answer in liters, those involved in the fuel calculation needed to know how to convert liters into kilograms.

When the ground crew determined that the existing 7682 liters of jet fuel were equal to 7682 x 1.77 = 13,597 kilograms, they were using the conversion number for :

POUNDS, not kilograms!!

The correct factor for converting liters to kilograms is .803 (kilograms per liter of jet fuel). Flight 143 had 7682 x .803 = 6169 kilograms of jet fuel already in its tanks, not 13,597 kilograms!

What flight 143 needed:

22,300 kilograms required minus 6169 kilograms already in tanks =
16,131 kilograms of jet fuel.

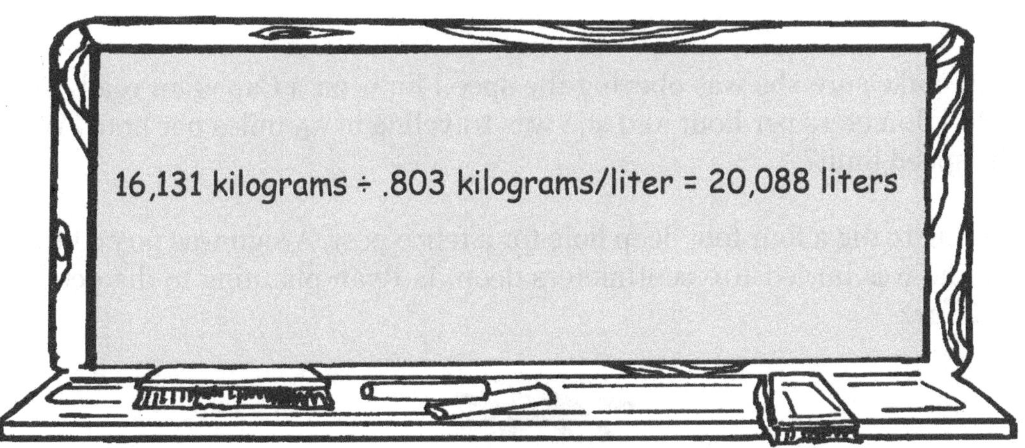

16,131 kilograms ÷ .803 kilograms/liter = 20,088 liters

Changing 16,131 kilograms to liters is easy. Using the correct conversion factor of .803, we find that Flight 143 needed 20,088 liters of additional jet fuel.

No wonder the jet ran out of fuel. It needed 20,088 liters, but due to the conversion error, only 4,917 liters were added before take-off!

Level 1

1) Holly wanted to make sure she was obeying the speed limit on a Canadian road. The speed limit was 80 kilometers per hour and she was traveling at 55 miles per hour. Was Holly obeying the speed limit?

2) Ryan was planning to dig a four foot deep hole for a fence post. A sign was posted that said an electrical line was buried 100 centimeters deep. Is Ryan planning to dig deeper than the electrical line?

3) One of the beautiful aspects to the metric system is that lengths, weights and volume are all connected. For example: One cubic decimeter of water is a liter of water and weighs one kilogram.

How much does the water weigh in an aquarium that is 20 decimeters high, 30 decimeters wide and 80 decimeters long?

Level 2

1) Light travels 186,000 miles per second. How many kilometers per second does light travel?

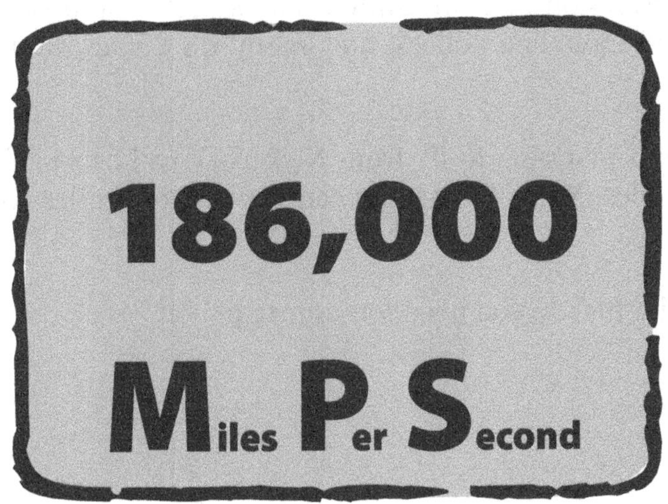

2) The flight crew for Air Canada Flight 143 knew that they needed a total of 22,300 kilograms of jet fuel for their flight.

After adding 4917 liters of jet fuel to the 7682 liters already in the tank, the jet held 12,599 liters of fuel.

If the flight crew had a basic knowledge of the metric system, they would know that a liter of water weighs one kilogram. The flight crew also knew that jet fuel is lighter than water.

Using this information, explain why the flight crew should have known that 12,599 liters of jet fuel was not 22,300 kilograms of jet fuel.

3) How many cubic centimeters are in a cubic meter?
(Remember, there are 100 centimeters in a meter.)

Level 3

1) If the price of gas is $4 per gallon, what is the cost per liter?

2) If the present conversion rate for United States money and Canadian money is one US dollar equals 1.08 Canadian dollars, how many US dollars would you receive for 85 Canadian dollars?

3) You are a pilot and planning to fly from New York to Los Angeles, a distance of approximately 3000 miles. Your Boeing 747 can travel 8350 miles with its 57,000 gallon fuel tank full.

How many liters of jet fuel do you need for your trip?

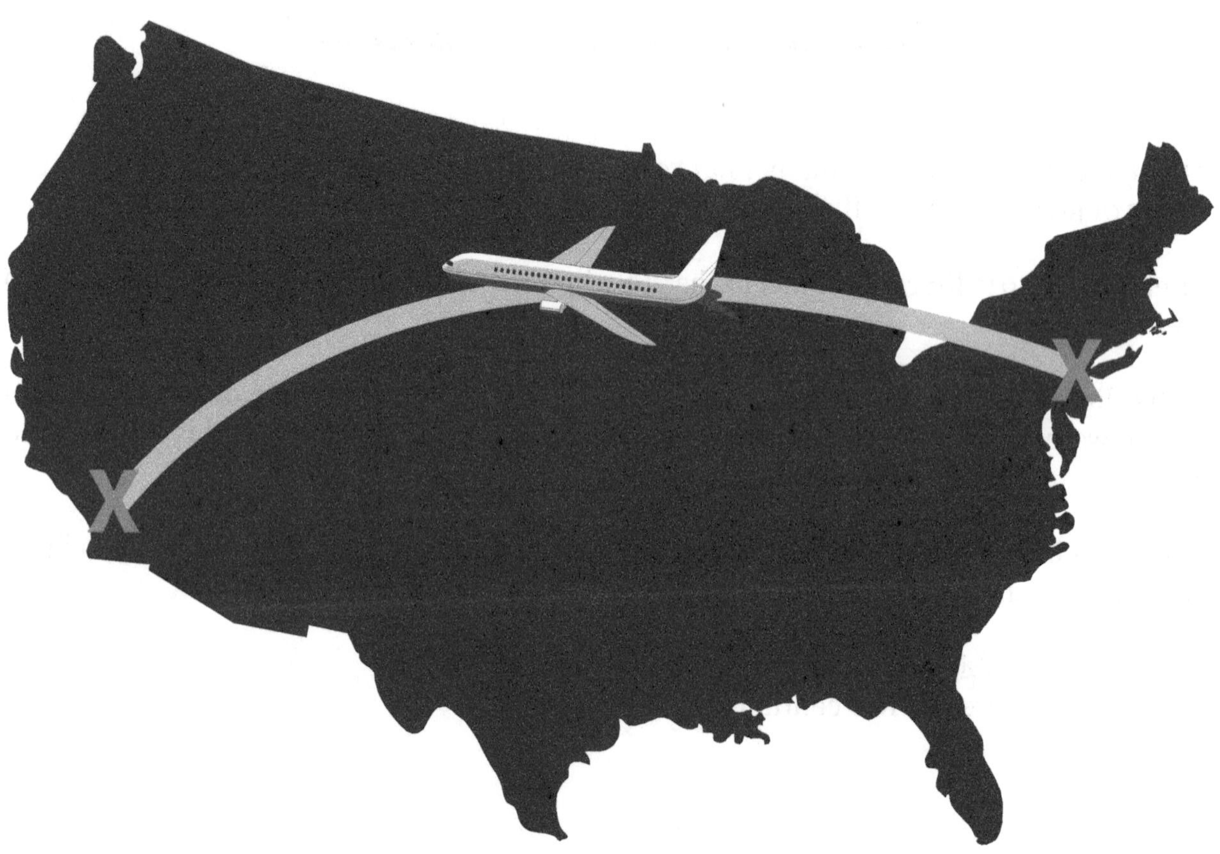

Here are the four ways. We'll look closely at each one and place them on your scale.

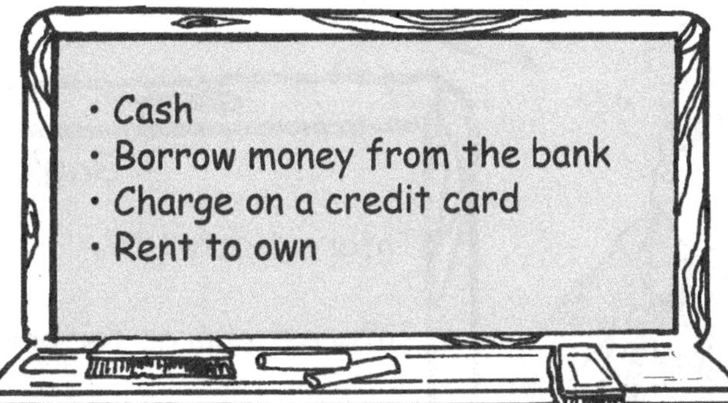

• Cash
• Borrow money from the bank
• Charge on a credit card
• Rent to own

Well, the first one is easy. I could save the $100 per week for 22 weeks and then just pay cash for the television. I think I know where to put this method on the scale.

CASH

→ **Very Responsible**

Not Too Bad

I'm a Little Bit Nervous

Bad Idea

What Was I Thinking

Why Don't I Just Burn Money in the Trash

Let me show you how borrowing money from a bank works. They will charge you 8% annual interest until you pay back the $2200.

Bank Borrowing

Interest rate: 8%

Interest charge for one year: .08 x $2200 = $176

Interest charge per week: $176 ÷ 52 = $3.39

Interest charge for 22 weeks: 22 x $3.39 = $74.58

Total cost of television: $2200 + $74.58 = $2274.58

To make the calculation easier, we will assume that you borrow the $2200 and then save $100 each week until you have enough to pay back the bank.

Actually, I need to save $100 plus the interest of $3.39 each week to have enough money saved in 22 weeks.

BANK

Very Responsible

→ **Not Too Bad**

I'm a Little Bit Nervous

Bad Idea

What Was I Thinking

Why Don't I Just Burn Money in the Trash

I'll put borrowing from a bank slightly lower than cash because if I don't save the money to pay back the bank, I will see my debt grow.

Remember, to borrow from a bank you must have good credit.
I think my credit is good because I always pay my bills on time.

Next we will see what happens when you pay for a television using a credit card with an annual interest rate of 22%. Again, we will save the money and pay it all off in 22 weeks. Credit card companies don't let you do this—they require money each month—but it will make our calculations easier.

Credit Card

Interest rate: 22%

Interest charge for one year: .22 x $2200 = $484

Interest charge per week: $484 ÷ 52 = $9.31

Interest charge for 22 weeks: 22 x $9.31 = $204.82

Total cost of television: $2200 + $204.82= $2404.82

CREDIT CARD

Very Responsible

Not Too Bad

I'm a Little Bit Nervous

→ **Bad Idea**

What Was I Thinking

Why Don't I Just Burn Money in the Trash

This method scares me a little because of the high interest rate and how quickly my debt will grow if I cannot make my payments.

Remember, if you are late with credit card payments or cannot pay what you owe, your interest rate might go up. You also will end up paying a penalty of $30-$40 each month that your payment is late.

Before we calculate the cost of a $2200 television when you use rent-to-own, let's look at what rent-to-own companies are.

Rent-to-own is a multi-billion dollar industry that sells televisions, refrigerators, washing machines, computers and furniture by making loans that are paid weekly or monthly.

The industry claims it rents and also allows the consumer to buy the rented item. To defend its position, the industry points to the fact that consumers can stop making payments and return the items.

Consumer groups respond to this statement by pointing out that most customers rent-to-own with the intent of eventually becoming the owner of the merchandise and rarely intend to really rent the item for a few weeks or months.

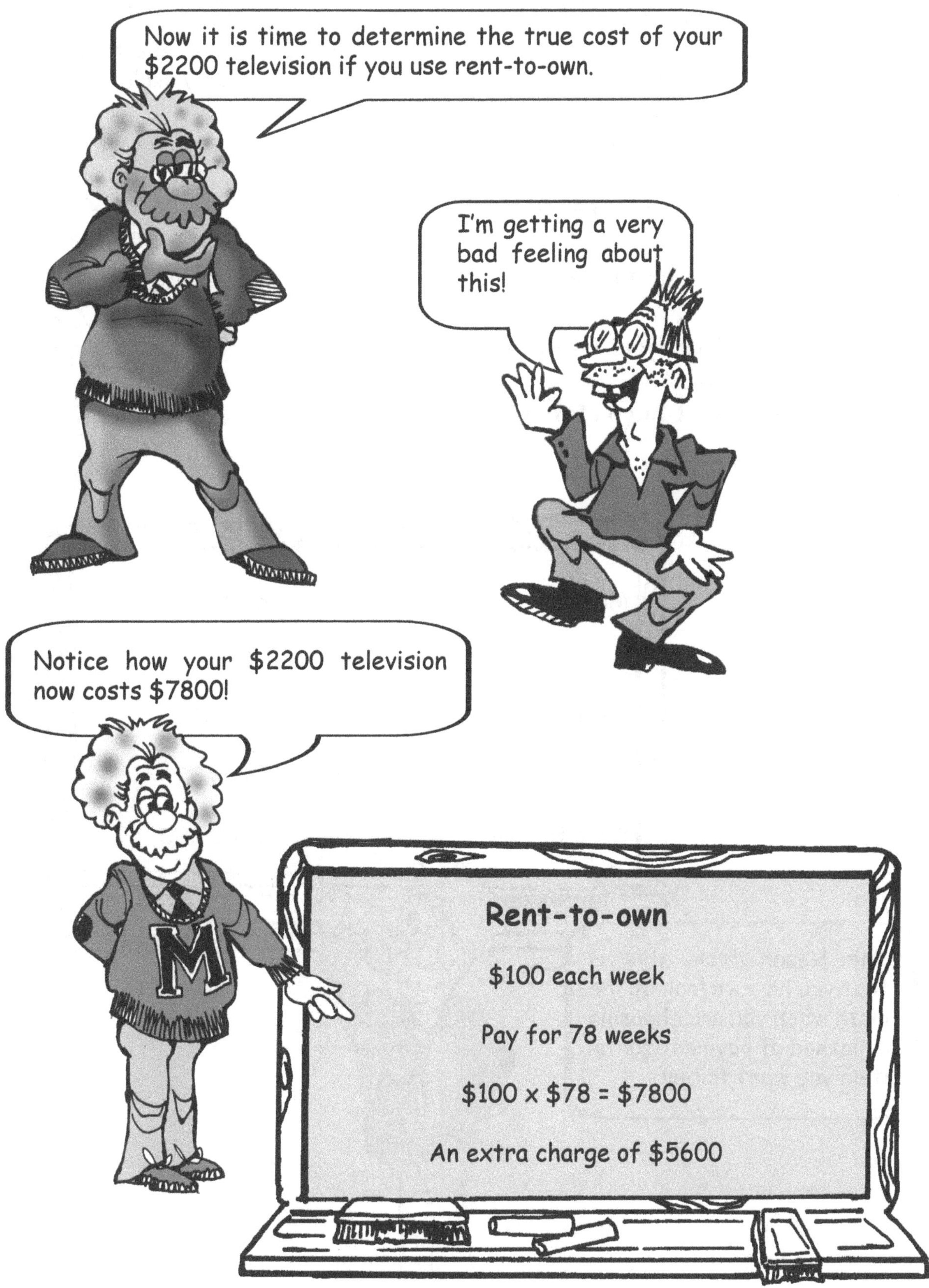
Now it is time to determine the true cost of your $2200 television if you use rent-to-own.
I'm getting a very bad feeling about this!
Notice how your $2200 television now costs $7800!
Rent-to-own
$100 each week
Pay for 78 weeks
$100 x $78 = $7800
An extra charge of $5600

RENT TO OWN

Very Responsible

Not Too Bad

I'm a Little Bit Nervous

Bad Idea

What Was I Thinking

→ **Why Don't I Just Burn Money in the Trash**

I think I know where to put rent-to-own on my scale.

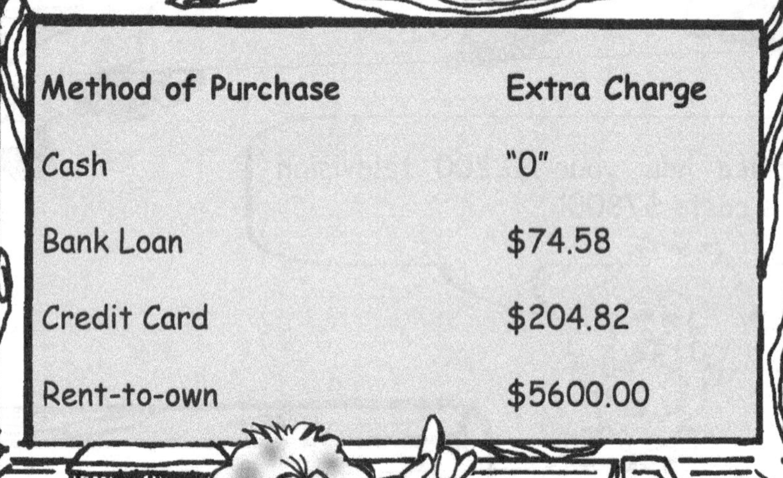

Method of Purchase	Extra Charge
Cash	"0"
Bank Loan	$74.58
Credit Card	$204.82
Rent-to-own	$5600.00

The lesson from this is that you have to look at the math when you are choosing a method of payment for an item you want to buy.

Level 1

1) What is the annual interest on a loan of $3000 with an interest rate of 27.9%?

2) Mark borrowed $4000 at an interest rate of 32.9%. After one year his loan grew to $5316 because he did not pay any of the interest charges. If Mark pays no payments his second year, what will his debt grow to by the end of year two?

3) If $1000 is borrowed at an annual interest rate of 25% and no payments are made, how many years until the debt doubles?

Level 2

1) Jay bought his furniture at a rent-to-own store. Look at his store contract and determine how much more he spent when compared to paying cash.

Item	Cost New	Weekly Cost	Number of Weeks
Washer & Dryer	$620	$39	78
Television 19 inches	$200	$12	87
Living Room Set	$2100	$85	78

2) Chris was offered a $1500 television through a rent-to-own store for $62 per week for 52 weeks. He decided to take out a $1500 loan from a bank with an 8% annual interest rate, save his money, and then pay the loan back in a year. How much money did Chris save by buying the television with an 8% bank loan when compared to the cost of using the rent-to-own store?

3) If a credit card company charges 32.9% annual interest, what percent is the interest charge for one month?

Level 3

1) Stephanie charged an $8000 grand piano on her credit card that charges 27.9% annual interest. If Stephanie pays her entire credit card bill when it arrives in the mail next month, she will not have to pay any interest.

Unfortunately, Stephanie forgot to mail her credit card payment until the day after it was due. The credit card company charged her a $30 late fee plus one month's interest on the $8000. How much money did Stephanie lose by forgetting to mail her bill on time?

2) Kelly has a credit card with an annual interest rate of 9.9%. Kelly charged a $3500 trip to Bermuda to her credit card.

Unfortunately, Kelly was late with a payment on another non-credit card bill and according to the fine print in her credit card contract, her annual interest rate increases to 32.9% if she is late with any other bill. How much did Kelly's monthly interest charge increase on her $3500 debt when the interest rate jumped from 9.9% to 32.9%?

3) Kristin's monthly interest charge went from $48.00 to $59.76 on a balance of $2400 because the interest rate charged on her credit card increased. If Kristin's annual interest rate started at 24%, what is her new interest rate?

Einstein

Luke bought an $1800 computer with his credit card that charged 27.9% annual interest. He never charged anything else to the credit card and always paid the minimum payment of $50 every month.

Every Christmas the credit card company would send Luke a check for $120, which he would cash.

When Luke cashed the check for $120, the amount he owed the credit card company would increase by $120.
M

If Luke always paid his credit card bill on time, how long will it take for the amount Luke owes to drop below $1000?

Chapter 9
Lawmakers Make Math Mistakes

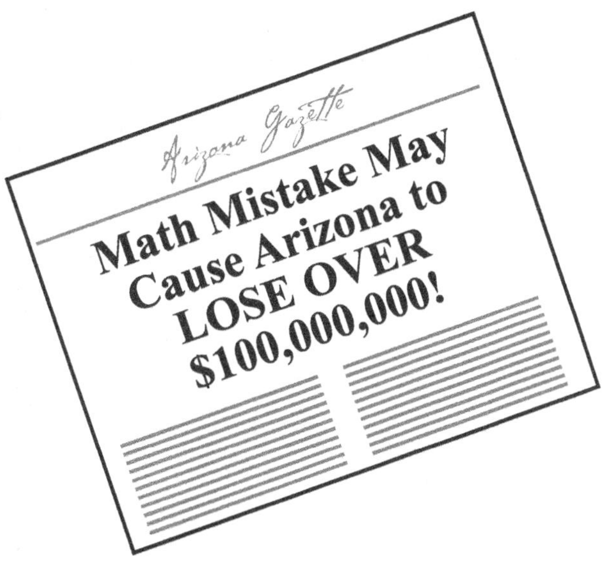
Arizona Gazette
Math Mistake May Cause Arizona to LOSE OVER $100,000,000!

Arizona lawmakers put a proposal before voters in 2006 to raise the tax on cigarettes to pay for early-childhood education and health programs. The tax passed, but a math mistake in the wording on the ballot caused headaches for lawmakers.

Lawmakers wanted to raise taxes on cigarettes by 80 cents. Look at the language on the ballot and see if that is what they wrote.
There will be an .80 cent/pack tax increase on cigarettes
YES NO

The wording on the ballot should have read 80 cents/pack. When it is written as an .80 cent/pack increase, it calls for an increase of .80 of a cent - not even a penny per pack!! (8/10 of a cent)

The state hoped to raise $186,000,000 for early-childhood programs. Now it may only take in 1.86 million dollars. This shows why you really have to be careful when you write and solve math problems.

The State of Arizona is by no means the only state to make math mistakes. In the questions at the end of this chapter, you will see that Hawaii and New York also made major math blunders.

Level 1

1) Jillian saw the following ad in the newspaper:

Jillian brought one dollar to the store and asked for 200 apples. The owner of the store replied that the ad said that she could only have two apples for the dollar. Who was right? Why?

2) Ruben wants to put an ad in the paper to sell earthworms for a dime each. Which of the following ads are written correctly? Why?

a) Earthworms for .10 cents each

b) Earthworms for $.10 each

c) Earthworms for 10¢ each

3) Legislators in Hawaii passed a cigarette tax increase designed to raise 8 million dollars each year for cancer research. They planned to do this by taxing each cigarette 1.5 cents. After the law was written and passed, the tobacco industry claimed that the way the law was written meant that they were only required to pay a total of 1.5 cents each year.

Look at the following sentence from the new law and explain what lawmakers did wrong.

"This law puts a total of 1.5 cents into a cancer research fund next year."

Level 2

1) A reporter writing about a math mistake in an Arizona ballot measure to raise the tax on cigarettes made a math mistake himself. Write a letter to the editor explaining why the reporter's math is incorrect.

What the reporter wrote:

"In Arizona, a ballot measure approved by voters meant to tax each pack of cigarettes by 80 cents. Unfortunately, the ballot measure added a period in front of the 80 cents → .80 cents – actually making it only 8 cents per pack. Legislators are going to collect the tax anyway, it will just be 90% less than they expected."

2) How many .01 cents will it take to make one dollar?

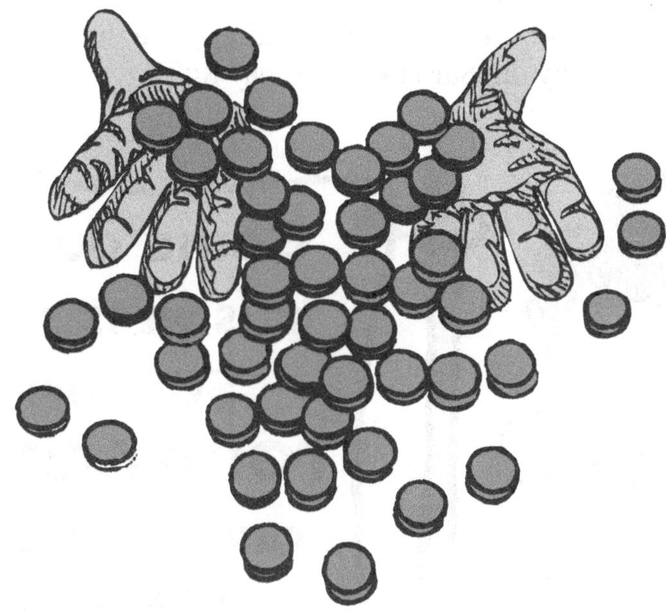

3) Put the following in order from smallest to largest.

2/3 cent

.07 cents

$.06

.05 dollars

Level 3

1) First prize in a radio contest is a partial college scholarship. The winner will have .50% of the $100,000 cost of college paid for. If Jasmine won the contest, how much is her scholarship worth?

2) Look at this excerpt from a science based internet site (October 2, 2006) and see if you can find a science mistake.

"While liquid hydrogen is the densest form of the fuel, keeping it at the required 480 degrees below zero in the on-board storage tank is expensive and difficult."

3) Sara saw this sign and took $100 worth of books to the sales counter and expected to pay $5. The clerk at the bookstore charged Sara a higher price than $5. What did the clerk charge Sara for the books? Why did Sara expect to pay $5?

GOING OUT OF
BUSINESS SALE
50% OFF
TODAY ONLY
TAKE ANOTHER
45% OFF

Einstein

Lawmakers in New York passed a new get-tough drunk driving law. The intent of the law was to stop plea bargains with prosecutors when the blood alcohol content of a driver's blood was significantly higher than the legal limit.

Look at the way the law was written and explain why it is IMPERATIVE that lawmakers fix their mistake.

> "Drivers with a blood-alcohol content higher than .18 grams are guilty of aggravated driving while intoxicated."

Chapter 10

The Eccentric Mathematician and the Lock That Would Not Open

An eccentric mathematician frequently went to a gym to work out. The other people he would meet in the locker room enjoyed talking to him, but sometimes they were very annoyed with a strange habit of his.

The eccentric mathematician would lock his wallet in a locker before he worked out, but he would tape the lock combination to his locker.

The eccentric mathematician's friends at the gym wanted to teach him a lesson about how dangerous it was to leave the combination for his lock taped to the locker. They decided that they would open the lock and hide the eccentric mathematician's wallet.

Unfortunately, when the eccentric mathematician's friends tried to open the lock, the combination taped to the locker did not open the lock. They spent several minutes thinking about why the combination wasn't working and possible ways to open the locker.

Base 10 has columns like this.
10,000
1000
100
10
1

We multiply by 10 each time to get the next larger column, so in base 9 we need to multiply by 9.

6561	729	81	9	1

Let's put the combination **8503** into the base 9 chart.

6561	729	81	9	1
	8	5	0	3

6561	729	81	9	1
	8	5	0	3

Now we can figure out what 8503 base 9 is in base 10.

8 groups of 729: 8 x 729 = 5832

5 groups of 81: 5 x 81 = 405

0 groups of 9: 0 x 9 = 0

3 groups of 1: 3 x 1 = 3

5832 + 405 + 0 + 3 = 6240

Now we know that 8503 base 9 is equal to 6240 in base 10.

Before we try the combination 6240, let's consider another possibility for the combination.

8503

6561	729	81	9	1
1				

8503 ÷ 6561 = 1 with 8503 - 6561 = 1942 left over

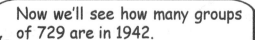

Now we'll see how many groups of 729 are in 1942.

6561	729	81	9	1
1	2			

1942 ÷ 729 = 2 with 484 left over.

Oh I see. We will now see how many 81's there are in 484 and so on.

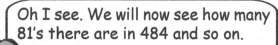

6561	729	81	9	1
1	2	5		

484 ÷ 81 = 5 with 79 left over.

I'll finish up.

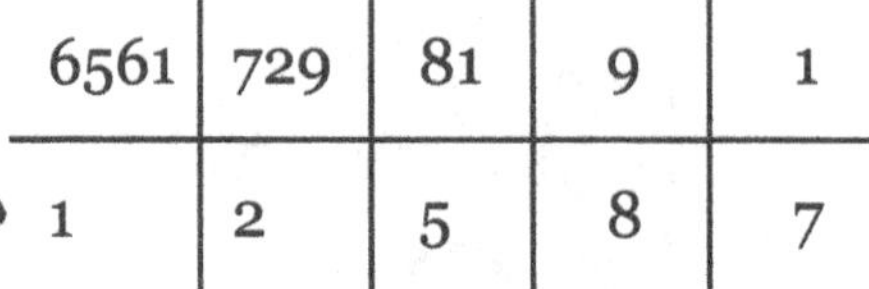

6561	729	81	9	1
1	2	5	8	7

79 ÷ 9 = 8 with 7 left over for the 1's column.

Now we know that 8503 base 10 is 12,587 in base 9.

Level 1

1) Change 582 base 9 into base 10.

2) Change 1111 base 9 into base 10.

3) Change 2002 base 5 into base 10.

Level 2

1) Change 845 base 10 into base 9.

2) Change 10 base 10 into base 9.

3) Change 100 base 10 into base 2.

Level 3

1) The columns for base 10 are shown below:

1000 100 10 1 . 1/10 1/100 1/1000 1/10,000

Write the columns for base 2.

2) The number 2.27 base 10 is equal to 2 $\frac{27}{100}$. What does the number 2.34 base 5 equal in base 10?

3) Change the base 10 number .999999 into base 2.

Einstein

Change 432.113 base 5 into base 10.

Chapter 11

The Power of Algebraic Thinking

Einstein was always able to impress his students with his mind-reading math tricks.

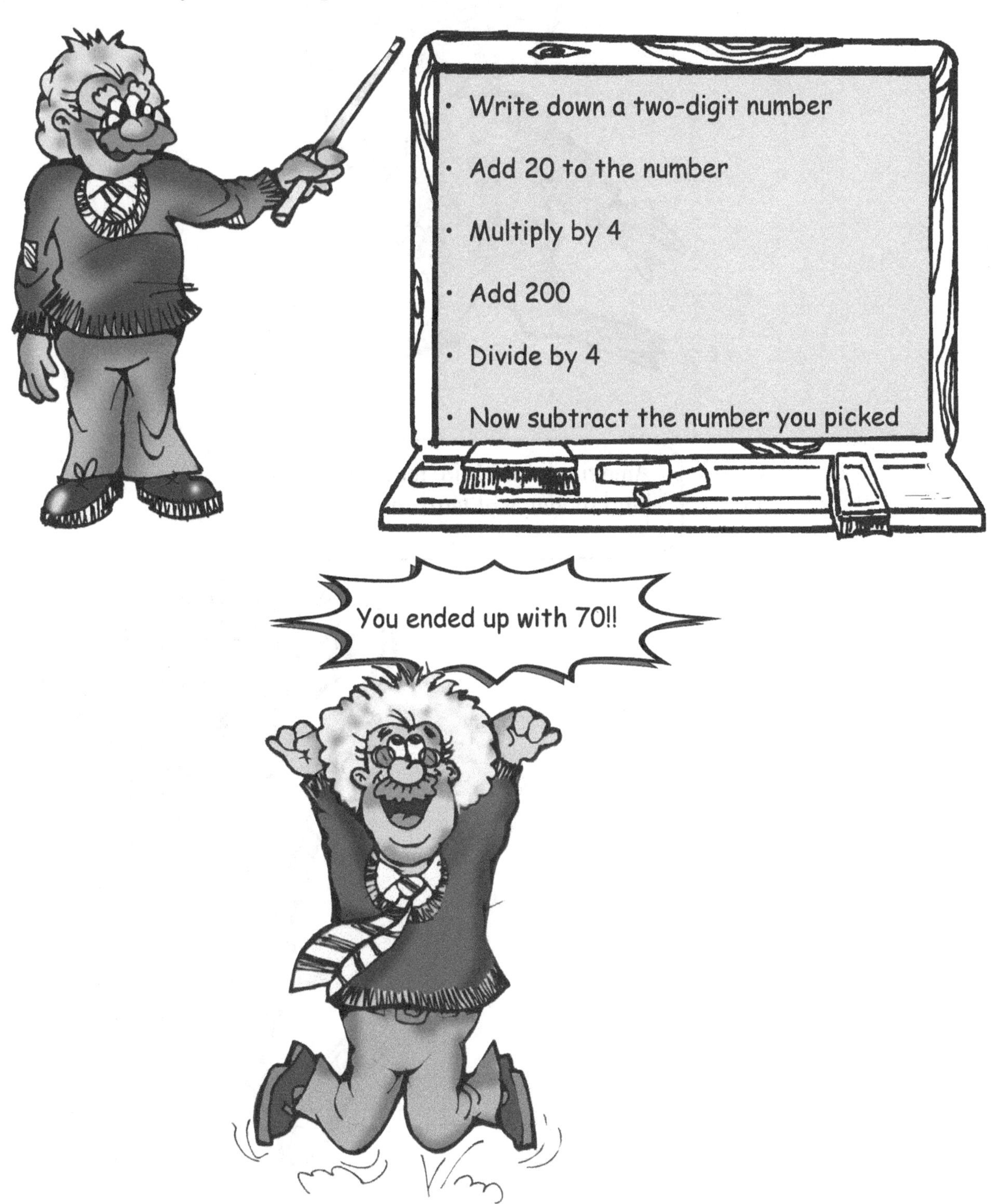

• Write down a two-digit number
• Add 20 to the number
• Multiply by 4
• Add 200
• Divide by 4
• Now subtract the number you picked
You ended up with 70!!

How did he do that?

Amazing! Einstein must have some kind of magical math powers.

Here's another one. Pick a number between 1 and 9 and enter it into your calculator. Now multiply by 3 and then multiply again by 37,037.
01234
1 2 3
4 5 6
7 8 9
0 =
You will now have a row of the number you picked on the calculator.
Genius! Brilliant!
M
Unbelievable! How in the world did he do that?

Then one day Einstein's students learned how to change math problems into the language of algebra.

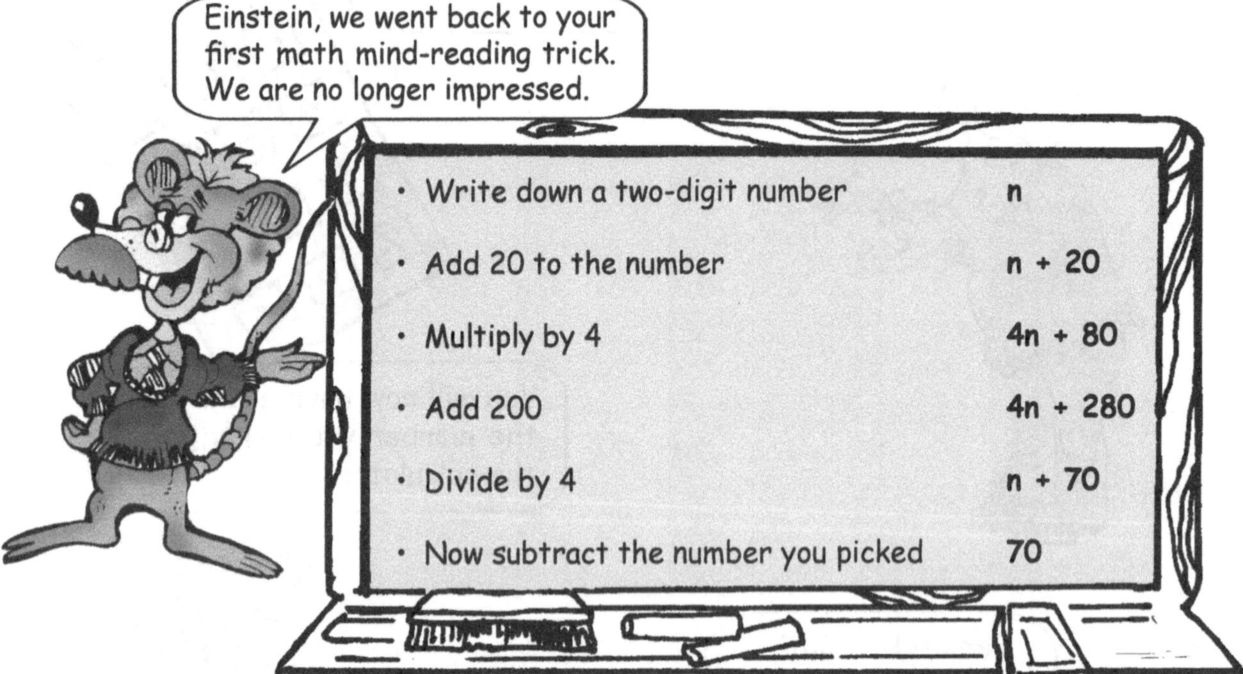

Einstein, we went back to your first math mind-reading trick. We are no longer impressed.
• Write down a two-digit number n
• Add 20 to the number n + 20
• Multiply by 4 4n + 80
• Add 200 4n + 280
• Divide by 4 n + 70
• Now subtract the number you picked 70

After we turned it into the language of algebra, it was very, very easy to see that the trick wasn't really that clever.

When Einstein's students changed the math trick into the language of algebra, it became clear that Einstein's goal during the trick was to get rid of ***n*** (The number selected) so he could control what number remained.

I suppose you also figured out my other trick.
As a matter of fact we did!!
• Pick a number between 1 and 9 n
• Now multiply by 3 3n
• Multiply again by 37,037 111,111n
If n is 2, then 111,111 x 2 = 222,222.
If n is 8, then 111,111 x 8 = 888,888.

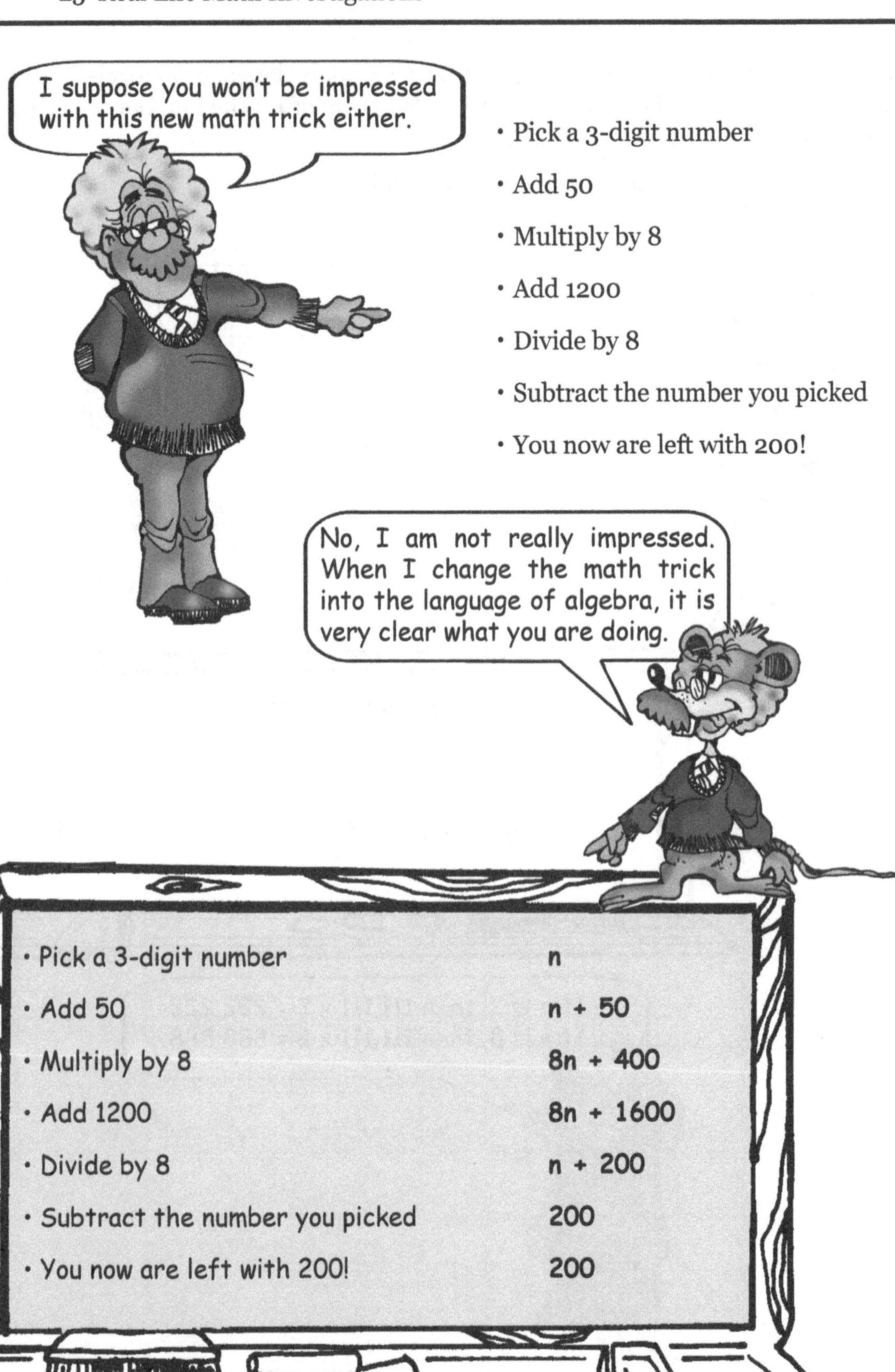
I suppose you won't be impressed with this new math trick either.
• Pick a 3-digit number
• Add 50
• Multiply by 8
• Add 1200
• Divide by 8
• Subtract the number you picked
• You now are left with 200!
No, I am not really impressed. When I change the math trick into the language of algebra, it is very clear what you are doing.
• Pick a 3-digit number n
• Add 50 n + 50
• Multiply by 8 8n + 400
• Add 1200 8n + 1600
• Divide by 8 n + 200
• Subtract the number you picked 200
• You now are left with 200! 200

Level 1

1) Change the following math magic trick into the language of algebra.

- Write down a 2-digit number
- Add 100 to the number
- Multiply by 10
- Subtract 40
- Divide by 10
- Subtract the number you picked
- You are left with 96!

2) A math magic trick was turned into the language of algebra. Change from the language of algebra back into the magic trick.

n

$n + 50$

$5n + 250$

$5n + 100$

$n + 20$

20

3) Change the following math trick into the language of algebra.

- Pick a number from 1 to 9 and enter it into your calculator
- Multiply by 18,518.5
- Now multiply by 6
- You will now have a row of the number you picked on your calculator!

Level 2

1) Change the following math magic trick into the language of algebra.

- Pick a 2 - digit number
- Add 102
- Multiply by 2
- Add 96
- Divide by 2
- Subtract 149
- Subtract your original number
- Divide by 9
- You are left with .11111

2) Change the following math magic trick into the language of algebra.

- Pick a number
- Multiply by 2
- Add 100
- Multiply by 8
- Subtract 400
- Divide by 16
- Subtract the number you picked
- You ended up with 25

3) Change the following math magic trick into the language of algebra.
"I will turn the number you pick into a kind of insect."

- Pick a 3-digit number
- Add 100
- Multiply by 7
- Subtract 28
- Divide by 7
- Add 159
- Subtract your original number
- Change the digits in the remaining number into letters.
(A = 1 B = 2 C = 3 D = 4 and so on)
- You now have spelled out BEE

Level 3

1) Turn the following math magic trick into the language of algebra.

- Pick two 3-digit numbers and add them.
- Add 850
- Multiply by 3
- Subtract 1440
- Divide by 3
- Subtract the sum of the two numbers you picked
- You are left with 370!

2) Rat Einstein was asked how old his car was. Instead of giving the answer in years, he gave the answer in minutes.

If the car is ***n*** minutes old, how many years old is the car in the language of algebra? (Hint: The car is n/60 hours old.)

3) Ian added ten consecutive odd numbers and ended up with a sum of exactly 10,000. What is the smallest of the ten consecutive odd numbers?

Einstein

On December 1st of a certain year, Marie Curie was twice as old as Franklin Roosevelt and 1.5 times the age of Albert Einstein. On this day, Sir Alexander Fleming was one year older than Franklin Roosevelt. On this same date, the total of all four of their ages was 81. How old was Albert Einstein on this December 1st?

Chapter 12
The Amazing Googolplex Challenge

Two large numbers that are fun to talk about are googol and googolplex. Googol is written with a one followed by 100 zeros.

Googol is easy to write, it just takes a little time.
10,000,000,000,000,000,000,000,000,000,000,
000,000,000,000,000,000,000,000,000,
000,000,000,000,000,000,000,000,000,
000,000,000,000,000,000
You can also write googol as 10^{100} if you want to use exponents.

Googolplex is also an interesting number. It is written with a one followed by a googol of zeros. Your challenge is to decide whether it is possible to write out all the zeros in googolplex. You are given three things to help you:

1) All the paper and blackboards you need for writing zeros.
(You can even have the entire highway system to write on if you decide that you need it.)

2) All the assistants you need to help you.
(Every person in the world will be at your disposal if you decide you need them.)

3) Unlimited time to accomplish your task.
(Eternity if you decide you need it.)

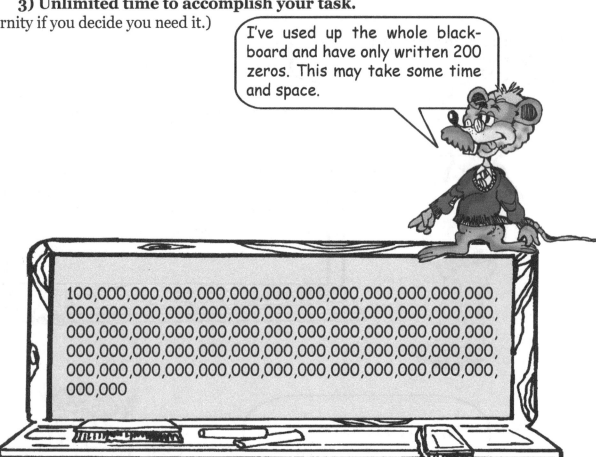

I've used up the whole blackboard and have only written 200 zeros. This may take some time and space.

100,000,000,000,000,000,000,000,000,000,000,000,000,
000,000,000,000,000,000,000,000,000,000,000,000,000,
000,000,000,000,000,000,000,000,000,000,000,000,000,
000,000,000,000,000,000,000,000,000,000,000,000,000,
000,000,000,000,000,000,000,000,000,000,000,000,000,
000,000

Before we talk about whether it is possible to write all the zeros in googolplex, we need to discuss some information about our universe.

This is a very important piece of information.
It has been estimated that there are 10^{87} atoms in the entire universe.
That is amazing! There are billions and billions of huge stars in our universe with a very large number of atoms in each. How can there be only 10^{87} atoms in the entire universe?
You are right—there is a lot of matter in the universe, but 10^{87} is a much larger number than you think!
I still don't see how that can be possible. I read in my astronomy book that there are 100 stars for every grain of sand on Earth. That's a lot of stars and therefore a whole lot of atoms!

Complicated way

Step 1: Number of zeros written with one piece of chalk.

Step 2: Number of pieces of chalk needed.

Step 3: The mass of the needed chalk exceeds the mass of the Earth.

Step 4: I think that proves that the task is impossible!

There is an easy way to determine whether all the zeros in googolplex can be written out. How many atoms are there in the entire universe?
You just told me that there are 10^{87} atoms in the entire universe.
How many zeros in googolplex?
That's easy! A googol of zeros or 10^{100} zeros.
10^{100} zeros are far more zeros than atoms in the universe. This shows very clearly that you cannot write out all the zeros in googolplex! It is impossible!
Wow!

You can also write googolplex with exponents.
Googolplex $10^{10^{100}}$

This really shows how exponents save time. Instead of spending millions of years trying to write out googolplex, I can simply write $10^{10^{100}}$

Level 1

Match each statement with a choice in the column on the right.

Length of a football field in yards	10^0
Number of millimeters in a meter	10^1
Number of kilograms in 22 pounds	10^6
Millimeters in a kilometer	10^2
Number of stars in the universe	10^3
Number of moons orbiting the Earth	10^{22}

Level 2

Match each statement with a choice in the column on the right.

If you weighed 70 pounds on Earth, how many pounds would you weigh on a neutron star?	10^{3}
Number of molecules in a little more than a cup of water.	10^{9}
If you weighed 37 pounds on Earth, how many pounds would you weigh on the sun?	10^{1}
If your weight on Earth is 150 pounds, how many pounds would you weigh on Pluto?	10^{4}
How many cubic millimeters in a cubic meter?	10^{25}
The weight of a grain of sand on Earth is 1/1,000,000 of an ounce. How many pounds does a grain of sand weigh on a neutron star?	10^{13}

Level 3

1) If there are 10^{18} molecules in one grain of sand, how many molecules are there in all 10^{20} grains of sand on Earth?

2) It has been estimated that there are 10^{20} grains of sand on Earth and 100 stars in the universe for every grain of sand on Earth.

If it is discovered in the future that there are only 10^{18} grains of sand on Earth, how many stars would there be for each of the 10^{18} grains of sand?

3) Googolplex has 10^{100} zeros and the universe has 10^{87} atoms. If you could turn every atom in the universe into a zero, how many universes would you need to have enough zeros for all the zeros in googolplex?

Einstein

The Richter Scale is used to measure the strength of earthquakes. As the numbers on the scale increase by one, the level of ground shaking increases 10-fold. For example, a magnitude 3 earthquake has 10 times the level of ground shaking as a magnitude 2 earthquake. This also means that a level 4 earthquake would have 100 times the level of ground shaking as a level 2 earthquake.

The amount of energy released as the Richter Scale climbs is different from the increase in ground shaking. Each whole number increase in the Richter Scale means 32 times as much energy would be released. A magnitude 3 earthquake releases 32 times the energy of a magnitude 2 earthquake. This also means the energy released from a magnitude 4 earthquake would be 32 x 32 = 1024 times the energy released from a magnitude 2 earthquake.

If a magnitude 1 earthquake releases the energy equivalent of 6 ounces of dynamite, how much dynamite would you need to detonate to release the energy equivalent of a magnitude 8 earthquake?

Chapter 13

The Strange Medical Test

Amyotrophic Lateral Sclerosis, or ALS, is a very serious disease that causes muscle weakness and atrophy. The disease, which affects 1 in every 10,000 people in the United States, eventually leads to an inability of the brain to control the muscles of the body.

ALS is commonly referred to as "Lou Gehrig's Disease" because it was the cause of death of the famous baseball player.

A blood test for ALS is not currently available, but for our discussion, we will pretend that a blood test has been developed that will identify those with ALS with an accuracy rate of 99.9%. This means that if the tested person does not have ALS, the test will be negative 99.9% of the time. Also, if the test is given to those with ALS, it will be positive 99.9% of the time. (When testing for diseases, negative means the disease does not appear to be present and positive results mean that the disease does appear to be present.)

Our test for ALS is now given randomly to 10,000 people across the United States and unfortunately our volunteer shown below has tested positive for ALS. What is the probability that our volunteer has ALS?

Before we get to the answer, look at the following situation.
There is a disease that only one person in the entire world has. The blood test for the disease is 99.9% accurate. If you test positive for the disease, what is the probability that you have the disease?
Now I see what is going on. There will be a large number of "false positives". There will be 1 in 1000 people who test positive, but do not have the disease.
Your chance of having the disease is still very small even though you test positive for the disease because only one in six billion people have the disease.

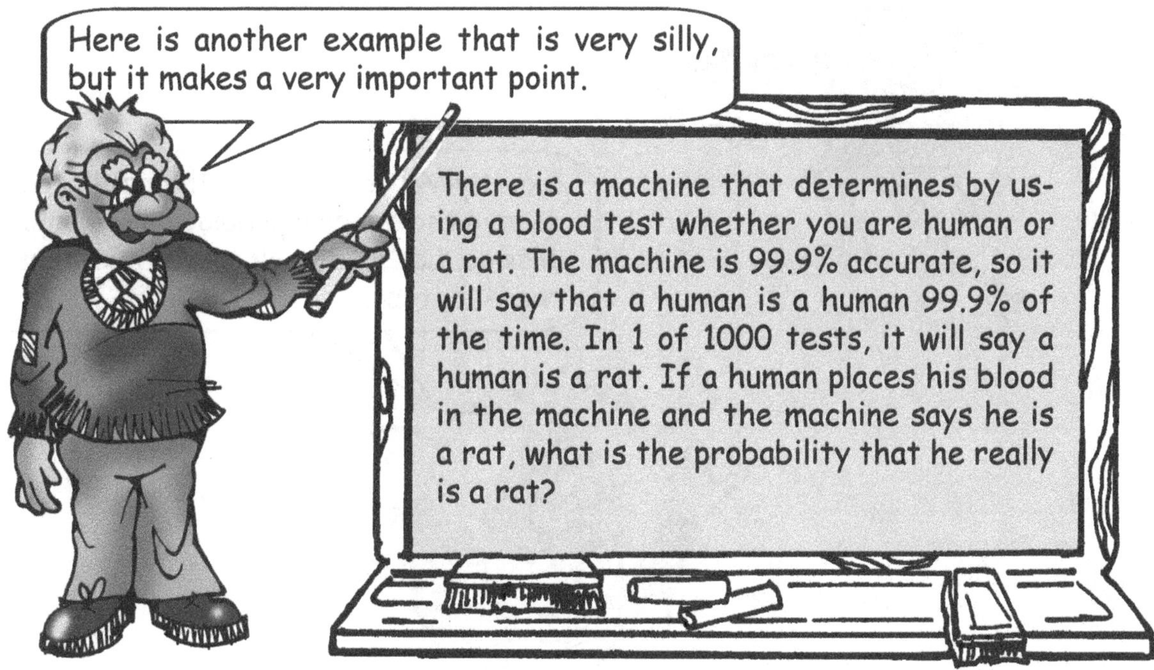
Here is another example that is very silly, but it makes a very important point.
There is a machine that determines by using a blood test whether you are human or a rat. The machine is 99.9% accurate, so it will say that a human is a human 99.9% of the time. In 1 of 1000 tests, it will say a human is a rat. If a human places his blood in the machine and the machine says he is a rat, what is the probability that he really is a rat?

Let's take a group of 10,000 people that we selected at random and test them for ALS. Because the test correctly identifies people without ALS 99.9% of the time, 999 out of 1000 tests accurately say that the person does not have ALS. But the test also identifies a healthy person as having ALS 1 out of 1000 tests.

Because 1 out of 1000 people are incorrectly told they have the disease, our group of 10,000 people will have 10 healthy individuals who the test says have ALS.

Because we know that ALS occurs at a rate of approximately 1 out of 10,000 people, there should be one person in this group of 10,000 who does have the disease. (Statistically speaking)

Using this information, we know that approximately 11 in 10,000 people will test positive for ALS, but only one person in this group really does have the disease.

Group of 10,000

Healthy but tests positive for ALS	Healthy but tests positive for ALS
Healthy but tests positive for ALS	Healthy but tests positive for ALS
Healthy but tests positive for ALS	Healthy but tests positive for ALS
Healthy but tests positive for ALS	Healthy but tests positive for ALS
Healthy but tests positive for ALS	Healthy but tests positive for ALS
Really does have ALS	

ANSWER to the question: The probability of having ALS after testing positive is 1 in 11. Before the test, each person tested had a 1 in 10,000 chance of having the disease. The people who tested positive now have a 1 in 11 probability of having ALS. Although a 1 in 11 probability is still very worrisome, it is much better than having a 99.9% probability of having the disease!!

Remember, there is not currently a test for ALS. We pretended that there was to explain statistics relating to medical tests.

Level 1

1) If a test has a reliability of 99.9% and 1000 people are tested, approximately how many receive incorrect results?

2) If a test has a reliability of 80% and 1000 people take the test, approximately how many will be given incorrect results?

3) There is a test that has been developed that will identify those with a certain disease with an accuracy rate of 99.9%. This means that if the tested person does not have the disease, the test will be negative 99.9% of the time. Also, if the test is given to those with the disease, it will be positive 99.9% of the time. (The disease affects 1 in every 10,000 people.)

Person A is randomly selected for the test and tests positive.

Person B goes to his doctor to be tested because he has symptoms of the disease. He also tests positive.

Do both people have a 1 in 11 chance of having the disease? Why or why not?

Level 2

1) A doctor performs a routine test on a symptom-free individual that is 99% accurate. (99% of healthy people test negative and 99% of sick people test positive.) The doctor also knows that 1% of the population has this disease. If the individual tests positive, what is the probability he has the disease?

2) A disease occurs at the rate of 1 in 100 people. A test for the disease is 95% accurate. (95% of healthy people test negative and 95% of sick people test positive.) An individual is selected at random, tested for the disease, and tests positive. What is the probability that he has the disease?

3) Let us assume that 5% of the population uses illegal drugs. A person is picked at random and given a drug test that is 98% accurate. (98 out of 100 who do not use illegal drugs test negative and 98 out of 100 who do use illegal drugs will test positive.) If this person tests positive for illegal drug use, what is the probability he really does use illegal drugs?

Level 3

Questions 1-3 refer to the following:

A blood test for Disease X has a 99.9% reliability. This means that 99.9% of healthy people test negative and 99.9% of sick people test positive. We also know that 1% of people have Disease X.

1) If 1,000,000 people are tested for Disease X, how many can we predict will test positive for the disease?

2) If 1,000,000 people are tested for Disease X, how many can we predict will test negative?

3) Predict how many of the 1,000,000 were given incorrect results?

Einstein

A medical test has a reliability of 99.99% for a disease that occurs in the general population at a rate of 1 in 10,000. What is the probability that a randomly selected individual who tests positive for the disease has the disease?

Chapter 14
Sometimes Probabilities Can Fool you

Well the answer is fairly obvious.....
Be very careful Einstein!! The obvious answer is not always correct.
?
E=M
E²=MC
E=M²C

Oh, I see what is going on. My brain tried to fool me! The answer is not $\frac{1}{2}$. To solve this problem, we need to see how many combinations there are for Rat's two children.

BOY BOY
BOY GIRL
GIRL GIRL
GIRL BOY

Because we know that Rat has at least one boy, only three of the combinations are possible.

BOY BOY
BOY GIRL
~~**GIRL GIRL**~~
GIRL BOY

The three remaining combinations have only one where Rat's other child is a boy. The probability that Rat's other child is a boy must be 1/3.
BOY BOY
BOY GIRL
GIRL BOY
How about a little credit for stopping your flawed thinking!

Level 1

1) If you roll a pair of dice, what is the probability that both will be the same number?

2) If you roll a pair of dice, what is the probability that you will get a pair of sixes?

3) If a couple has three children, what is the probability that they will all be boys?

Level 2

1) Monica flipped a coin 4 times and it was heads each time.

Monica knew that it is very difficult to get five heads in a row.

$$\frac{1}{2} \times \frac{1}{2} \times \frac{1}{2} \times \frac{1}{2} \times \frac{1}{2} = \frac{1}{32}$$

From this information, Monica determined that there was a 1/32 chance of flipping a head on her next coin toss. Is Monica's thinking correct? Why or why not?

2) The State of Iowa has a lottery in which the player picks three numbers from 0 to 9. In this game, each number you pick can be any number from 0 to 9. Here are some sample picks:

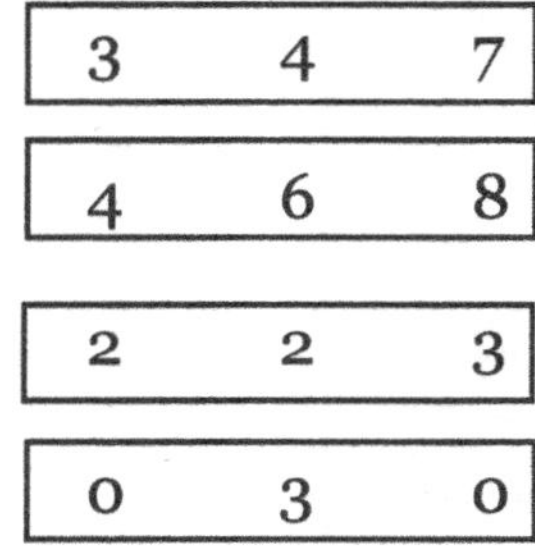

If your numbers match the winning numbers in the exact order, you win $600.

What is the probability of winning this game if you buy one ticket?

3) Rolling five dice and getting all the same number is a very high scoring roll in a game called Yahtzee. What is the probability of rolling five dice and getting all the same number?

Level 3

1) The Iowa Lottery offers a game where the player must pick five different numbers from 1 to 39. The player cannot pick the same number twice. The player must then pick one "hot ball number" from 1 to 19.

Sample ticket:

2	5	7	18	38	7 (Hot ball number)
1	10	15	16	39	10 (Hot ball number)

To determine the winning combination, five ping pong balls are picked from a box containing 39 ping pong balls. (Each numbered from 1 to 39.)

Then one extra ball – the hot ball – is picked from a box containing 19 ping pong balls. (Each numbered from 1 to 19.)

The order picked for the five ping-pong balls does not matter.

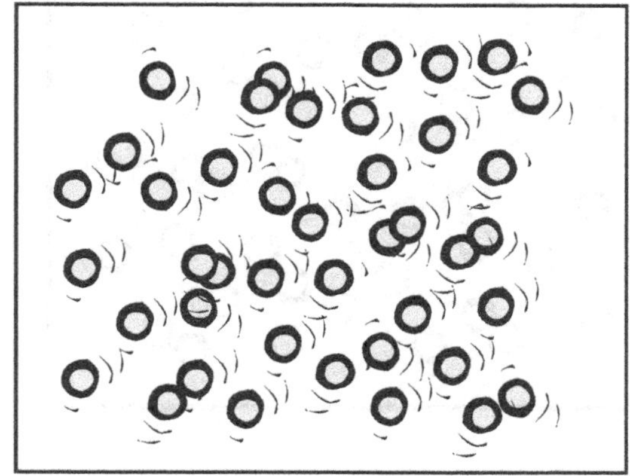

Box with balls 1-39

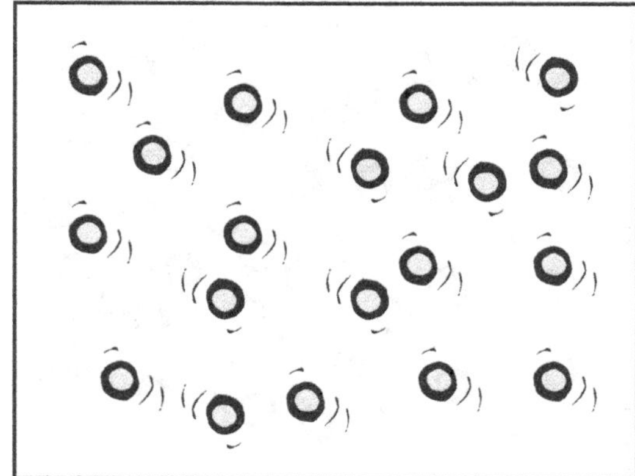

Box with balls 1-19

To win the lottery, you must have all five numbers correct plus the correct "hot ball". What is the probability of winning this lottery?

2) There is a lottery that is played in several states called Powerball. To play this lottery, the player must pick five different numbers from 1 to 55.

The player cannot pick the same number twice. For example:

(3, 7, 15, 18, 54) is okay

(3, 9, 13, 51, 13) is not allowed because 13 was picked twice.

After the five different numbers are picked, the player must pick a Powerball number from 1 to 42. (The Powerball number is allowed to match one of the five numbers the player previously picked.)

To determine the winning combination, five ping-pong balls are picked from a box containing 55 ping-pong balls. (Each numbered from 1 to 55.)

Then one extra ball – the Powerball– is picked from a box containing 42 ping-pong balls. (Each numbered from 1 to 42.)

The order picked for the five ping-pong balls does not matter.

Box with 55 ping-pong balls (1-55)

Powerball (1-42)

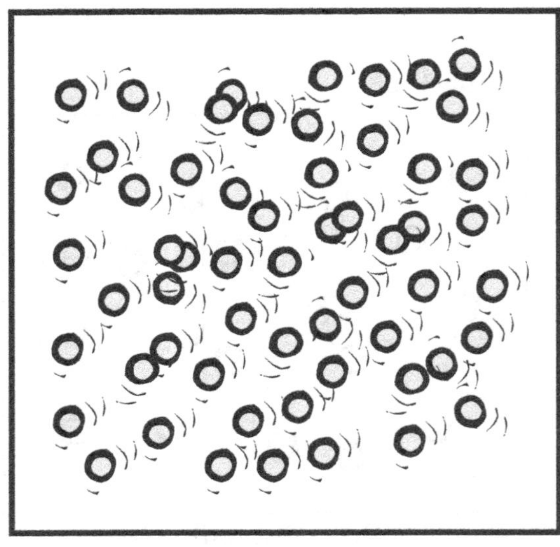

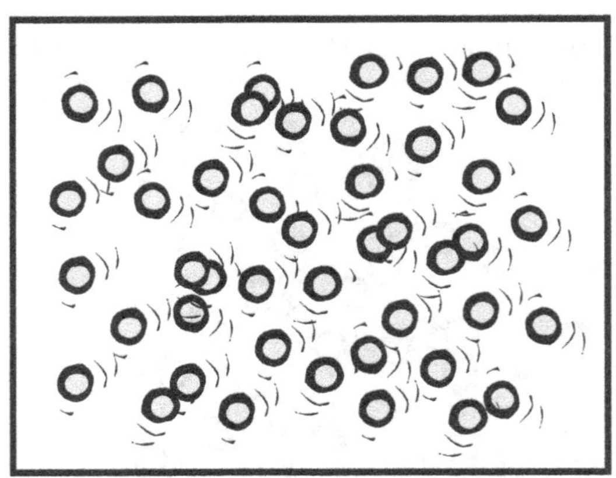

Pick 5 balls

Pick one ball

To win the lottery, you must have all five numbers correct plus the correct "Powerball". What is the probability of winning this lottery?

3) A royal flush is a very rare poker hand. It consists of the ace, king, queen, jack, and the 10 of the same suit. If you are dealt five cards from a standard 52-card deck, what is the probability that you will be dealt a royal flush?

Einstein Level

You meet an old friend and discover that she has three children. You ask her if at least two of her children are boys. She is surprised by the strange question, but answers that yes, at least two of her children are boys.

What is the probability that all three of her children are boys?

Chapter 15
Can I Afford to Buy That House?

Harold is disabled and survives on Social Security checks of $1600 each month. Harold bought a $150,000 house with a loan that carried an interest rate of 8.75%.

Unfortunately, after a few months, Harold could not afford the house payments and the bank took his house. Did Harold make a wise decision buying this house? Why was Harold unable to afford the house payments?

Is there some way to tell how much you can afford to pay each month when you are buying a house?
I was hoping there was an equation or rule you could use to help guide your decision making. It's really sad to get kicked out of your home!

There is a very good rule to use when you are buying a house. Those who follow this rule rarely lose their house. Those who do not follow this rule often get into financial trouble and some lose their home.
Here's the rule.
Rule For Buying a House
Your house payment should not exceed 22% of your gross income.

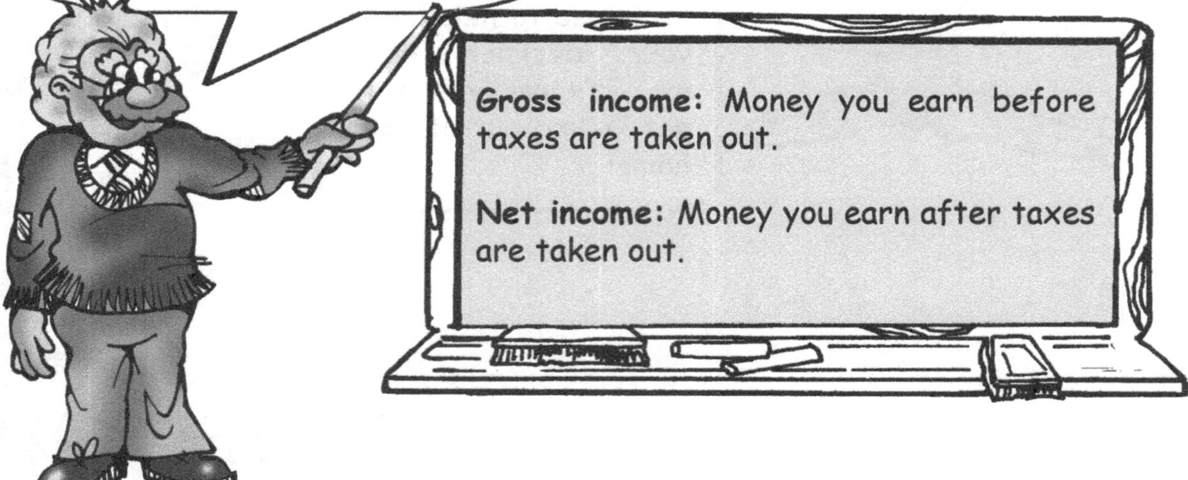
Before we talk about what a house payment is, let's define what gross income is.
Gross income: Money you earn before taxes are taken out.
Net income: Money you earn after taxes are taken out.

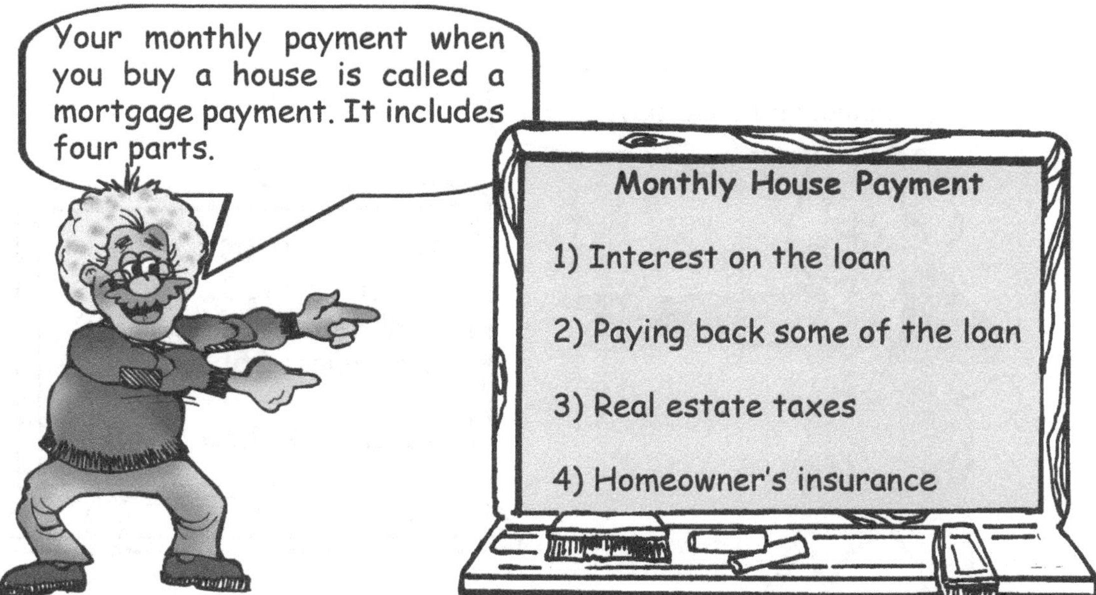

Your monthly payment when you buy a house is called a mortgage payment. It includes four parts.
Monthly House Payment
1) Interest on the loan
2) Paying back some of the loan
3) Real estate taxes
4) Homeowner's insurance

Let's look at Harold's loan and see if we can see why he had problems.

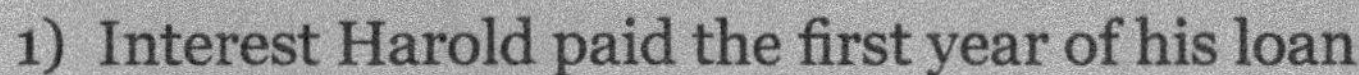

1) Interest Harold paid the first year of his loan.

The interest payment is the bank's charge to use the $150,000 for a year.

8.75% of 150,000 *.0875 x $150,000 = $13,125*

$13,125 ÷ 12 = $1093.75 each month in interest charges

2) Paying back some of the loan.
(This is called paying the principal.)
The interest payment is the bank's charge to use the $150,000 for a year. Harold must also start to pay back the $150,000 loan each month. We will have Harold start by paying $100 each month.

3) Real estate taxes for Harold are $180 each month.
Real estate taxes are taxes that pay for police, fire protection, schools and many other services.

4) Homeowner's insurance costs Harold $55 each month.
Homeowner's insurance is important because it pays for fire damage, tornado damage, theft, etc.

Now we can determine Harold's house payment.
Interest: $1093.75
Principal: $100
Real Estate Taxes: $180
Insurance: $55
Total: $1428.75
Let's see if Harold followed the rule of keeping his house payment below 22% of his gross salary.
22% of $1600 (Harold's monthly income)
.22 x $1600 = $352
No wonder Harold lost his house! He was supposed to limit his house payment to $352 each month, but paid $1428.75 each month!

Just for fun, I am going to see what percent of Harold's income was used for his house payment.
$1428.75 (House payment) ÷ $1600 (Monthly income) = 89%

When buying a house, try to keep your house payment below 22% of your monthly gross income. Harold paid 89% and because he couldn't make his payments, he lost his home.

Level 1

Gross Income: Total wages before taxes are taken out.

Net Income: What you are paid after taxes are taken out.

Remember, your house payment should not exceed 22% of your gross income.
(House payments include payments on the loan, interest, property taxes and insurance.)

1) If Laura earns $3500 each month, what is her upper limit for a house payment each month?

2) Dave earns $72,000 per year. What is the upper limit for his monthly house payment?

3) April bought a house for $180,000. Her monthly costs are listed below:

Insurance: $55
Property taxes: $220
Interest on loan: $1050
Payment of principal: $100

If April's gross pay is $2100 each month, did she keep her loan within the financial safety limit for home loans? Why or why not?

Level 2

1) Lauren was told by a loan officer that her monthly interest and principal payment (combined) on a $220,000 loan would be ½% of the total loan amount.

What was Lauren's monthly interest and principal payment?

2) Warren really wanted to buy a house whose price would mean Warren would have to pay significantly more each month than 22% of his gross salary.

Warren's house payment each month would be $1800 and his gross annual salary was $63,000. What percent of Warren's gross monthly salary is an $1800 house payment?

3) The annual interest rate for Rachel's $140,000 loan is 9%. What does Rachel pay in interest each month on this loan if this is an interest only loan?

Level 3

Remember, your house payment, which includes payments on the loan, interest, property taxes and insurance, should not exceed 22% of your gross salary.

1) Ruben took out a $100,000 loan from a bank with a 5.75% interest rate. Ruben now owes the bank $100,000. Ruben wanted to start paying off the loan, so he paid $4200 to the bank after one year. What is the balance on Ruben's loan at the end of one year? (What will Ruben owe the bank at the end of one year?) *Hint: $350.00 each month does not even pay the interest owed on the loan.*

2) Daniel has an annual gross salary of $51,000. He needs to determine the highest cost house he can afford.

The insurance cost will be $60 per month and property taxes will be $180 per month. Payments on the loan will be $100 each month and the interest rate will be 6%. What is the highest price house that Daniel can afford?

3) Jacob is trying to determine how expensive a house he can afford. Jacob earns $11.50 per hour and works 40 hours per week. The monthly property tax is $100, insurance is $50 each month, and the principal payment will be $75 each month.

Which of the following housing price ranges can Jacob afford if the loan interest rate will be 6%?

a) $40,000 - $50,000

b) $70,000 - $80,000

c) $100,000 - $110,000

d) $110,000 - $120,000

Einstein

Martha borrowed money for a house with an interest rate that can increase each year. The loan also was a special kind of loan where no principal is paid the first few years.

Martha's loan started with an interest rate of 4.5% and then jumped to 9.5% after one year.

Martha stayed in the safety range when the loan was 4.5% annual interest, but when the loan jumped to 9.5% interest, Martha could not make the payments and went bankrupt.

Martha's annual gross salary was $38,400 and her loan was for $102,400. What percentage of Martha's gross salary was the 4.5% loan and what percent of Martha's gross salary was the 9.5% loan?

Property taxes: $2.8\frac{1}{8}\%$ of house price

Insurance: $80 each month

Chapter 16
Why Did the Bank Take My House?

I bought a house for $180,000 and I was making monthly payments of $800. Two years later my monthly payments increased to $1325!

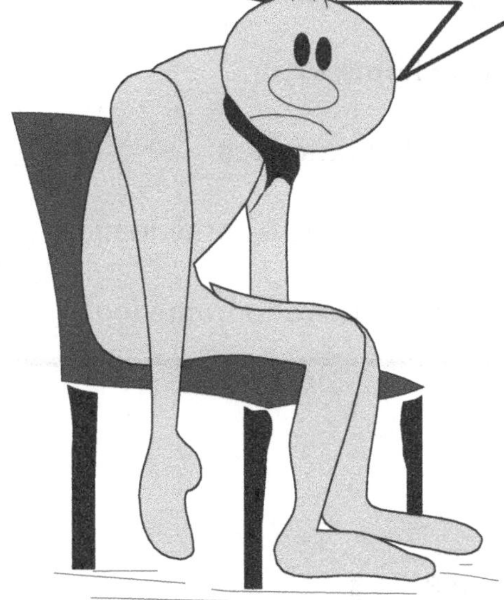

$180,000 Loan

Monthly payments

- Start: $800 per month
- 2 years: $1325 per month
- Now: $2025 per month

I could barely afford the $800 each month and the $1325 is impossible without working two jobs. Now I am told that my monthly payments will increase to $2025. I am going to lose my house! What happened to me?

Before I can explain what happened to this unfortunate homeowner, I need to let you know about four different kinds of loans.

Types of House Loans

1) Fixed-rate home loan

2) Interest-only home loan

3) Variable interest rate home loan

4) Negative amortization home loan

Don't be scared by the fancy names, they are really pretty easy to understand. I am going to rename them so they don't seem so scary.

Types of House Loans

1) Fixed-rate home loan
(My monthly payments stay the same)

2) Interest-only home loan
(I pay only the interest on the loan)

3) Variable interest rate home loan
(The interest rate changes and so do my monthly payments)

4) Negative amortization home loan
(With each payment I make, I owe more)

Fixed-Rate Home Loan

(My monthly payments stay the same)

This kind of loan is the safest kind of loan you can use when you buy a house.

The interest rate stays the same for all the years of the loan so you do not have to worry about your house payment increasing dramatically.

These loans are usually paid back over a 30-year time span. Let's look at a 5% fixed-rate home loan of $100,000 and see what happens.

Fixed-Rate Home Loan of $100,000 at 5% Interest

Interest for first year: 5% of $100,000 = $5000

Monthly interest payment: $5000 ÷ 12 = $416.67

Monthly principal payment: $100

(Remember that the principal payment is used to start paying back the $100,000 that you owe.)

As you can see, after one year we have paid some of the loan back to the bank. The $100,000 that we owed the bank will be approximately $98,800 after year one. The entire $100,000 that we owe will gradually drop to zero over the 30 year life of the loan.
M
Amount owed at start : $100,000
Amount owed after one year:
$100,000 - $1200 = $98,800

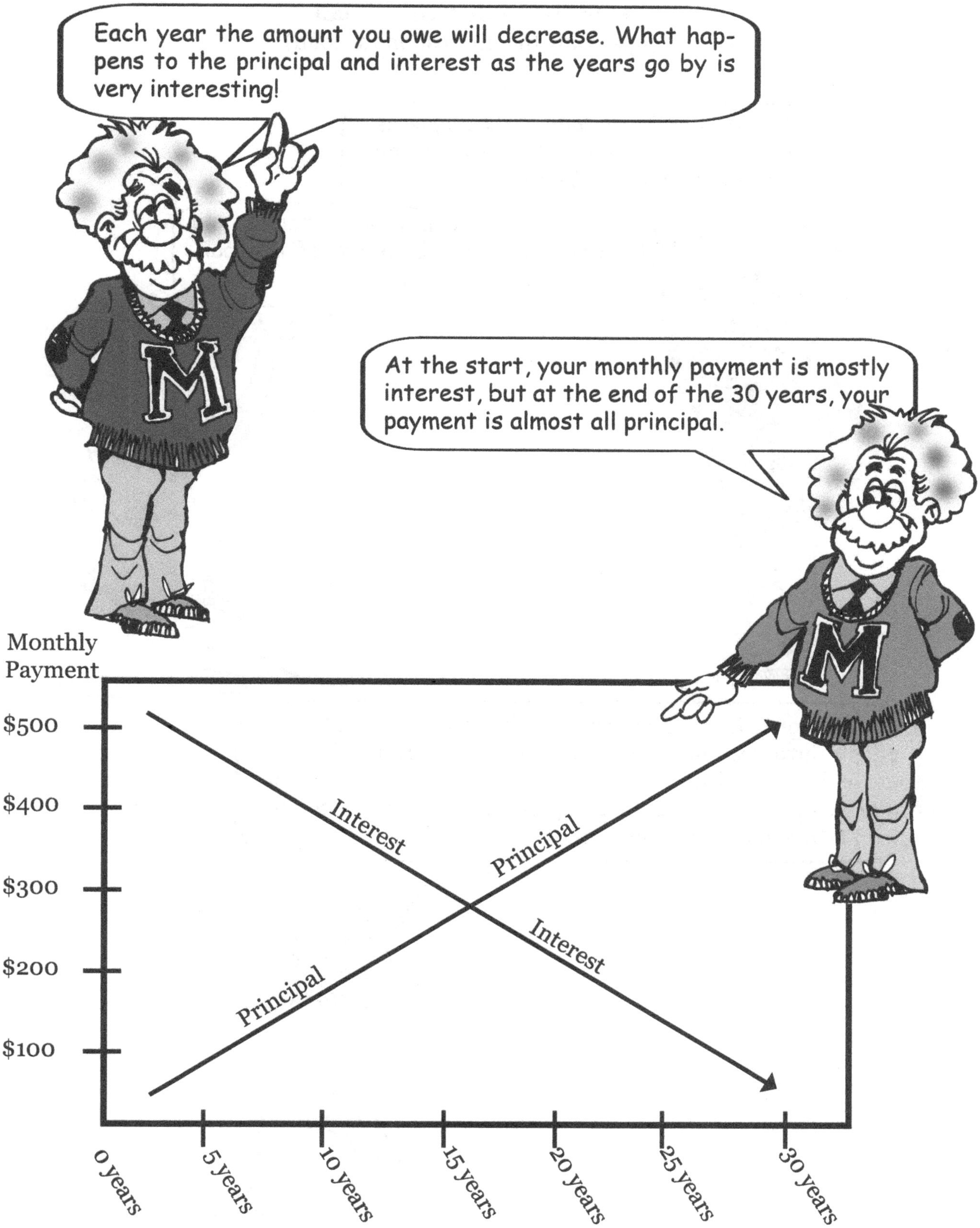

Each year the amount you owe will decrease. What happens to the principal and interest as the years go by is very interesting!

At the start, your monthly payment is mostly interest, but at the end of the 30 years, your payment is almost all principal.

Interest-Only Home Loan

(I pay only the interest on the loan)

This kind of home loan is as simple as its name. You only pay the interest on the money that you borrow.
Because you pay no principal, you will never pay back any of the loan. How does that work?

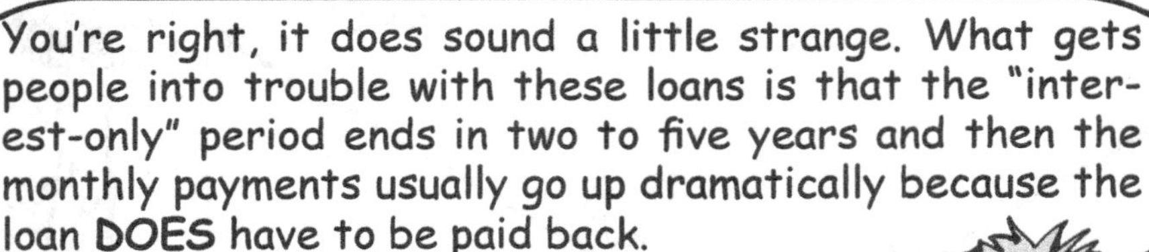

You're right, it does sound a little strange. What gets people into trouble with these loans is that the "interest-only" period ends in two to five years and then the monthly payments usually go up dramatically because the loan DOES have to be paid back.

The following example will show you how dangerous these loans can be.

Two years ago, Nancy and Rich found their dream home. They signed an interest-only loan for the $290,000 they needed to buy the house. With the interest rate set at 7.25%, their monthly interest payment was $1752.

The interest-only period is now ending and they are terrified. Not only do they have to start paying principal, but the interest rate on the loan is jumping to 12.25%!

By the way, home loans are called mortgages.

New Monthly Payment

Annual interest at :
12.25%: .1225 x $290,000 = $35,525

Monthly interest: $35,525 ÷ 12 = $2960

Principal payment: $250

Total monthly payment: (Without taxes and insurance) $2960 + $250 = $3210

Unfortunately, Nancy and Rich will probably lose their dream home.

Part of most interest-only loans is an interest rate that changes. This is what led to Rich and Nancy's home loan nightmare. Let's talk a little more about changing interest rates.

Variable Interest Rate Home Loan

(The interest rate changes and so do my monthly payments)

Variable rate loans are loans where the interest rate does not stay the same. (Like it does on fixed-rate home loans where the interest rate is the same for 30 years.)

Can the interest rate drop instead of climb?

The interest rate can drop, but it rarely does. Variable rate loans typically start with a low interest rate so buyers can afford to buy a house, but then the rates climb.

Shouldn't loan companies and people who use these loans look at what the payment will be at the higher interest rate to judge whether it is wise to buy a house?

You would think so, but loan companies make thousands of dollars when they make a loan so they sometimes ignore the fact that people will not be able to afford the house they are buying when the interest rate increases.

Also, the people taking out the loan often don't understand the loan or develop wishful thinking about their ability to make payments on the loan.

Just for fun I made a chart with interest payments each month for different interest rates when $250,000 is borrowed. I am shocked at how high the monthly payments go when interest rates increase.

$250,000 Loan	
Interest Rate	Monthly Payment (interest only)
1%	$208
2%	$417
4%	$833
6%	$1250
8%	$1667
10%	$2083
12%	$2500

If you took out a loan at 4% interest, your monthly interest payment would be only $833.

If the interest rate climbed to 12%, it would be quite a shock to have to pay $2500 interest each month!!

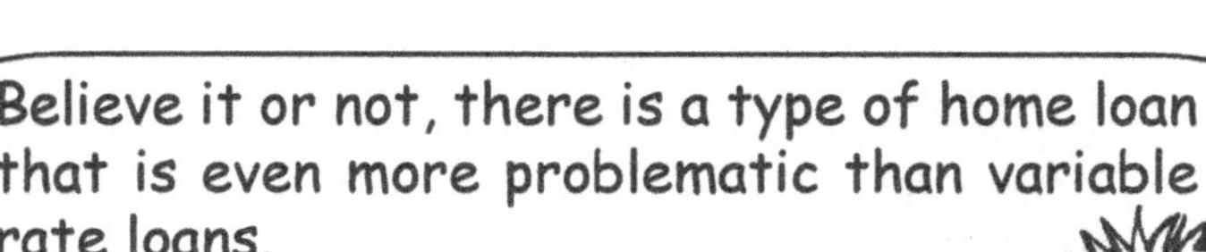

Believe it or not, there is a type of home loan that is even more problematic than variable rate loans.

Negative Amortization Home Loan

(With each payment I make, I owe more)

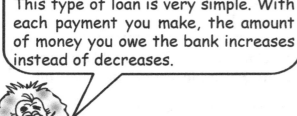

Don't be scared by the fancy name. This type of loan is very simple. With each payment you make, the amount of money you owe the bank increases instead of decreases.

How in the world can that happen?

Let's say you take out a loan for $100,000 at 6% interest. This means the annual interest you will pay is 6% of $100,000 or $6000.

I see that. I also remember that there are two parts of a loan payment----the interest payment and the principal payment. (There are also insurance and tax payments, but we will ignore them for now.)

• Interest Payment
• Principal Payment
(Paying back the loan)

For a normal loan, we would pay interest each month. $6000 ÷ 12 = $500 payment each month. We would also pay some of the principal, so the $100,000 we owed would get smaller each year. A typical payment on principal for this loan would be $200.

Amount of principal paid in one year:
12 x $200 = $2400

Amount of interest paid in one year:
12 x $500 = $6000

Amount owed at start of year:
$100,000

Amount we owe after one year:
$100,000 - $2400 = $97,600

Let's say that instead of paying $500 each month for the interest owed on the $100,000 loan, that you pay only $200. In a year's time you would have paid 12 x $200 = $2400 of the $6000 that you owed for interest.

I owed $6000 in interest for the year, but I only paid $2400. Who pays the other $3600?

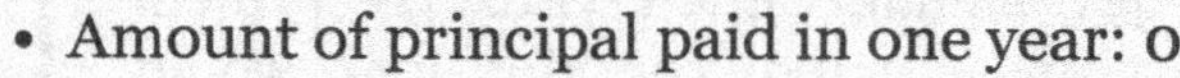

It gets added to the amount you owe on the loan. "With each payment you owe more, not less".

- Amount of principal paid in one year: 0
- Amount of interest paid in one year: 12 x $200 = $2400
- Amount of interest we should have paid in one year, but didn't: $6000 - $2400 = $3600
- Amount owed at start of year: $100,000
- Amount we owe after one year: $100,000 + $3600 = $103,600

That is really scary! I don't think I would ever use that kind of loan.

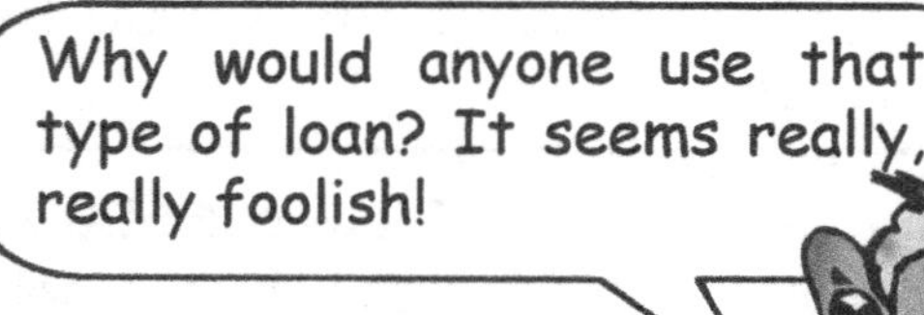

Why would anyone use that type of loan? It seems really, really foolish!

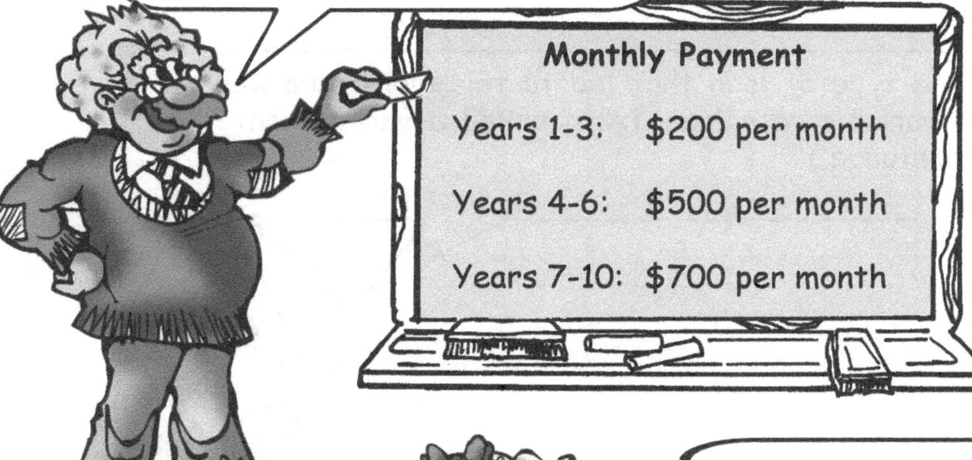

The reason some people use these loans is because the payment is small in the first few years, but then it goes up dramatically.

Years 1-3: $200 per month
Years 4-6: $500 per month
Years 7-10: $700 per month

I guess the only time to use this kind of loan is if you are sure your salary is going to increase dramatically in a few years.

That's right, but a large number of people use this type of loan because they can't afford higher loan payments and they really want to buy a house. They then get into a real financial bind and lose the house because they can't afford the payments when they increase.

Now let's look at why the unfortunate homeowner had his house payments increase so much that he was unable to pay and lost his home.

The type of loan that led to this nightmare was a variable-rate loan. (Also called a variable-rate mortgage.)

Monthly Payments for a $180,000 Loan

	Interest	Principal	Property Taxes	Insurance	Total
Start:	$600	$0	$150	$50	$800
2 years:	$1125	$0	$150	$50	$1325
Now:	$1525	$300	$150	$50	$2025

The first year the interest rate was 4%. In two years it went to 7.5%. The final increase to $2025 each month happened because the interest rate climbed to 10.5% and the principal had to start being paid back.

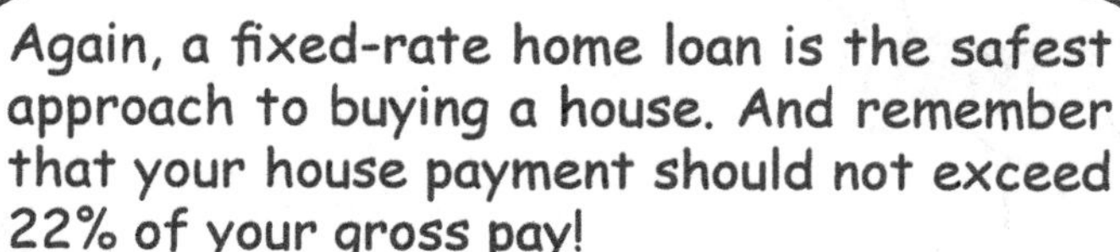

Again, a fixed-rate home loan is the safest approach to buying a house. And remember that your house payment should not exceed 22% of your gross pay!

We will ignore the monthly insurance and tax payments in this chapter's questions.

Oh no! I love that part.

Okay, but they will make the problems more tedious.
E=m
E2=mc
E=m2c

Oh---Sorry. We can ignore the tax and insurance payments.

Level 1

1) What is the monthly interest payment for an interest-only loan of $240,000 at 8% annual interest?

2) If the annual interest rate is 8%, what is the monthly interest rate?

3) If the annual interest charge for a $280,000 loan is $25,200, what is the annual interest rate?

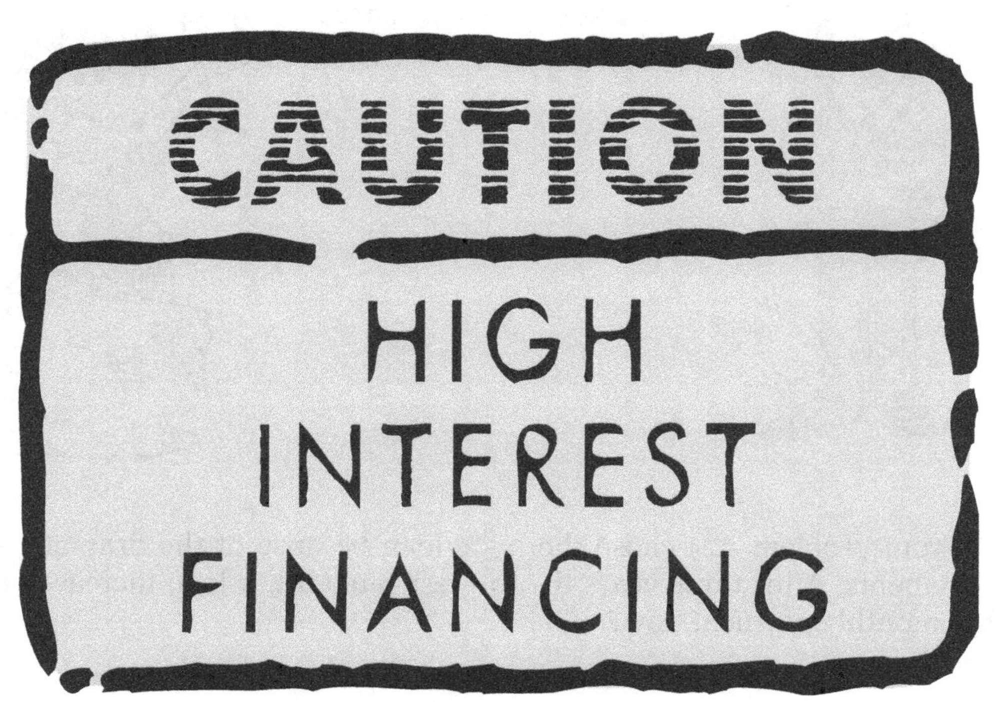

Level 2

1) Steve had a good credit rating so he was able to borrow $180,000 at an interest rate of 5.75%. Jasmine had a lower credit rating so her interest rate for a $180,000 loan was 7%. How much more does Jasmine pay in interest charges each month than Steve pays?

2) Laura is trying to decide between a 6.75%, fixed-rate loan and an interest-only, variable rate loan that charges 3.5% interest the first three years. If the loan will be for $240,000, how much money will she save each month with the interest-only loan during those three years?

The principal payment for the fixed-rate loan will be $100 each month.
Remember, variable rate loans are ones whose interest rates can go up.

3) Laura (From problem #2) chose the 3.5% loan because of the dramatic savings in monthly payments. After three years the interest rate on her loan increased to 10.75%. What is her monthly payment now?

Level 3

1) *Actual Internet Ad*

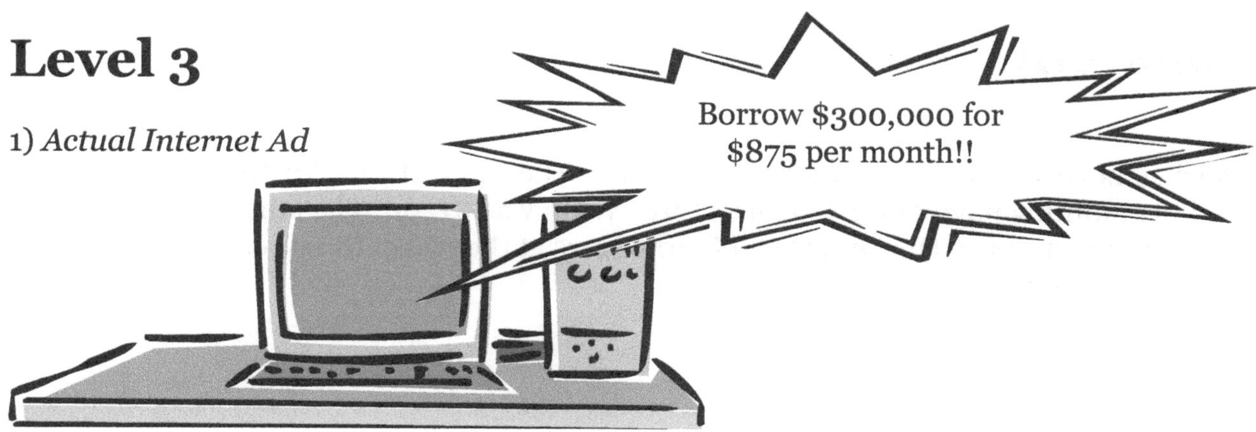

Borrow $300,000 for
$875 per month!!

This ad for a loan was on the internet. In the fine print you will find that the interest rate is 7.5%.

Is this a negative amortization loan? (With each payment I make, I owe more.)

If it is a negative amortization loan, the $300,000 debt will grow each year. What will you owe at the end of the first year?

2) *Actual Internet Ad*

Borrow $500,000 for
only $1498 per month!

If you sign a contract for this loan, the amount you owe will grow with each payment that you make. The amount you owe at the beginning of the loan is $500,000. How much will you owe at the end of one year if the fine print informs you that the interest rate is 8.2%?

3) *Actual Internet Ad*

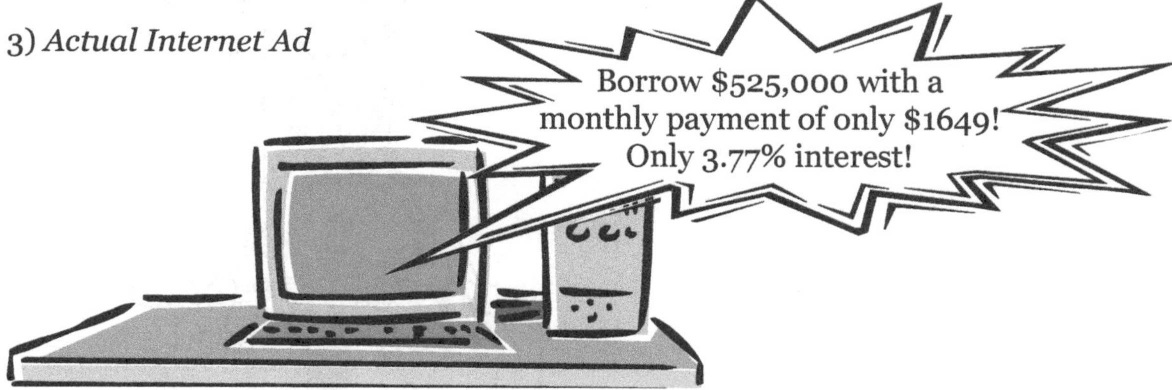

Borrow $525,000 with a
monthly payment of only $1649!
Only 3.77% interest!

The low interest rate for this loan is only good for three months. The interest rate will then increase to 9.25%. What will be the monthly payments after three months?

Einstein

Markus borrowed $400,000 for a new house. The interest rate for the loan was 7.25% and his monthly payment for the first three years was $1200. The amount Markus owed started at $400,000. How much will Markus owe at the end of three years? (Round to the nearest thousand.)

Chapter 17
The True Story of Teenage Drivers

(The names have been changed)

Dr. Jones and his wife always had a hard time balancing protecting their daughter Arlene while at the same time helping her develop independence. Arlene was 16 years old and was always very responsible. She was a talented artist, excellent student, and was known for her infectious smile.

Arlene was excited one Friday afternoon because a boy she knew invited her out for ice cream. Arlene's parents hesitated, but eventually agreed to let Arlene go out for a few hours. They expected Arlene to obey some strict rules that night including not disturbing the young driver, being home by her curfew and wearing her seatbelt.

During the evening trip for ice cream, the young driver lost control of his car and hit a utility pole. Arlene, who was wearing a seatbelt, was killed instantly.

Arlene's heartbroken parents have now spent countless hours trying to lower the number of deaths caused by teenage drivers.

We are going to look at the math and science behind teenage driving to see if teenagers have been unfairly labeled as unsafe drivers.

To do this, we first need to look at the deaths per 100,000 teenage drivers. I have broken these statistics down by state so each teenage driver can predict his or her risk.

Number of auto fatalities each year among drivers aged 16 to 20 per 100,000 teen drivers, according to the National Safety Council and the group End Needless Death on Our Roadways.

District of Columbia -- 127

North Carolina -- 104

Mississippi -- 97

Delaware -- 96

Louisiana -- 96

Nevada -- 95

Florida -- 93

Arizona -- 92

Missouri -- 91

Kentucky -- 90

Georgia -- 90

West Virginia -- 85

Texas -- 83

New Mexico -- 82

Arkansas -- 82

Montana -- 76

Hawaii -- 76

Alabama -- 76

South Carolina -- 74

Tennessee -- 74

South Dakota -- 74

Colorado -- 73

Pennsylvania -- 73

Rhode Island -- 71

Wyoming -- 68

Oregon -- 67

Wisconsin -- 66

Indiana -- 66

Oklahoma -- 65

Idaho -- 65

Maine -- 65

Minnesota -- 62

North Dakota -- 62

California -- 62

Maryland -- 60

Virginia -- 60

Kansas -- 60

Iowa -- 59

Nebraska -- 58

Ohio -- 56

Illinois -- 55

Washington -- 52

Michigan -- 51

Alaska -- 51

Vermont -- 47

Utah -- 45

New York -- 43

Connecticut -- 41

New Jersey -- 40

Massachusetts -- 36

New Hampshire – 36

Nationwide, this works out to approximately 67 deaths per 100,000 teenage drivers.

To show you how dangerous a teenage driver is, look at the number of deaths each year for police officers.

All on-duty deaths for police officers

(Including heart attacks, accidents and other causes.)

20.4 deaths per 100,000 police officers

Even though police deaths make the news, a police officer is not among the most dangerous occupations.

Now let's compare being a teenage driver to some of the most dangerous occupations.

America's Most Dangerous Jobs
(Bureau of Labor Statistics)

**Deaths per 100,000 employed*

Job	Number Of Fatalities	Fatality Rate*
Timber Cutters	105	122.1
Fishermen	52	108.3
Pilots	230	100.8
Structural Metal Workers	47	59.5
Extractive Occupations	69	53.9
Roofers	65	30.2
Construction Workers	288	28.3
Truck Drivers	852	27.6
All occupations		4.3

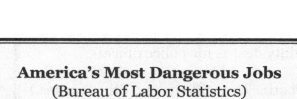

When you look at these statistics, it is clear that 67 deaths per 100,000 drivers is very scary. Why are teenagers such dangerous drivers?

Inexperience of course, but recently the National Institute of Health took brain scans of teenagers' brains and found that they are not fully developed.

The portions of the brain that regulate risk-taking and impulse control were not fully developed. This fact means that the parts of the brain that are crucial for driving are not equipped to properly deal with the challenges of driving.
What can be done?

Many people think raising the driving age to 18 is the proper response to try to lessen the carnage on the roads. The driving age of most countries in Europe is 18 and fatalities are significantly lower there.

It is unlikely that the driving age in the United States will be raised to 18, so many states are enacting Graduated Drivers License Programs to try to lower the number of teenage driving deaths.

Another fact that is pushing states to adopt Graduated Drivers License Programs is that 16 year old drivers crash an astonishing 15 times more often than 20-24 year old drivers!

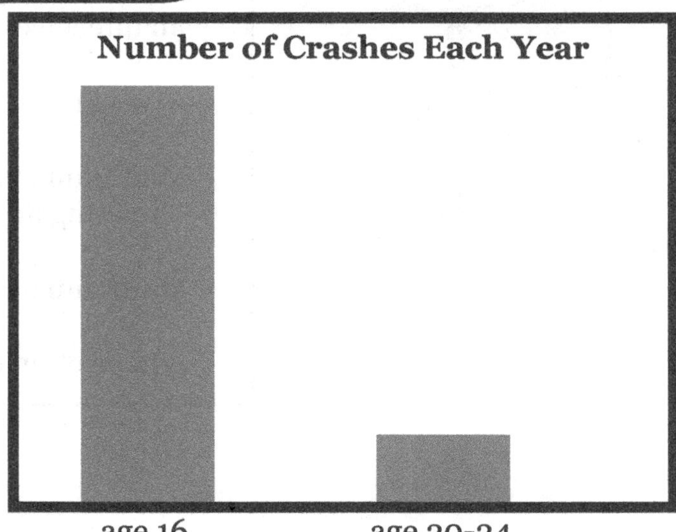

Many teenagers are upset about the restrictions they face under Graduated Drivers License Programs, but these programs really do save lives.

A study by the Center for Disease Control and Prevention found that states with these restrictions had a 20% reduction in fatal crashes.

- Minimum age of 15.5 for obtaining a learner's permit
- Waiting period after obtaining a learner's permit of at least three months before applying for an intermediate license.
- A minimum of 30 hours of supervised driving
- Minimum age of at least 16 years old before obtaining an intermediate license
- Minimum age of 17 years old for full licensing
- A restriction on carrying passengers

The math is a very clear warning
to young drivers ---you must heed
that warning and be very careful!

Level 1

1) If "teenage driver" was an occupation, what rank would it occupy in the list of "America's Most Dangerous Jobs"?

2) There were far more on-the-job deaths for truck drivers when compared to fishermen. Why are fishermen rated as an occupation that is far more dangerous than truck drivers?

3) How many times more likely is it that a roofer will die on the job than the average worker?

Level 2

1) Jillian is a 16 year old driver who did research on the number of accidents in several different age groups. She found that drivers under 20 years of age were involved in 2,490,000 accidents and drivers 35-44 years old were involved in 3,420,000 accidents. She concluded that it was a myth that teenagers are more at risk driving than other age groups. Why is Jillian's reasoning flawed?

2) If you were a teenage driver in Texas, how many times more likely are you to be fatally injured in a car accident than a police officer is likely to die while on duty?

3) If graduated driving licenses were required in all states, the death rate for drivers who are 16-20 years old would drop by close to 20%. The current rate is 67 deaths per 100,000 drivers. Predict what the new rate would be.

Level 3

1) The probability of getting tails with a coin flip: ½

    The probability of rolling a 5 with one die: 1/6

    The probability of a pilot dying while on the job in a one year time span: 1/?

2) The probability of a teenage driver in the District of Columbia dying in a car accident during a one year time span is one in how many? 1/?

3) There were 105 timber cutters who died at work during a one year span. The rate was 122.1 per 100,000. How many timber cutters did not die on the job that year?

Einstein

Jackie is just starting her freshman year of high school in North Carolina. Her high school has 2200 students. In each of the four years Jackie will attend high school, there will be 1500 of the students who will have their driver's license.

Using the statistics on automobile fatalities for drivers aged 16-20, predict how many students in Jackie's high school will lose their lives while driving during her four years of high school.

Chapter 18
Intriguing Math and Science Questions

1) A penny is 1/16 inch thick. If one million pennies are stacked on top of each other, how tall would the stack be?

(a) As tall as a football field is long

(b) The stack would reach the moon

(c) It would be approximately one mile in height

(d) It would be as tall as the Empire State Building

2) At what temperature are Centigrade and Fahrenheit the same?

(a) 100 degrees

(b) Zero

(c) Absolute zero

(d) -40 degrees

3) How many Earths would fit into the sun?

(a) 10

(b) 100

(c) 1000

(d) 1,000,000

4) The weight of a penny on a neutron star is closest to:

(a) Weight of an African Elephant on Earth

(b) Weight of the Empire State Building on Earth

(c) Weight of a person on Earth

(d) Weight of a bowling ball on Earth

5) The amount of time it would take light to travel from one end of our galaxy to the other end:

(Light travels one million miles in a little more than 5 seconds.)

(a) 100,000 years

(b) 10 years

(c) Less than a second

(d) 10 seconds

6) What is the temperature at the center of the Earth? What is the temperature at the center of the sun?

(a) 1000 degrees/one million degrees

(b) 7000 degrees/15,000,000 degrees

(c) -100 degrees/Infinity

(d) 212 degrees/ 10,000 degrees

7) 10^{110} is how many times larger than 10^{10} ?

(a) 100 times bigger

(b) 100 x 1000 times bigger

(c) A googol times bigger

(d) Infinitely bigger

8) 10^6 is how many times larger than 10^{-6} ?

(a) 1,000,000,000,000

(b) 12 times bigger

(c) 36 times bigger

(d) -1 times bigger

Einstein

If light travels 186,000 miles in one second, how long does it take light to travel one inch?

Chapter 19
How People Lie With Statistics

"Through clever and constant application of propaganda, people can be made to see paradise as hell, and also the other way around - to consider the most wretched sort of life as paradise."

- Adolf Hitler

"Propaganda," Goebbels once wrote, "has absolutely nothing to do with truth."

"In a time of universal deceit, telling the truth is a revolutionary act."

- George Orwell

In August of 2003, a television pundit attempted to show that U.S. casualties in Iraq were not as bad as they appeared. He used mathematics to put some perspective on the dangers soldiers in Iraq were facing.

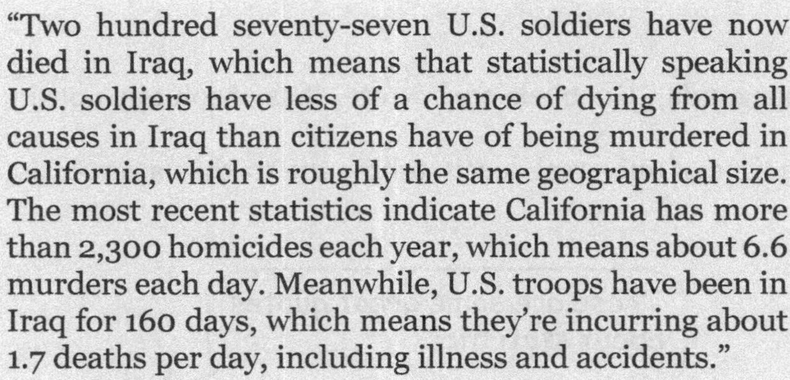

"Two hundred seventy-seven U.S. soldiers have now died in Iraq, which means that statistically speaking U.S. soldiers have less of a chance of dying from all causes in Iraq than citizens have of being murdered in California, which is roughly the same geographical size. The most recent statistics indicate California has more than 2,300 homicides each year, which means about 6.6 murders each day. Meanwhile, U.S. troops have been in Iraq for 160 days, which means they're incurring about 1.7 deaths per day, including illness and accidents."

That is impressive thinking. I guess it IS more dangerous to live in California than to be a soldier in Iraq.

Get me out of California!! I want to go to Iraq where it is WAY safer!

Before you get too excited, look closely at the comparison that is being used.
But they are both about the same size.
They are very similar in size, but I think we need to know how many soldiers are in Iraq and also how many people live in California.

Lets see if you want
to go to Iraq now

U.S. Population in California and Iraq

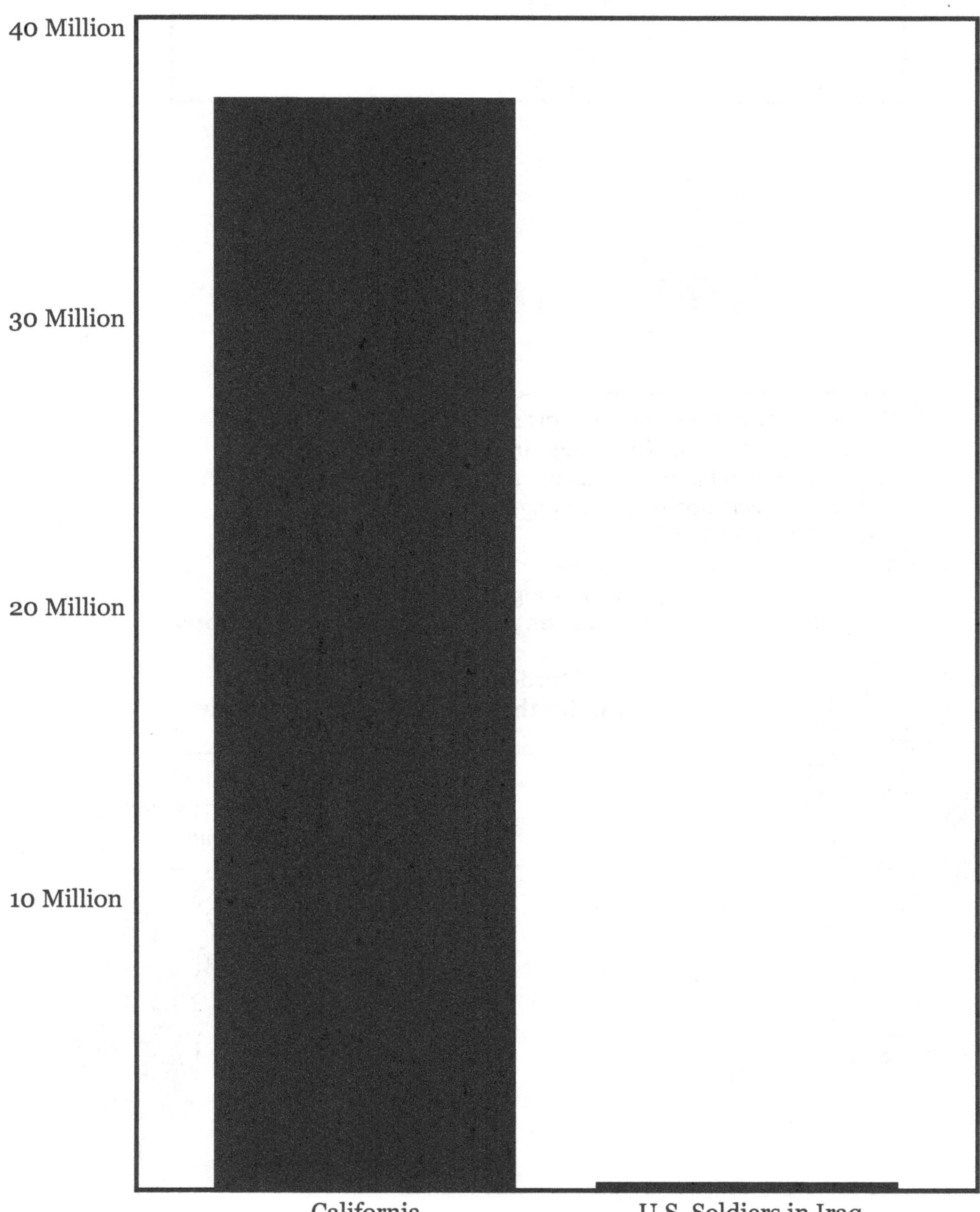

Population of California **36 million** U.S. soldiers in Iraq **150,000**

Of course the television pundit's comparison of U.S. fatalities in Iraq and the number of murders in California was not only meaningless, it was ridiculous!

U.S. troops in Iraq death rate per day:
1.7 deaths per day for 150,000 troops

Murders in California per day:
6.6 deaths per 36,000,000 people

Look at a fair analysis of U.S. troop casualties and murders in California.
M

Now we need to find out how many deaths would occur if there were 36,000,000 U.S. soldiers in Iraq!
We need to multiply 150,000 soldiers by 240 to get to 36,000,000 soldiers.
Now we will multiply the 1.7 daily deaths by that same 240:
1.7 x 240 = **408 daily deaths**

The death rate for U.S. soldiers is comparable to 408 citizens of California being murdered each and every day.

From this information, we can now make a meaningful comparison.

Murder rate California: $\frac{\textbf{6.6 per day}}{\textbf{36,000,000}}$

Deaths U.S. troops from all causes: $\frac{\textbf{408 deaths}}{\textbf{36,000,000}}$

When you look at it fairly, it is very clear that U.S. troop deaths are **62 times higher** than murders in California!!

By the way, when the television pundit was confronted by a reporter for his unfair comparison, he made an interesting statement.
"Admittedly it was a crude comparison, but it was illustrative of something."

I know what it is illustrative of, but I am too polite to say it.

Level 1

1) Death records show that over 99% of the people who voted for Roosevelt in the 1932 election have died. There must be some kind of curse against those who voted for Roosevelt! Fair or unfair? Why?

2) Janelle found that 67% of people who die are in a bed when they die. Janelle now sleeps on a couch. Is there a problem with Janelle's reasoning?

3) Matthew and Brian were twin brothers who were very competitive. They took part in a contest and when their father asked them how they did, Brian stated proudly and accurately:

"I came in second and Matthew came in next to last."

Matthew did better than Brian in the contest, so how could Brian's statement be true?

Level 2

1) The Bureau of Labor Statistics reported in the year 2000 that 852 truck drivers lost their lives while on the job while only 105 timber cutters died at work. Jay decided that he would be a timber cutter instead of a truck driver because truck driving was 8 times more dangerous than being a timber cutter. Is Jay's logic flawed? Why or Why not?

2) Sam is reporting on how the use of safety belts can help reduce hospitalizations after car accidents. He noted that approximately one in six people who were using a safety belt were hospitalized after an accident while one in three unbelted occupants required hospitalization. He used these statistics as evidence that seat belt use helps prevent injuries. Is Sam using statistics fairly?

3) The insurance institute for highway safety reports on driver deaths for different makes and models of vehicles.

The Chevy Astro had only 7 driver deaths per million registered vehicle years while the Lincoln Town Car had 91 driver deaths per million registered vehicle years.

Would these statistics strongly point toward the Chevy Astro as being a vehicle that is safer to drive than a Lincoln Town Car?

Level 3

1) Florida repealed its helmet requirement for motorcyclists on July 1, 2000. The next year "unhelmeted deaths" went up sharply. This fact is being used by those who favor helmet requirements to bolster their case for reinstating the helmet law. Is this a fair use of statistics?

2) A company that sells oats proclaims the cholesterol lowering power of oats in the magazine ad shown below:

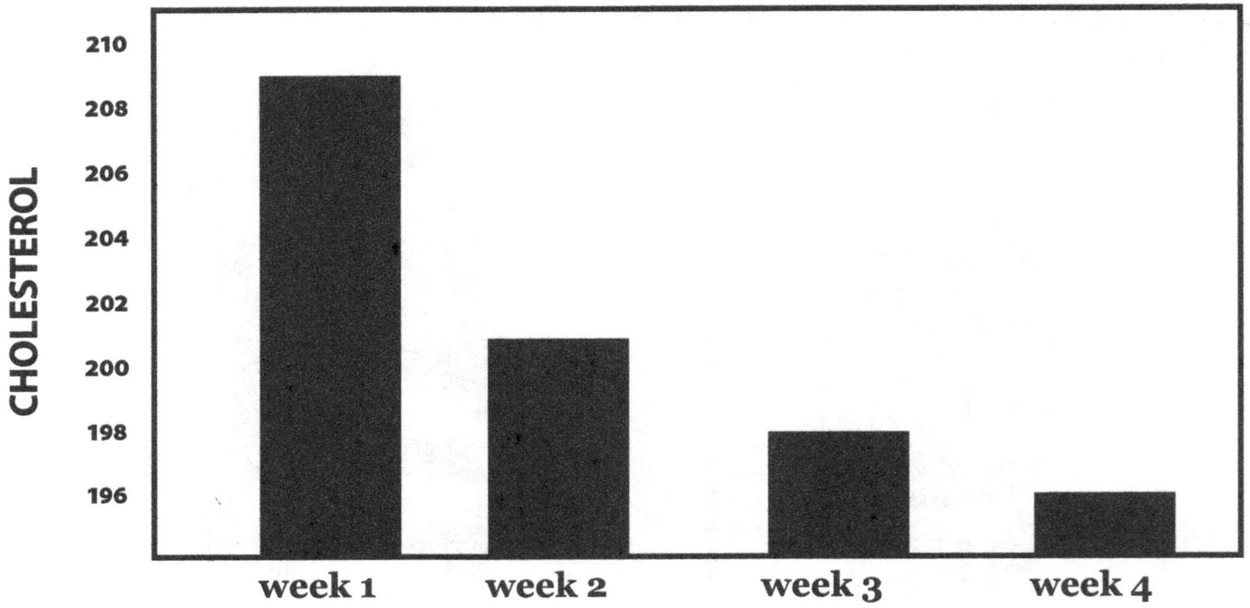

Is this a fair ad? Why or why not?

3) The same oat company mentioned in question #2 attempts to make a 4% drop in cholesterol seem significant by asking if paying 4% more in taxes is significant.

Comment on comparing a 4% drop in cholesterol to paying 4% more in taxes. Look at the information below about a cholesterol lowering drug called Crestor and then comment on the significance of oats causing a 4% drop in cholesterol.

Crestor lowered bad cholesterol by up to 52% in an experiment.
(The placebo lowered cholesterol by 7%.)

Einstein

A new heart medicine was studied (Medicine A). The group that took the heart medicine had .3% of its participants die of fatal heart attacks while the control group had .4% of its participants die of fatal heart attacks.

Another heart medicine was studied (Medicine B). The group that received the new medicine had a 25% lower occurrence of fatal heart attacks than the control group.

Both studies were properly done with thousands of participants. If you are a doctor, which heart medicine would you want for your patients? Why?

Chapter 20
The Power of Interest Rates and Money

How much money do you want to have each year when you retire?
It would be great if I could have $75,000 per year, but I think that is an unrealistic dream. How much money will my $10,000 grow to in 65 years?

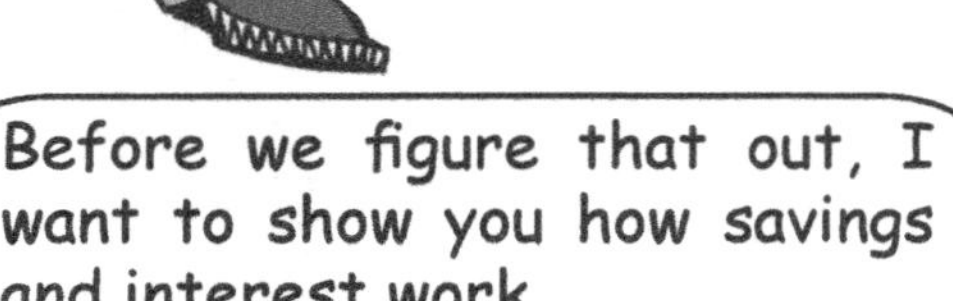
Before we figure that out, I want to show you how savings and interest work.
Look at how much your savings certificate was worth after one year.

Interest in one year: 9% of $10,000
.09 x $10,000 = $900
Savings Certificate now worth $10,900

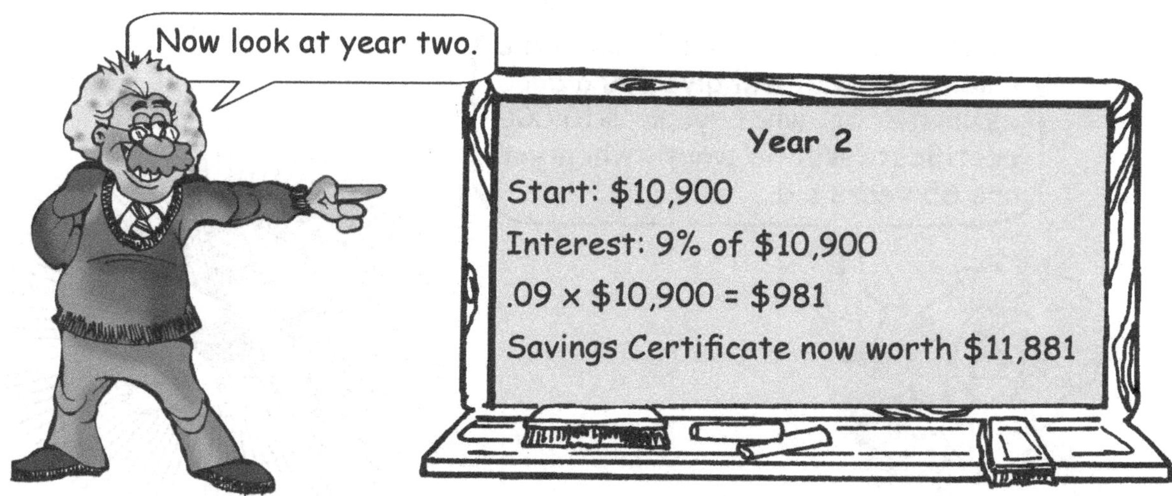

Now look at year two.

Start: $10,900
Interest: 9% of $10,900
.09 x $10,900 = $981

We can take a shortcut to find the new value of your savings certificate by multiplying each year by 1.09. This saves adding the interest each year.

Year 3: 1.09 x $11,881 = $12,950.29

Year 4: 1.09 x $12,950.29 = $14,115.82

Year 5: 1.09 x $14,115.82 = $15,386.24

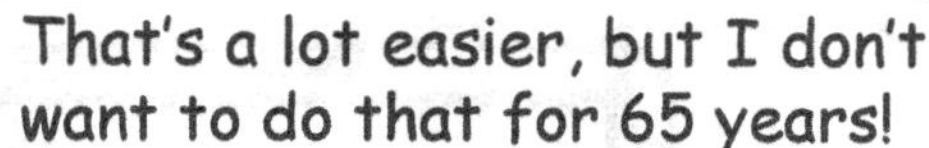

That's a lot easier, but I don't want to do that for 65 years!

There is a very neat trick called the rule of 72 that will give you a good estimate of what your $10,000 certificate will be worth when you are 65 years old.

Rule of
72

Simply divide 72 by your interest rate. That will tell you how many years until your money doubles.
72 ÷ 9 = 8 years
Your money will double in 8 years!

Okay, that seems much easier. I'll just double my $10,000 every 8 years.

Money Will Double Every 8 Years

0 years:	$10,000
8 years:	$20,000
16 years:	$40,000
24 years:	$80,000
32 years:	$160,000
40 years:	$320,000
48 years:	$640,000
56 years:	$1,280,000
64 years:	**$2,560,000**

Wow!

It is amazing how much money grows when left in a high interest savings account.

Let me show you another easier way to see how $10,000 grows in 65 years.

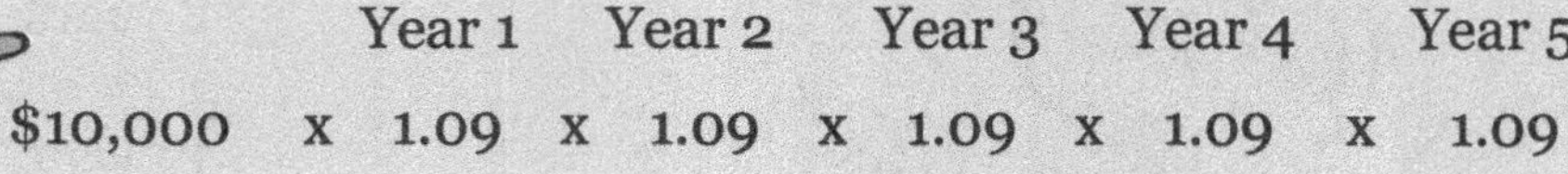

	Year 1		Year 2		Year 3		Year 4		Year 5
$10,000 x	1.09	x	1.09	x	1.09	x	1.09	x	1.09

You can see that you must multiply $10,000 by 1.09 → 65 times. That is the same as...

$$\$10{,}000 \times (1.09)^{65} = \$2{,}708{,}500$$

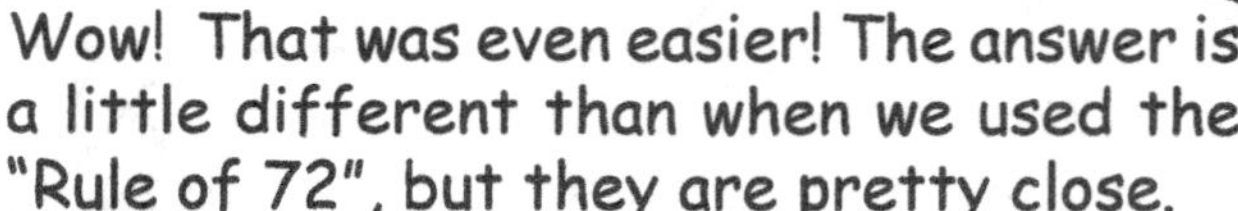

Wow! That was even easier! The answer is a little different than when we used the "Rule of 72", but they are pretty close.

What is interesting about having 2.5 million dollars at the age of 65 is the interest you will earn each year.

.09 x $2,500,000 = $225,000

That is amazing! I never spend any of the 2.5 million dollars and I am paid $225,000 a year. I am going to have a great retirement.

Let's say you wanted to be paid monthly when you retire. Look at how easy it is to determine monthly interest.
Year: .09 x $2,500,000 = $225,000
Monthly: $225,000 ÷ 12 = $18,750
I have really nice grandparents!

Level 1

1) How much interest would be earned if $15,000 was invested for one year at an interest rate of 4%?

2) Barack invested $1000 in the stock market at the age of 18. If the return on his money is 12% each year, how much money will his $1000 grow to by the time Barack retires at age 66? (Approximately)

3) Barack's grandmother put $1000 into the stock market when Barack was born. This money was not to be touched until Barack reaches the age of 66. If the return on the $1000 will be 12% each year, how much will the $1000 grow to when Barack reaches the age of 66?

Level 2

1) How much interest would you earn with a $5000 certificate of deposit at 5% annual interest for 7 months? (Round to the nearest dollar.)

2) How much interest would you earn with a $40,000 certificate of deposit at 11% annual interest for 11 months? (Round to the nearest dollar.)

3) Determine the value of a $100,000 certificate of deposit after three years if the annual interest rate is 6% and the interest is added to the certificate of deposit every year.

Level 3

1) Mitt and Rudy each have $10,000. Mitt invests his money in a savings account that pays 1.5% annual interest. Rudy invests his $10,000 in a certificate of deposit that pays 5.25% annual interest. After 10 years, how much more money will Rudy have than Mitt?

2) Hillary invested $100,000 in a very safe investment that paid 6% interest each year. Dennis invested his $100,000 in a risky investment that he hoped would earn a much higher rate of return. Unfortunately, Dennis lost 5% of the value of his money each year. At the end of 20 years, how much more money does Hillary have than Dennis?

3) Christopher was given a penny on the day he was born, two pennies on his first birthday, 4 pennies on his second birthday, 8 pennies on his third birthday, 16 pennies on his fourth birthday and so on. How much money will Christopher be given on his 65th birthday?

(Amount doubles every birthday.)

Einstein

After their first child was born, a couple immediately put \$3000 into a college savings account and then decided to add \$3000 every year until their child reached the age of 18. Their final payment into the account will be \$3000 on the child's 18th birthday.

If the projected cost of college is \$100,000 and the interest earned is 6% each year, will the couple have enough money when their child reaches the age of 18? How much money will they have? *(Round to the nearest thousand.)*

(The savings account is tax free.)

Chapter 21
Help the Rats Escape

Five teams are sitting at long tables to see what the last challenge will be to determine the winner of a 2007 math challenge. At each of the five tables are boxes with the numbers 1-12 written on the boxes.

Each team also has a cage containing 12 rats.

Your task today is to put the 12 rats into the boxes in whatever distribution you would like.

You can put them all in one box, one in each, two in some, none in some, and so forth. Any distribution you would like.

I will then roll a pair of dice and add the numbers. If you have any rats in that box, one will be set free.

For example, if a 2 and 3 are rolled, then one rat from your box 5 will be set free--if you have any rats in box 5.

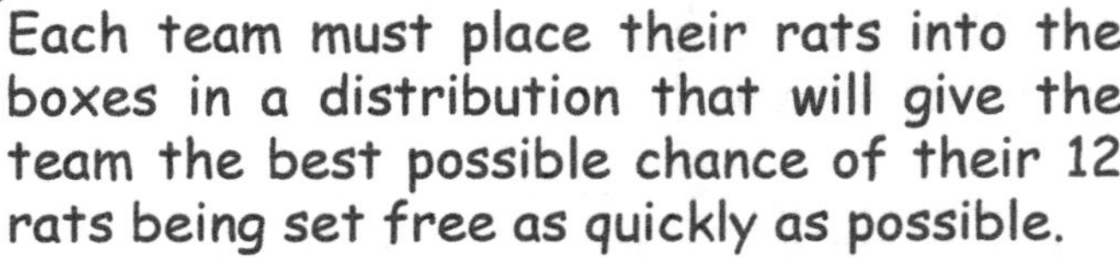

Each team must place their rats into the boxes in a distribution that will give the team the best possible chance of their 12 rats being set free as quickly as possible.

The team who sets their rats free first is the winner of the math competition. Remember that when the dice are rolled and added, each team can only set 1 rat free. (If they have any rats in the right box.)

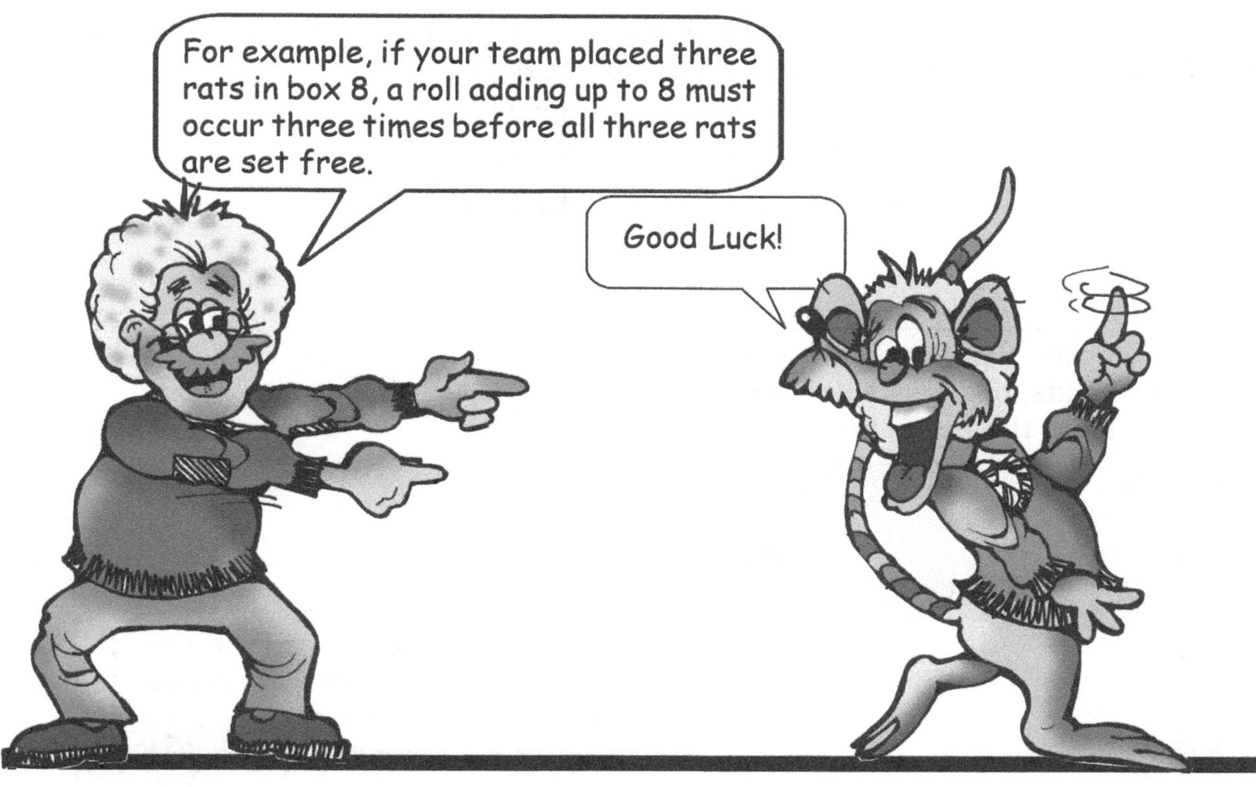
For example, if your team placed three rats in box 8, a roll adding up to 8 must occur three times before all three rats are set free.
Good Luck!

Before we determine mathematically the best way to distribute the rats to give us the best chance of winning, we will look at some other situations.
These will be easier and will help us develop proper thinking.

Situation A

Each team is given 10 rats, which they must place in two boxes. They can distribute the rats in any way they would like between the two boxes.

Heads
Tails
I will flip a coin. If it is heads, one rat is set free from the heads box.
If a team put all their ten rats in the "tails" box, then your flip of heads would not free any of the rats.
How would you distribute the ten rats to give you the best chance of freeing your rats before the other teams free theirs?

5 rats in the heads box and 5 rats in the tails box
or
10 rats in the heads box and zero in the tails box

????????????????????

This game is easy. I can predict mathematically that heads and tails will each be flipped half the time. I will place five rats in each box.
Heads: ½ of 10 = 5
Tails: ½ of 10 = 5
That is correct! This doesn't guarantee that you will win, but it is the best mathematical way to distribute the rats. Now look at a slightly more complicated situation.
A
B
C
D
D
A
C
B

Each team is given 8 rats which they must place in 4 boxes. Again, they can distribute the rats in any way they would like.

The spinner will be spun and whatever letter it lands on will mean one rat can be removed from that numbered box and set free. Whatever team frees all 8 rats first wins.

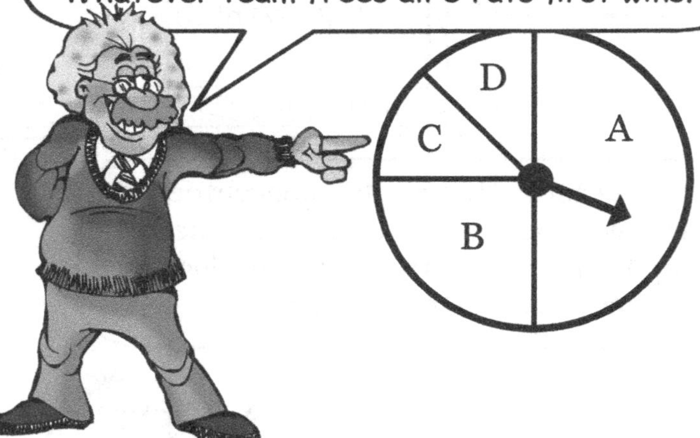

My first thought was to put all the rats in Box A, but I know that is not correct. I'll determine the probability of each letter being pointed to by the spinner.

A is $\frac{1}{2}$ of the circle: 50%

B is $\frac{1}{4}$ of the circle: 25%

C is 1/8 of the circle: 12.5%

D is 1/8 of the circle: 12.5%

Now I can easily determine how to distribute the rats.

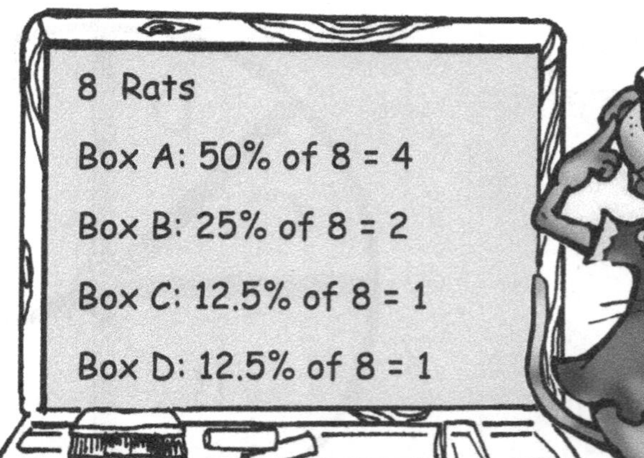

8 Rats
Box A: 50% of 8 = 4
Box B: 25% of 8 = 2
Box C: 12.5% of 8 = 1
Box D: 12.5% of 8 = 1

Again, this does not mean you will definitely win, but it gives you the best possible chance of winning.
A
B
C
D
Now we are ready to look at the math challenge from the beginning of the chapter.
Let's look at all possible outcomes when two dice are rolled.
1-1 2-1 3-1 4-1 5-1 6-1
1-2 2-2 3-2 4-2 5-2 6-2
1-3 2-3 3-3 4-3 5-3 6-3
1-4 2-4 3-4 4-4 5-4 6-4
1-5 2-5 3-5 4-5 5-5 6-5
1-6 2-6 3-6 4-6 5-6 6-6

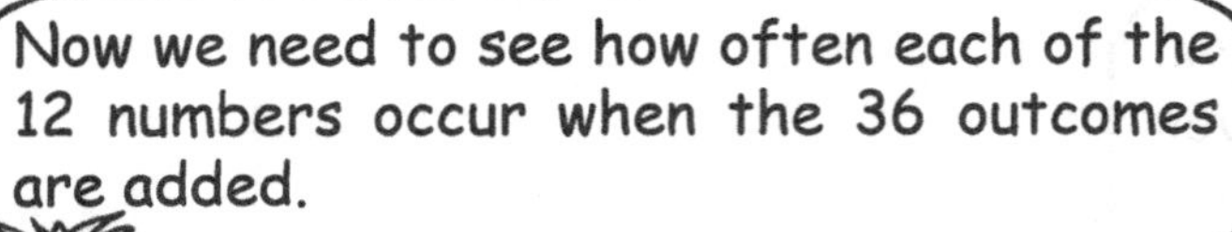

Now we need to see how often each of the 12 numbers occur when the 36 outcomes are added.

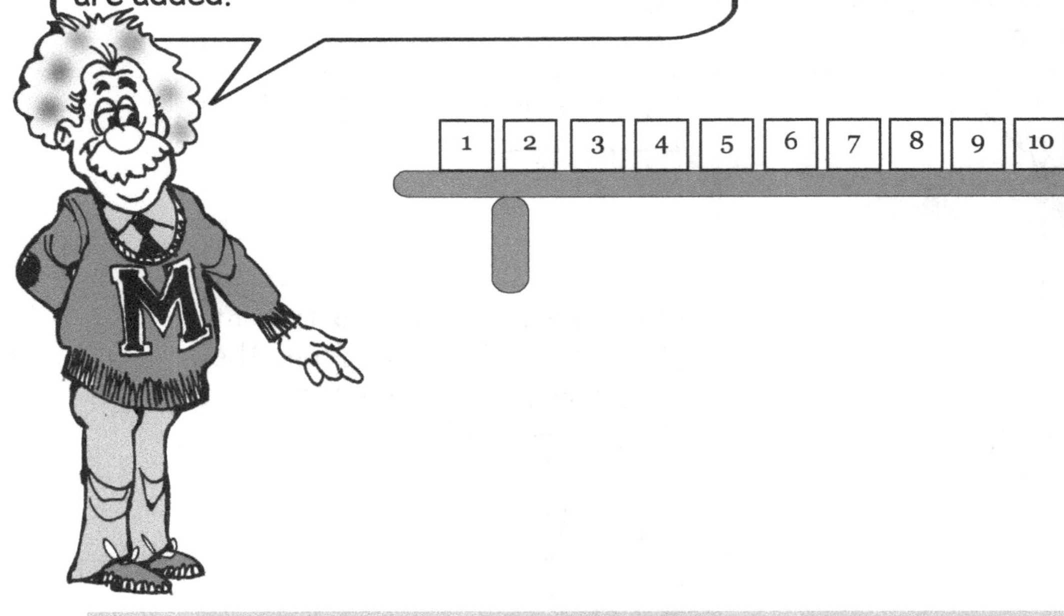

1: Never						
2: 1 of 36	1+1					
3: 2 of 36	1+2	2+1				
4: 3 of 36	1+3	3+1	2+2			
5: 4 of 36	1+4	4+1	2+3	3+2		
6: 5 of 36	1+5	5+1	4+2	2+4	3+3	
7: 6 of 36	1+6	6+1	2+5	5+2	3+4	4+3
8: 5 of 36	2+6	6+2	5+3	3+5	4+4	
9: 4 of 36	6+3	3+6	4+5	5+4		
10: 3 of 36	6+4	4+6	5+5			
11: 2 of 36	5+6	6+5				
12: 1 of 36	6+6					

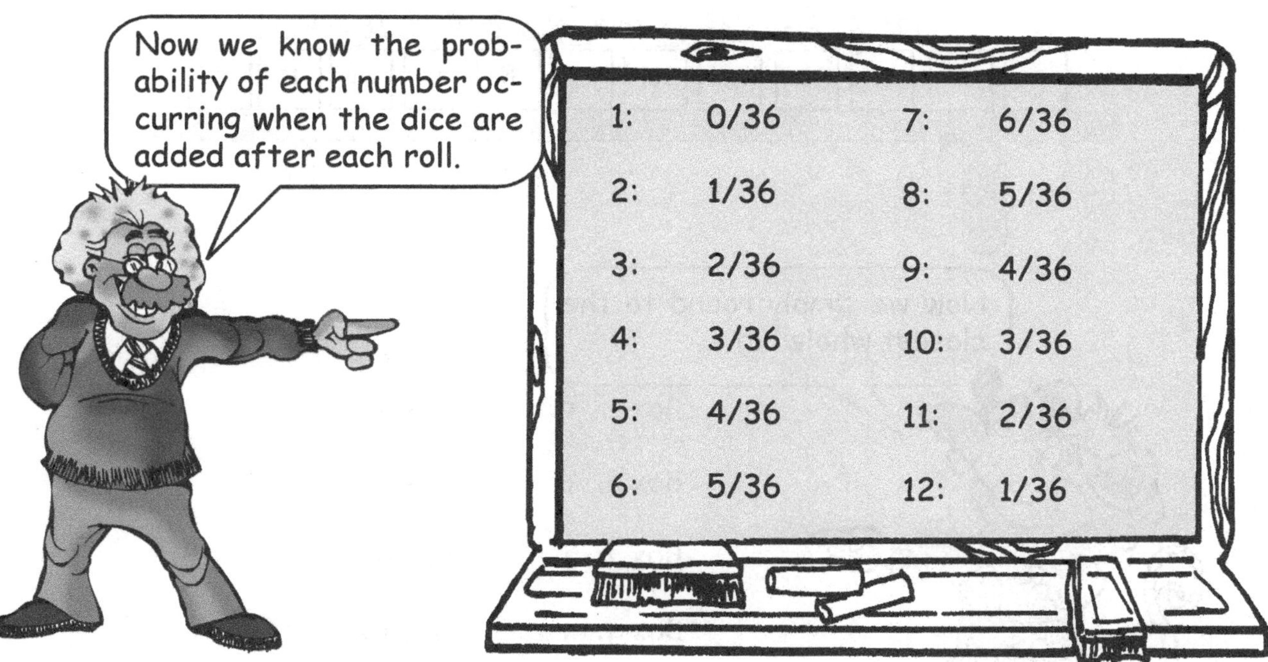

Now we know the probability of each number occurring when the dice are added after each roll.
1: 0/36
2: 1/36
3: 2/36
4: 3/36
5: 4/36
6: 5/36
7: 6/36
8: 5/36
9: 4/36
10: 3/36
11: 2/36
12: 1/36

Because we have 12 rats to place in the boxes, we simply multiply the probability of each number occurring by 12 to find the correct number of rats to place in each box.

Box 1: 0/36 x 12 = 0 rats

Box 2: 1/36 x 12 = 1/3 rat

Box 3: 2/36 x 12 = 2/3 rat

Box 4: 3/36 x 12 = 1 rat

Box 5: 4/36 x 12 = 1.33 rats

Box 6: 5/36 x 12 = 1.67 rats

Box 7: 6/36 x 12 = 2 rats

Box 8: 5/36 x 12 = 1.67 rats

Box 9: 4/36 x 12 = 1.33 rats

Box 10: 3/36 x 12 = 1 rat

Box 11: 2/36 x 12 = 2/3 rat

Box 12: 1/36 x 12 = 1/3 rat

Now we simply round to the closest whole rat.

Box 1: 0	Box 7: 2
Box 2: 0	Box 8: 2
Box 3: 1	Box 9: 1
Box 4: 1	Box 10: 1
Box 5: 1	Box 11: 1
Box 6: 2	Box 12: 0

Good luck! The proper mathematical placement of the rats doesn't mean you are going to win, but it will give you the best possible chance of winning.

Level 1

1) Rolling one die has six possible outcomes. Rolling a pair of dice has 36 possible outcomes. How many possible outcomes are there when three dice are rolled?

2) In the game of Risk, the attacking country usually throws three dice. The best roll would be 6-6-6. What is the probability that the attacking country will roll three sixes?

3) What is the probability the spinner will land on section A?
(The size of A and C are equal.)

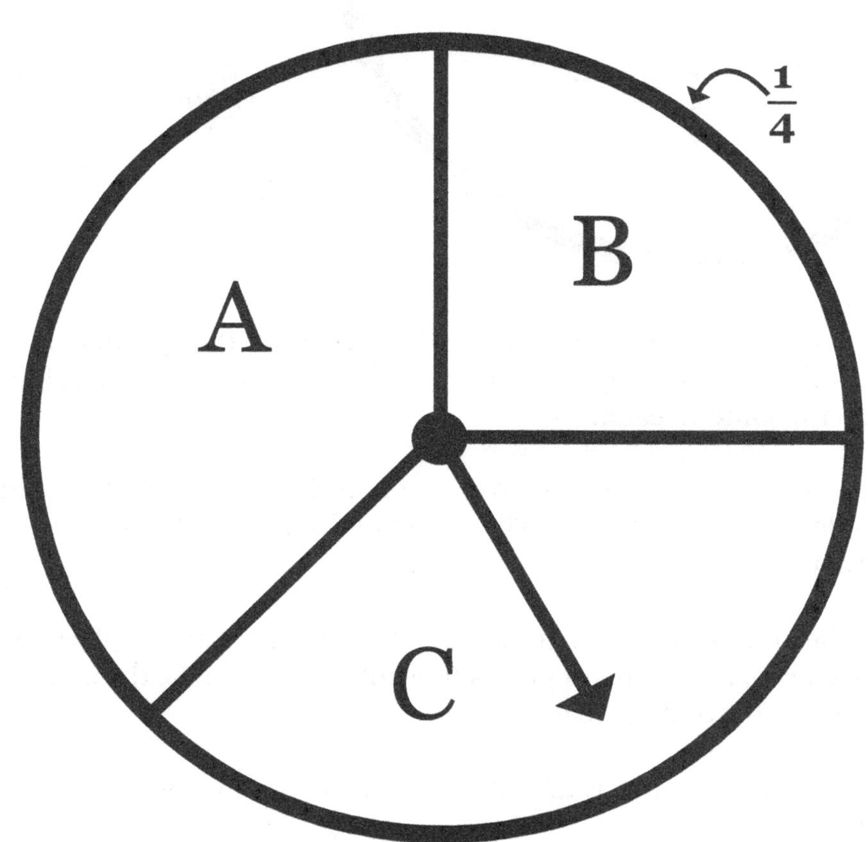

Level 2

Questions 1-3 refer to the spinner below

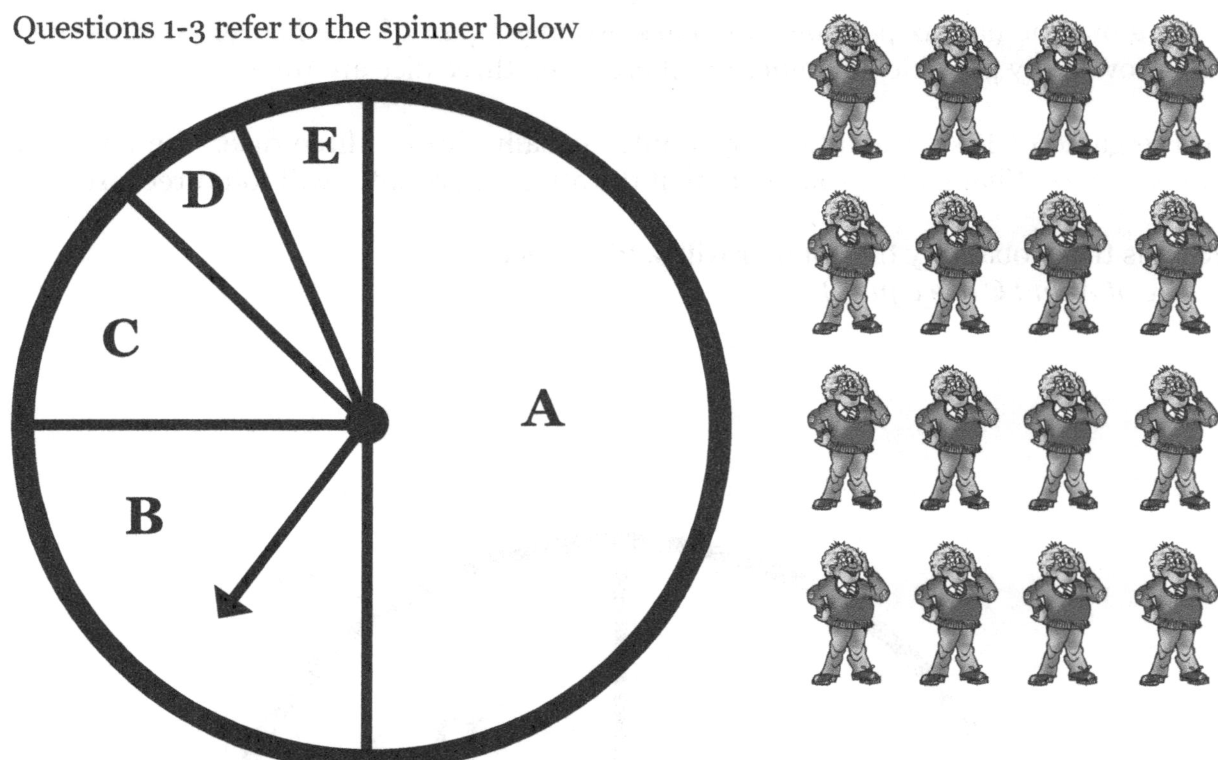

1) Five teams are each given 16 Einstein Dolls to place on the spinner. Teams are allowed to place their dolls in any arrangement they would like on the spinner. (All in one section or spread out with some in each.)

Each time the spinner is spun, if you have a doll in the area where the spinner lands, one of your team's dolls will be removed. The object of the game is to have all your team's dolls leave the spinner first.

Remember, if the spinner lands on a section where your team has placed several Einstein dolls, only one leaves. If your team places five dolls in section C, the spinner must land on C five times before all five dolls leave.

How would you distribute the Einstein dolls on the spinner to give your team the best chance of winning?

2) What is the probability that the spinner will land on section A 16 times in a row?

3) If each team had 4 Einstein dolls to place on the spinner, what distribution would give the best chance of winning?

Level 3

1) If you rolled a pair of dice 100 times, predict mathematically how many more 7's you would roll than 6's.

2) Remember, there are 36 possible outcomes when you roll two dice.

If you rolled two dice, picked one card from a 52-card deck, flipped a coin, and then spun the spinner shown below, how many possible outcomes would there be?

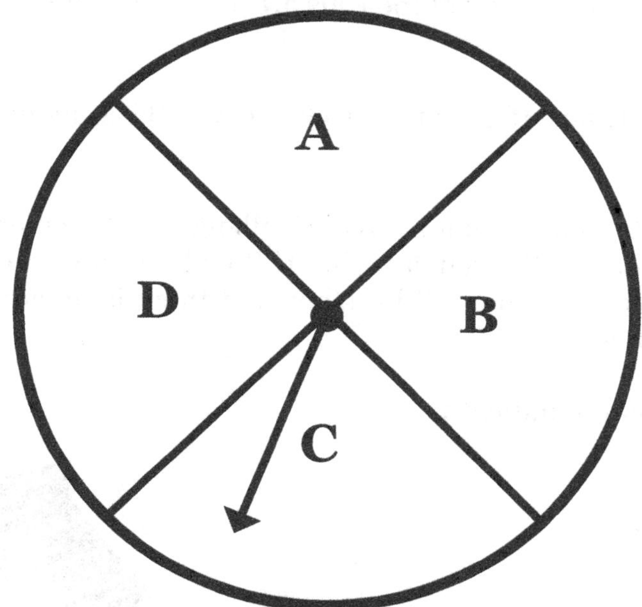

3) The four aces and four kings are taken from a deck of cards and placed in a pile.

The pile of eight cards is shuffled thoroughly and four cards are randomly chosen. What is the probability that all four cards will be aces?

Einstein

An eccentric mathematician decided that she would give a college scholarship to a math student if he/she won a math challenge. To further test the mathematical skills of the student, the eccentric mathematician decided to give the student a choice between two different challenges.

Challenge A:
Roll one die four times and if any of the rolls are a "6", the student wins the scholarship.

Challenge B:
Roll a pair of dice 24 times. If any of the rolls are 6-6, the student wins the scholarship.

Your job is to advise the math student. Will Challenge A or Challenge B give this student the best chance of winning the scholarship? If they both have an equal chance, put the math student's mind at ease and tell him/her that there is no advantage to picking one challenge over the other.

Defend your advice mathematically.

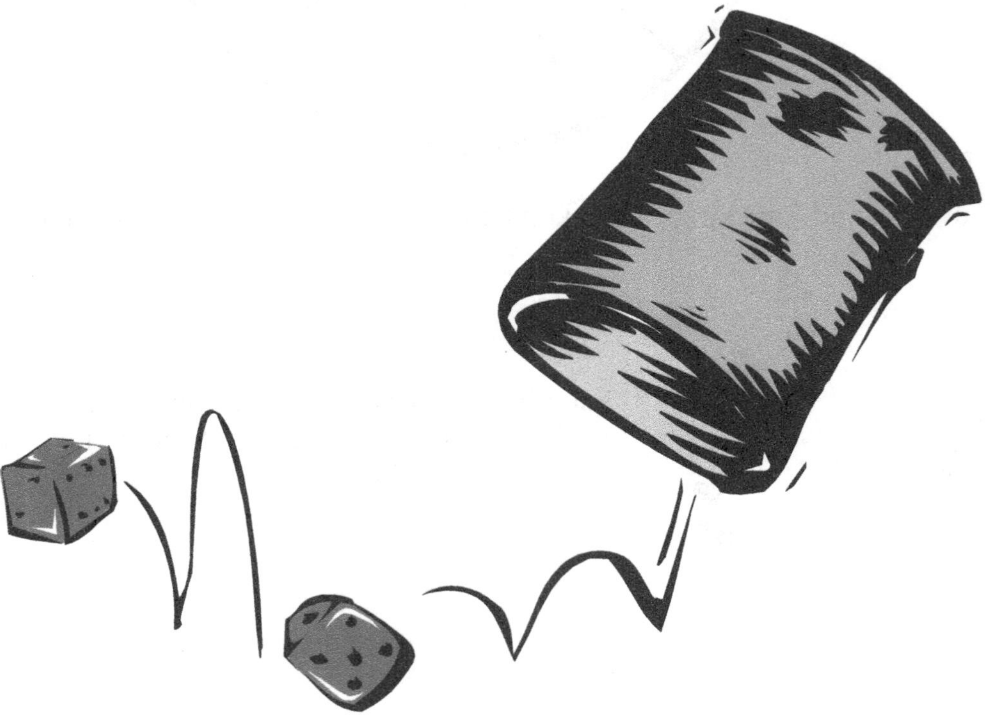

Chapter 22

Trigonometry For Those Who Never Understood It

I want to find out how tall this tree is, but it is cloudy and there is no shadow.
It is easy to find the height of a tree when there is a shadow by using ratios, but what can we do if there is no shadow?

Now is the time to put trigonometry to use! Don't be scared by the name - it is really quite easy.

Trigonometry
Greek for
"to measure a triangle"

Trigonometry is used for all kinds of things in the real world.

Uses of Trigonometry

- Finding the distance to the moon
- Digging tunnels
- Finding the distance a ship is from shore

Before we learn trigonometry, we have to first talk about triangles.

Look at these right triangles. Because the two sides are both the same, angles A and B must be equal and therefore 45° each.
B
A
1 inch
1 inch
B
A
5 inch
5 inch
That makes sense because there are 180 degrees in a triangle.
We are very interested in angle A for reasons you will see later.
That makes sense. No matter how big or small the right triangle is, if the legs are the same, both angles have to be the same.
Rule: When the ratio of the two legs of a right triangle is 1:1, angle A must be 45°. It doesn't matter if the triangle has sides of one inch or one mile.

Let's turn part of the triangle into a tree. When angle A is 45°, side a and side b must be the same.

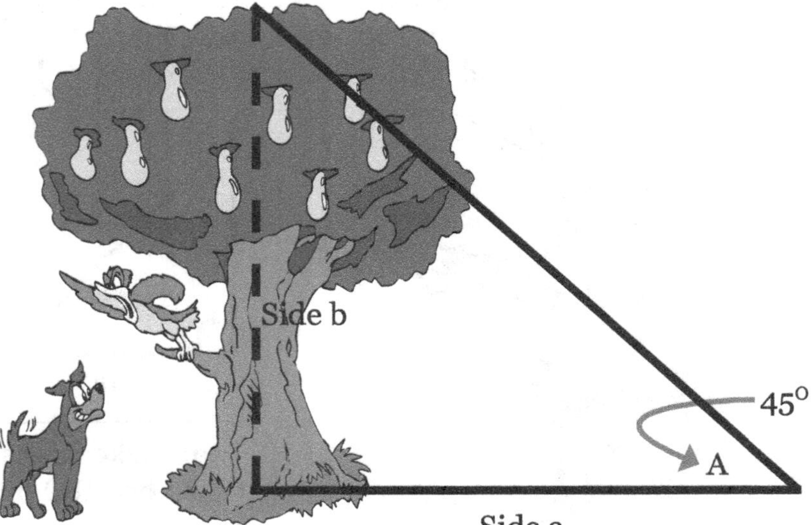
Side b
45°
A
Side a

We will now make a simple trigonometry tool to find angles. This tool is made from a protractor, a straw, thread and a washer.

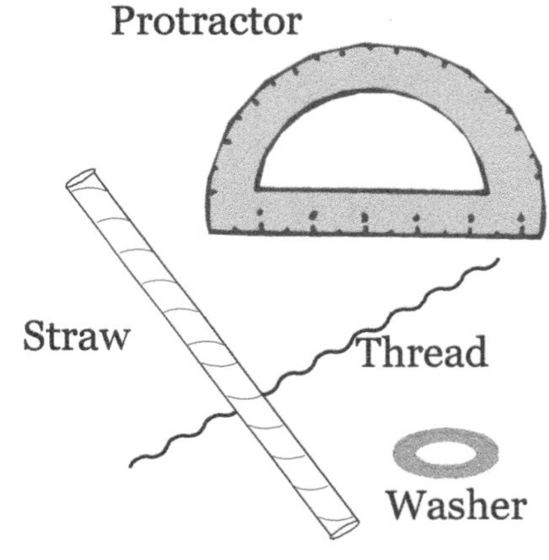
Protractor
Straw
Thread
Washer

Steps to make trigonometry tool

1) Drill hole as shown

2) Tie heavy thread through hole and attach washer

3) Attach straw to the top of the protractor with tape

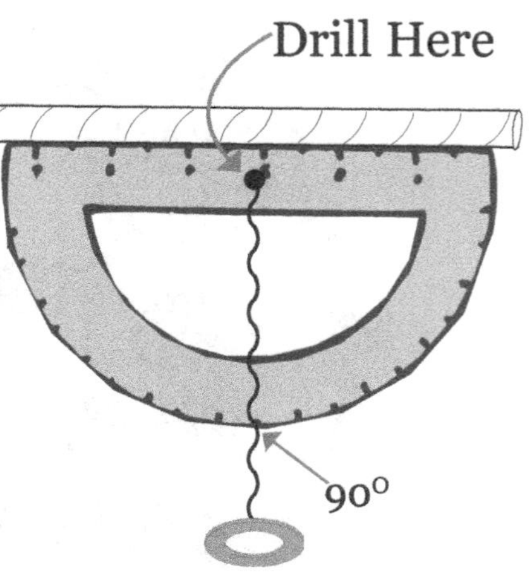
Drill Here
90°

Now all you need to do is lie down on the ground and be part of side a.
Side b
Side a
Move right
or
move left
Find the top of the tree through the straw. Keep moving until your protractor's hanging thread is at a 45° angle.
45°
90 100 110 120 130 140 150 160 170 180
It should look like this. From 90° to 135° is 45 degrees.

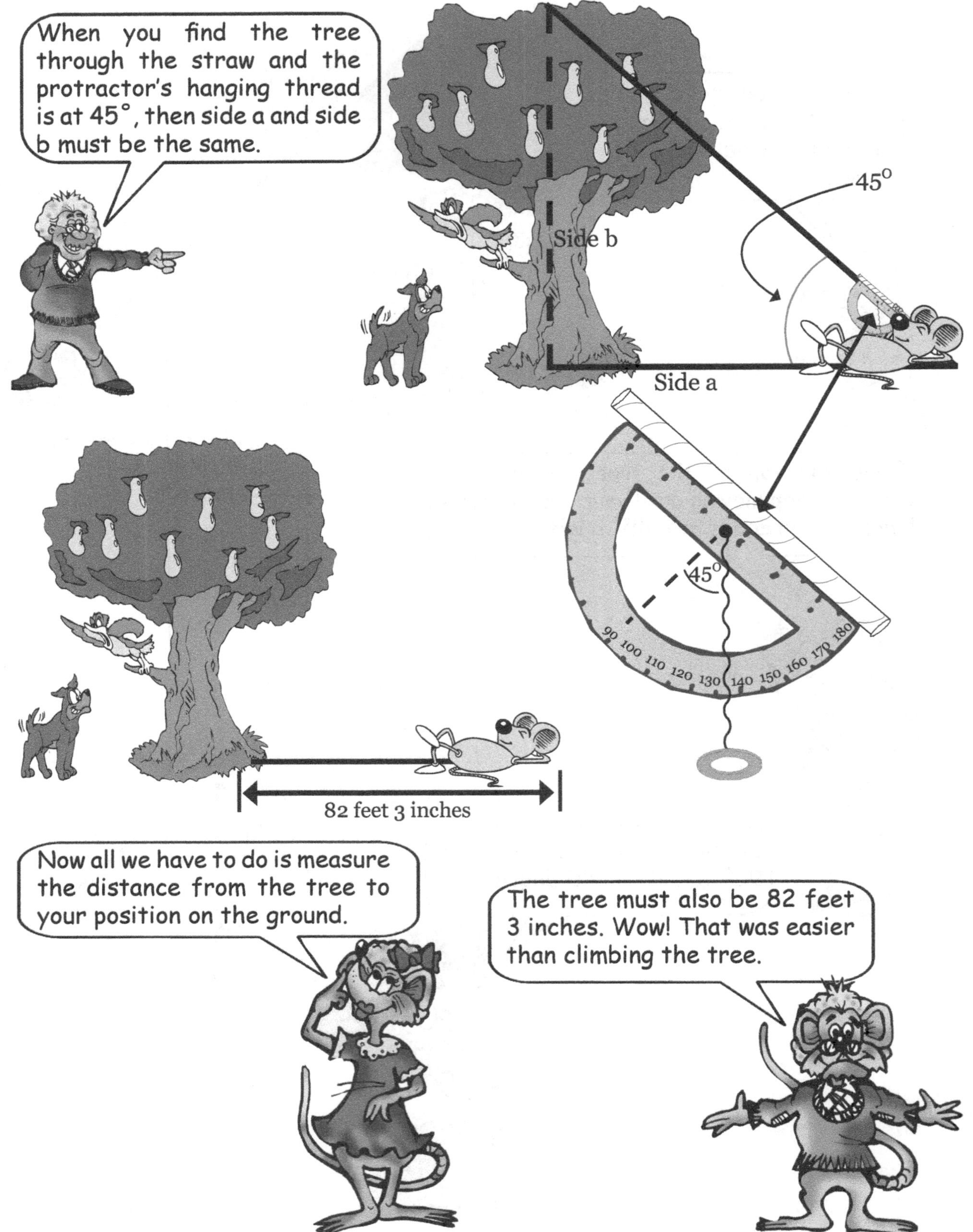

When you find the tree through the straw and the protractor's hanging thread is at 45°, then side a and side b must be the same.
Side b
45°
Side a
45°
90 100 110 120 130 140 150 160 170 180
82 feet 3 inches
Now all we have to do is measure the distance from the tree to your position on the ground.
The tree must also be 82 feet 3 inches. Wow! That was easier than climbing the tree.

Very important!
We want to know this angle. 152° - 90° = 62°

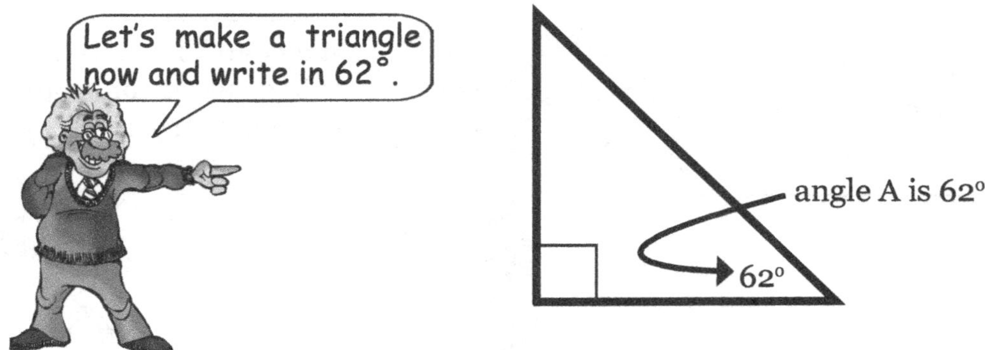

Remember when an angle of 45° meant that the legs of the right triangle were equal?

Every angle means something different about the legs of the triangle.

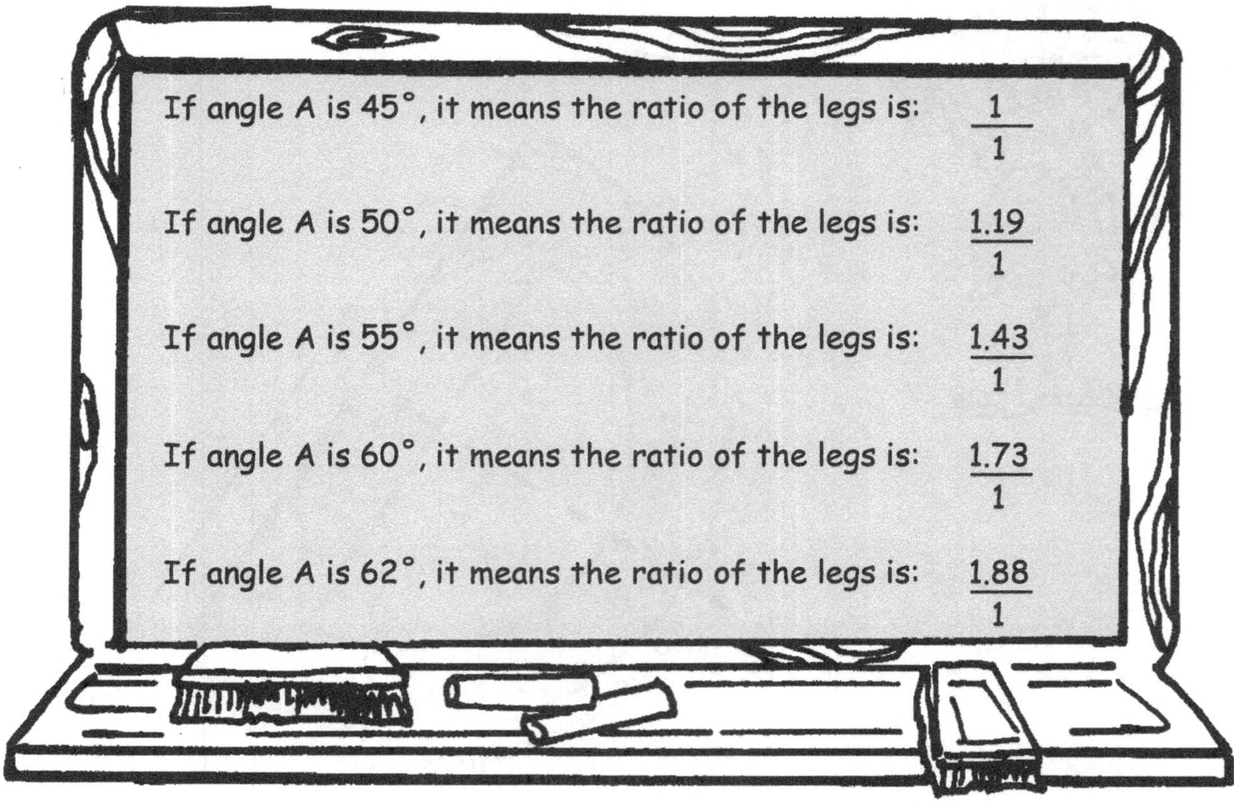

If angle A is 45°, it means the ratio of the legs is: $\frac{1}{1}$
If angle A is 50°, it means the ratio of the legs is: $\frac{1.19}{1}$
If angle A is 55°, it means the ratio of the legs is: $\frac{1.43}{1}$
If angle A is 60°, it means the ratio of the legs is: $\frac{1.73}{1}$
If angle A is 62°, it means the ratio of the legs is: $\frac{1.88}{1}$

When we talk about the ratio, we mean: $\dfrac{\text{the side opposite the angle}}{\text{side next to angle}}$

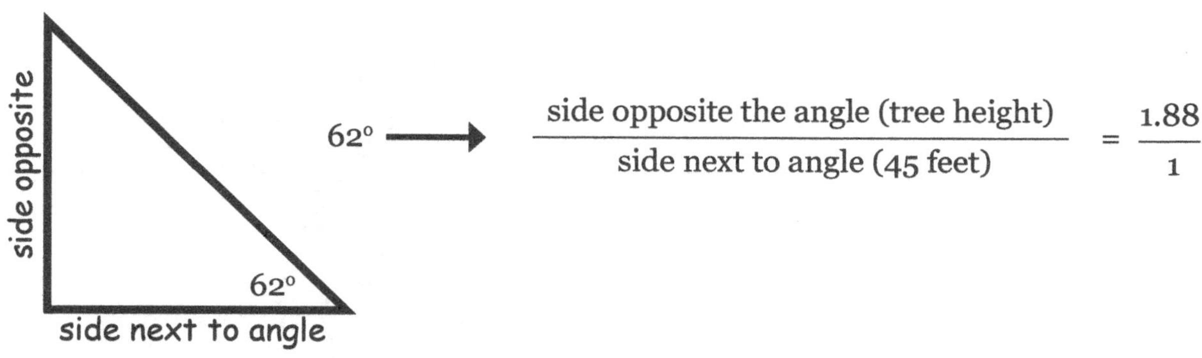

Cross-multiply: Tree height x 1 = 1.88 x 45 feet

Tree height = 84.6 feet

You used trigonometry to find the height of the tree!

Every angle has a special ratio. They are on the opposite page.

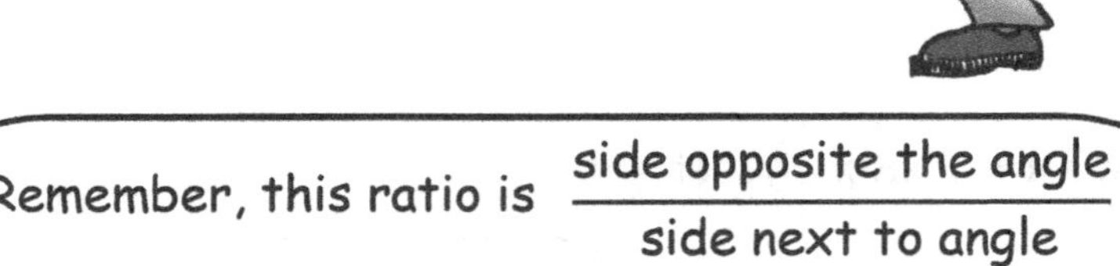

Remember, this ratio is side opposite the angle / side next to angle

There is a fancy name for this ratio. It is called the tangent.

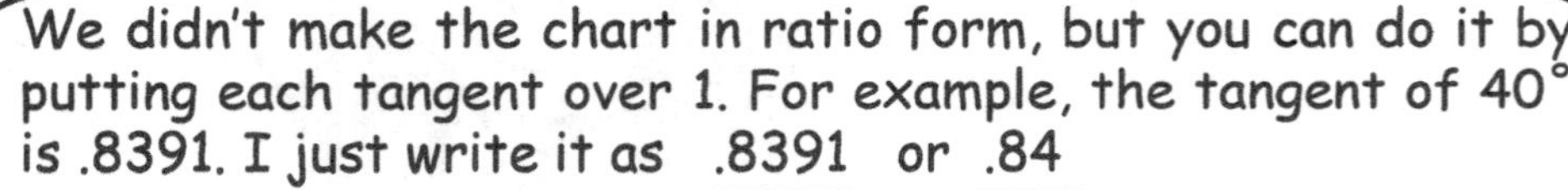

We didn't make the chart in ratio form, but you can do it by putting each tangent over 1. For example, the tangent of 40°
is .8391. I just write it as

Special Ratio:

$$\frac{\textbf{side opposite the angle}}{\textbf{side next to angle}}$$

Trigonometry Table

Angle	Tangent	Angle	Tangent	Angle	Tangent
1°	.0175	31	.6009	61	1.8040
2	.0349	32	.6249	62	1.8807
3	.0524	33	.6494	63	1.9626
4	.0699	34	.6745	64	2.0503
5°	.0875	35°	.7002	65°	2.1445
6	.1051	36	.7265	66	2.2460
7	.1228	37	.7536	67	2.3559
8	.1405	38	.7813	68	2.4751
9	.1584	39	.8098	69	2.6051
10°	.1763	40°	.8391	70°	2.7475
11	.1944	41	.8693	71	2.9042
12	.2126	42	.9004	72	3.0777
13	.2309	43	.9325	73	3.2709
14	.2493	44	.9657	74	3.4874
15°	.2679	45°	1.000	75°	3.7321
16	.2867	46	1.0355	76	4.0108
17	.3057	47	1.0724	77	4.3315
18	.3249	48	1.1106	78	4.7046
19	.3443	49	1.1504	79	5.1446
20°	.3640	50°	1.1918	80°	5.6713
21	.3839	51	1.2349	81	6.3138
22	.4040	52	1.2799	82	7.1154
23	.4245	53	1.3270	83	8.1443
24	.4452	54	1.3764	84	9.5144
25°	.4663	55°	1.4281	85°	11.4301
26	.4877	56	1.4826	86	14.3007
27	.5095	57	1.5399	87	19.0811
28	.5317	58	1.6003	88	28.6363
29	.5543	59	1.6643	89	57.2900
30°	.5774	60°	1.7321	90°	infinity

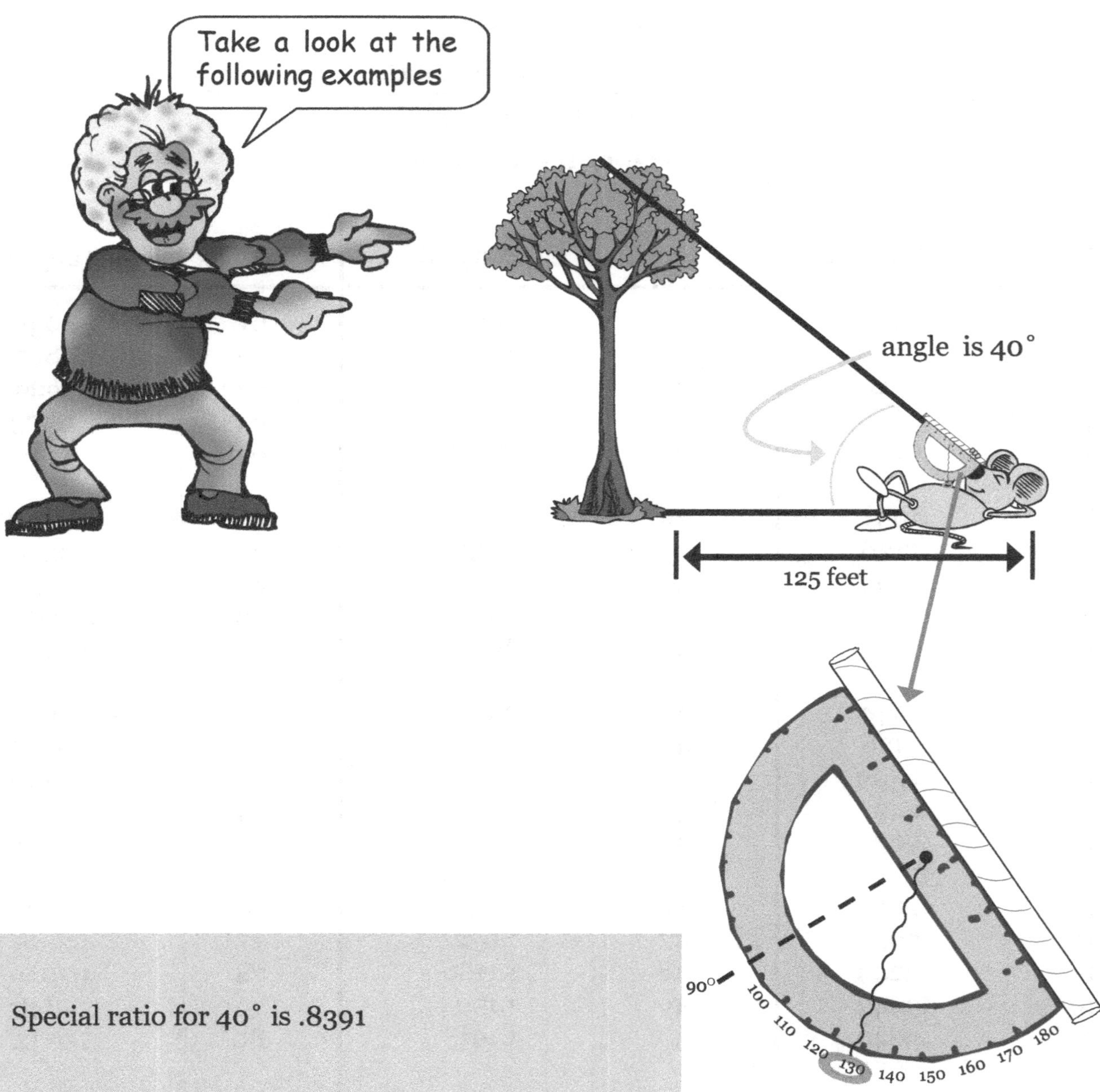

Special ratio for 40° is .8391

$$\frac{\text{Tree Height (call } n\text{)}}{\text{Side next to angle (125 feet)}} = \frac{.84}{1}$$

Cross-multiply: n = .84 x 125 feet

n = 105 feet

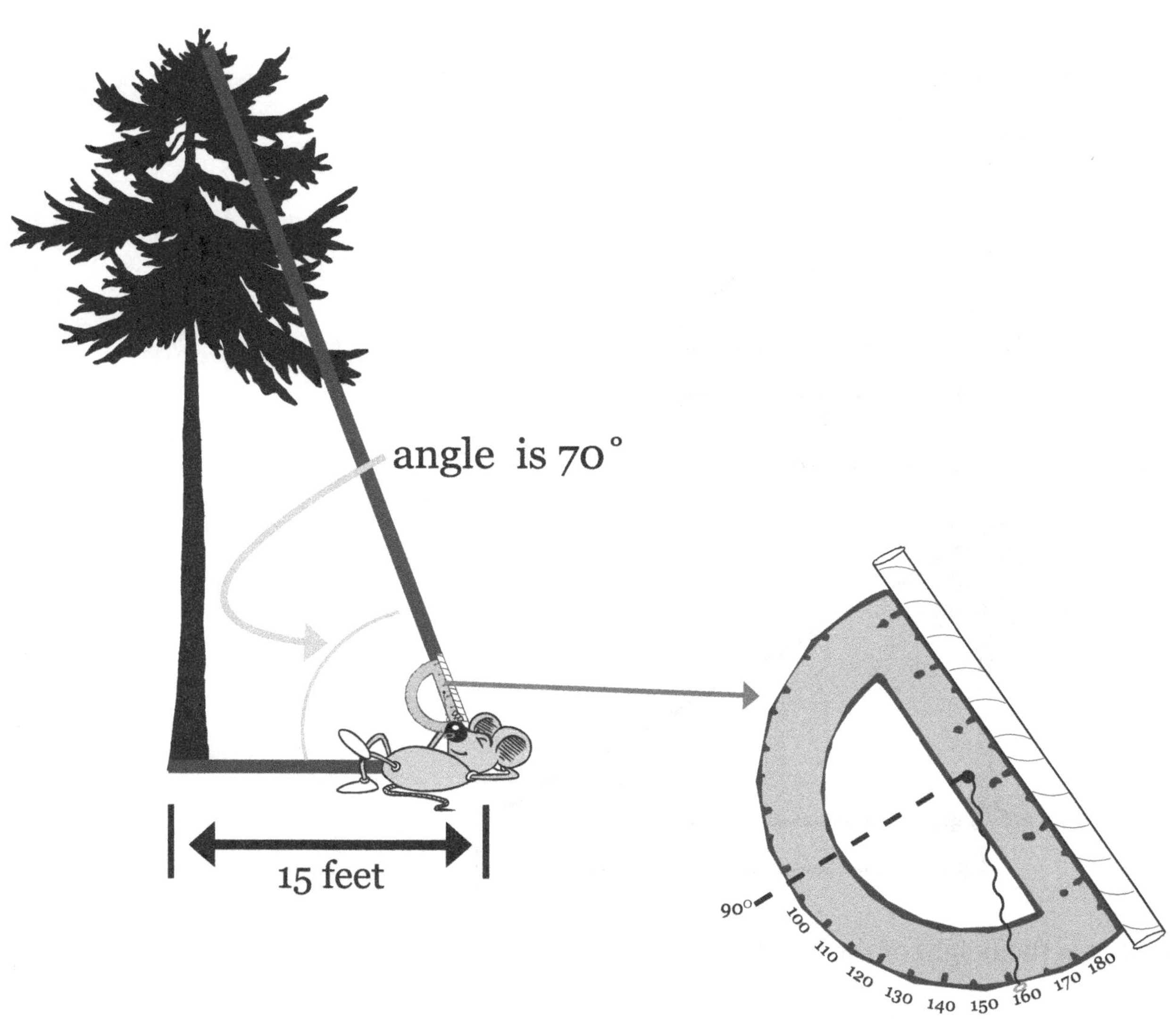

Special ratio for 70° is 2.7475

$$\frac{\text{Tree Height (call } n)}{\text{Side next to angle (15 feet)}} = \frac{2.75}{1}$$

Cross-multiply: n = 2.75 x 15

n = 41.25 feet

Level 1

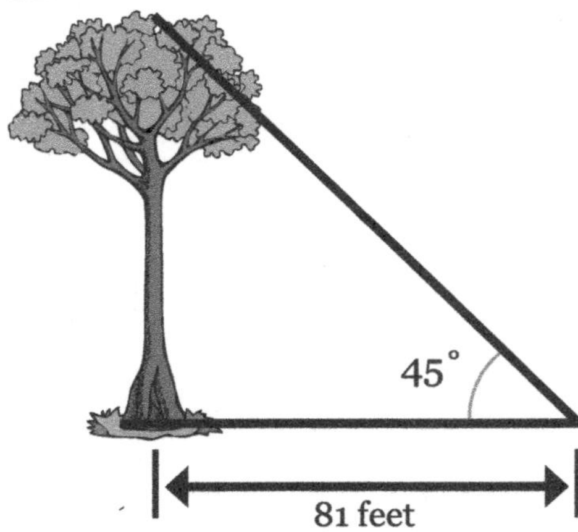

1) What is the height of the tree?

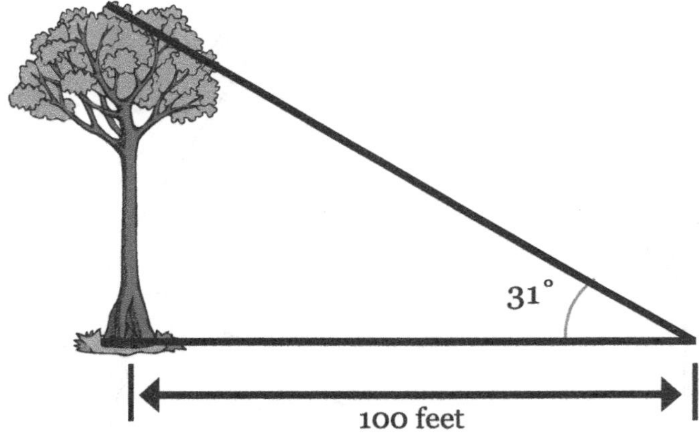

2) What is the height of the tree? (Round to the nearest whole number.)

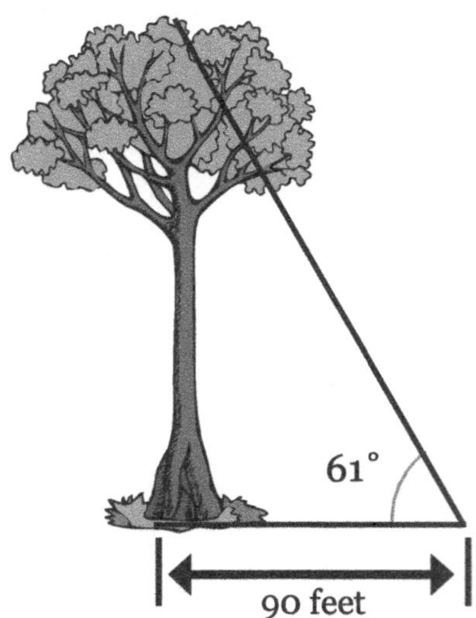

3) What is the height of the tree? (Round to the nearest whole number.)

Level 2

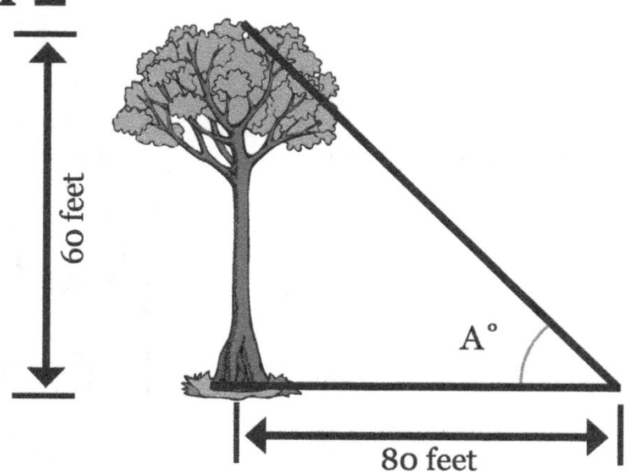

1) If you know that the height of the tree is 60 feet and the side next to the angle is 80 feet, how many degrees is angle A?

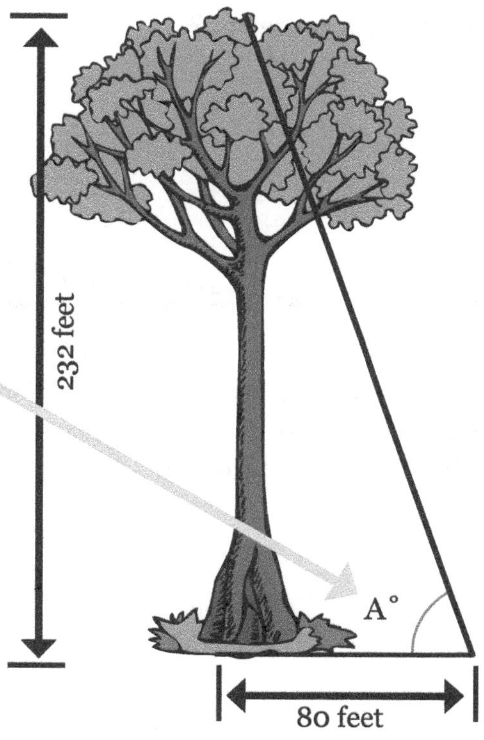

2) How many degrees is angle A?

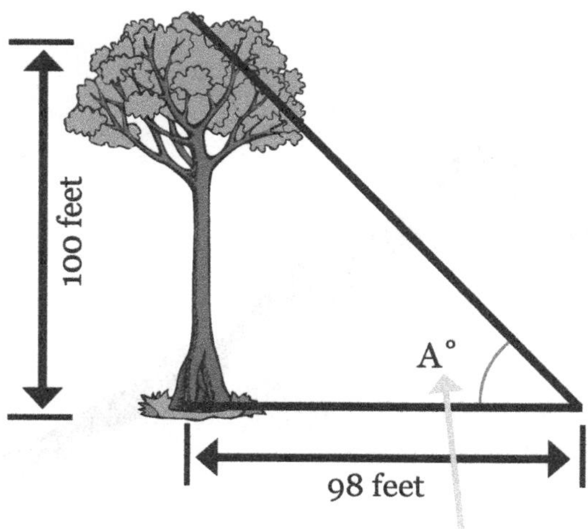

3) How many degrees is angle A?

Level 3

1) A ladder is leaning against a house.
The top of the ladder is two feet below the top of the house.
How tall is the house?

2) A ramp needs to be under 6° so wheelchairs can easily roll up and down the incline. Is this ramp under 6°?

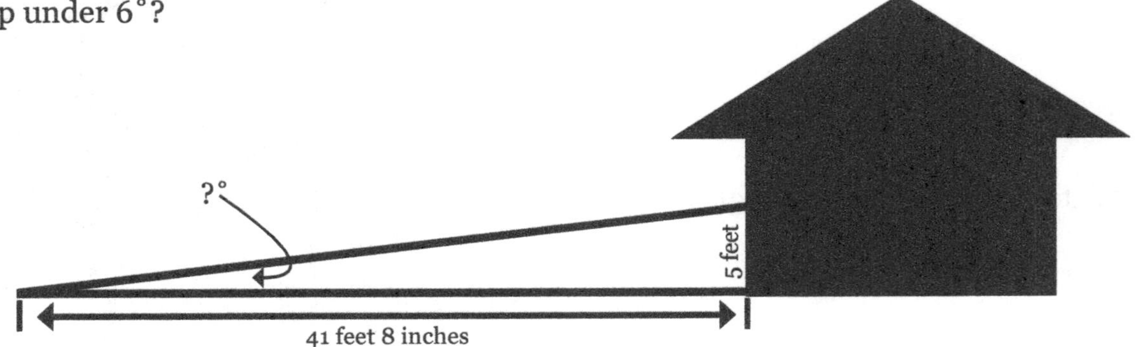

3) A tunnel through a mountain is one mile long. If Angle A is 30° and the top of the mountain is directly over the halfway point of the tunnel, how tall is the mountain? (Round to the nearest hundred.)

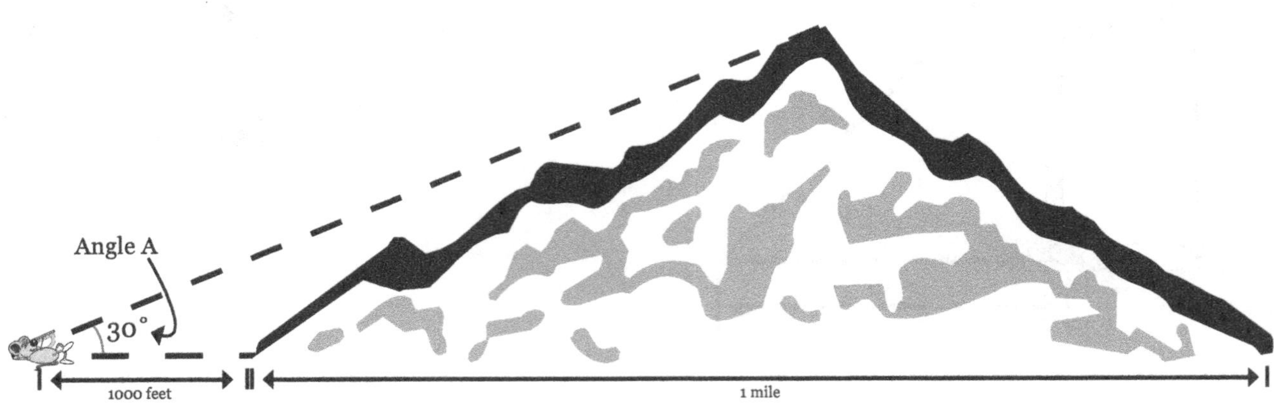

Einstein

You are attempting to find the distance across a river. There is a tree on the other side that you know is 42 feet high. The tree is growing at the waters edge and you are six feet tall.

When you lie down on the opposite side of the river and use your trigonometry tool, you find that the angle to the top of the tree is 9°. How wide is the river?
(Round to the nearest foot.)

Chapter 23
The Mathematics Hidden Within Music

Before we can answer the question of why some notes sound good together and others sound awful, we need to find out what sound really is and what happens when we hear it.

Have you ever dropped a rock into the water? What happens to the surface of the water?

When I throw a rock into the water, there are waves that travel away from the rock across the surface of the water.

Exactly! Sound is just like that, only in air. Whenever a sound is made, the air "splashes" just like in water, and waves travel through the air to reach your ears. These waves, which vary in pattern and strength, are called "sound waves".

BARK
BARK
BARK
That's a powerful and disturbing sound wave!
Look at how disorganized and random those sound waves are. No wonder they are unpleasant to listen to.
I agree! They are all over the place and not organized at all.
So what makes music different than other sounds?

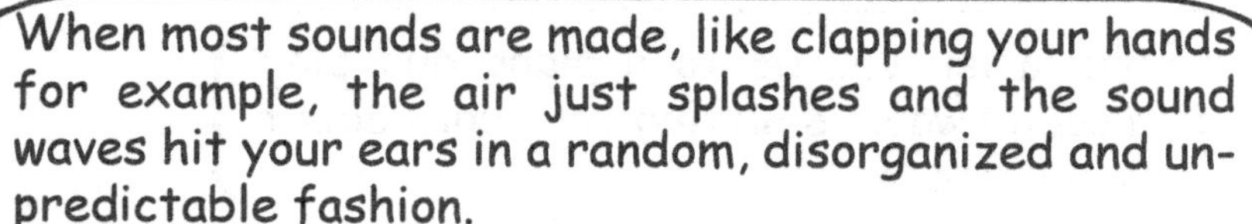

When most sounds are made, like clapping your hands for example, the air just splashes and the sound waves hit your ears in a random, disorganized and unpredictable fashion.

When a musical note is played by an instrument, like a piano, something very special happens to these sound waves. They organize themselves, get in line, and hit your ear steadily, predictably, and very, very fast!

For example, when you go to a piano and play middle C, a sound wave is hitting your ears about 262 times each second.
That sounds good.

These are some organized and predictable sounds. That dog could learn a lesson from the piano!

I don't think a dog's bark is meant to be pleasing. I think it wants to make you nervous and uncomfortable.

If musical sounds are so organized, why do some combinations of notes sound good and others sound bad?

Let me take over for a minute, Einstein. In order to answer that, we need to talk about "frequency". The frequency of a note is how many times it is hitting your ear in one second. We talk about a note's frequency with a measurement called "hertz". Middle C, remember, creates sound waves that hit your ear about 262 times each second.

So we would say that middle C has a frequency of about 262 hertz. Different notes have different frequencies, and the mathematical relationship between them is very interesting. Below is a chart of notes from a piano's middle C to the next highest C. I have included all their frequencies. (I have rounded the numbers a little bit.)

Note	Frequency in Hertz
C	262
C#	278
D	294
D#	312
E	330
F	350
F#	371
G	393
G#	416
A	441
A#	467
B	495
C	524

That's really exciting, but what does that have to do with good combinations and bad combinations of notes?

When you play two notes at once, C and G for example, you are creating both of those frequencies at the same time. Those sound waves are hitting your ears 262 times per second and 393 times per second. We can use math to predict whether or not the relationship between these two numbers is a simple and elegant one or a complicated and difficult one.

Let's do some experimenting. Go to a piano or keyboard and play both C notes together. Does that combination sound good? Yes it does. Now look at the chart. What is the frequency of the lower C? The higher C? Do you notice anything special about those two numbers?

The high C has a frequency that is twice that of the low C. So the mathematical relationship between the high C and the low C is 2 to 1 or as a fraction 2/1. I see now why the two notes sounded so good together---they have a very nice, clean, elegant ratio.

Note	Frequency in Hertz
C	262
C#	278
D	294
D#	312
E	330
F	350
F#	371
G	393
G#	416
A	441
A#	467
B	495
C	524

Let's do another one. Play C and G together. Does that combination sound good? Yes it does. Let's look at the chart to see why.

I can get the relationship between the two notes by dividing G's frequency by C's frequency.

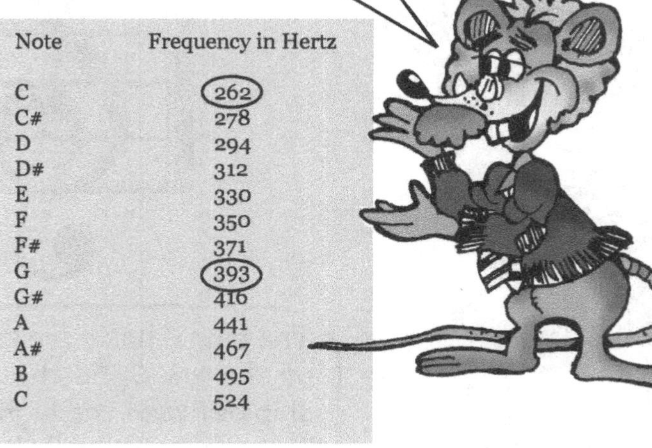

Note	Frequency in Hertz
C	262
C#	278
D	294
D#	312
E	330
F	350
F#	371
G	393
G#	416
A	441
A#	467
B	495
C	524

When you divide, you end up with 1.5 or 3/2. This is another very nice, clean, elegant ratio.

Let's try one more. Play C and C# together. Does that combination sound good? No, it is obviously not a pleasant sound. To find out why, look at the frequencies of the two notes.
When I divide 278 by 262, I get approximately 1.06 or 53/50. This is not a very clean, nice, elegant ratio and that is why it sounds so bad.

You can usually predict how good a pair of notes will sound based on the mathematical relationship between their frequencies. Good luck with the questions. Remember that these frequencies are not exact, and when you divide, you may have to round a little bit.

Level 1

1. Without playing anything, calculate the mathematical ratio between E and B. Do you think this will sound good? What is the ratio? Go play it - were you correct?

2. Without playing anything, calculate the mathematical ratio between C and F. Do you think this will sound good? What is the ratio? Go play it - were you correct?

3. Without playing anything, calculate the mathematical ratio between E and A#. Do you think this will sound good? What is the ratio? Go play it - were you correct?

Level 2

1. What two notes have a ratio of about 5/4? Remember, frequencies and ratios are approximate, and there are many correct answers. Does this combination sound good? Do you know the musical term for this ratio?

2. Which two notes have a ratio of about 47/25? Does this sound good? What very elegant ratio is this close to?

3. We can also apply this to groups of three notes. Play a low C, a G, and a high C all at once. Does it sound good? What are all of the ratios that are possible between these notes? What are the musical terms for all possible ratios?

Level 3

1. We can use math to calculate the frequencies of notes that may not be listed on the chart we have in front of us. Go to a piano, and play both C's on the chart. Remember what that sounds like. Now play those 2, along with the next highest C. Play all three at once. Do they sound good? What do you think the frequency of that higher C is? What about the one above that?

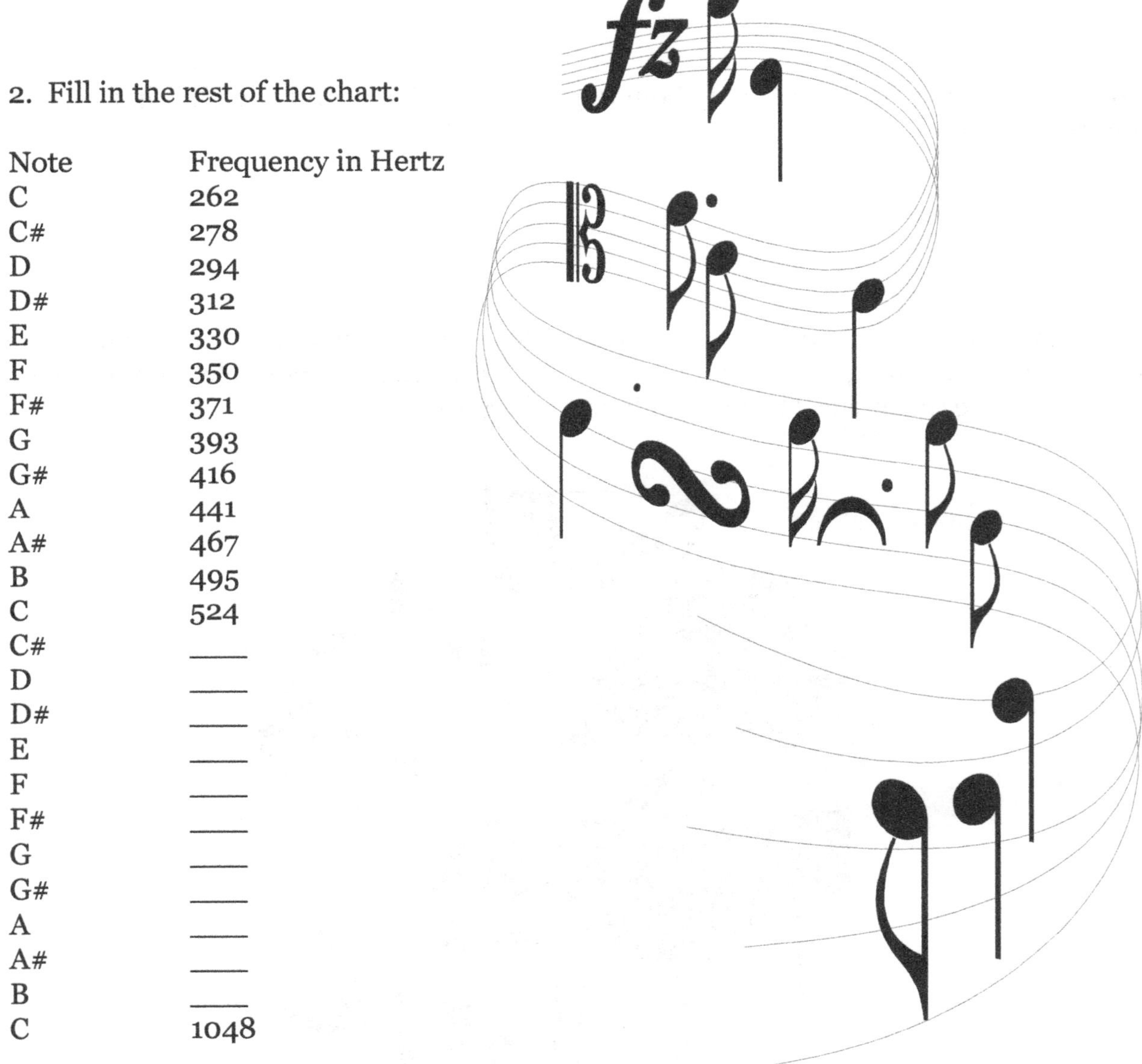

2. Fill in the rest of the chart:

Note	Frequency in Hertz
C	262
C#	278
D	294
D#	312
E	330
F	350
F#	371
G	393
G#	416
A	441
A#	467
B	495
C	524
C#	____
D	____
D#	____
E	____
F	____
F#	____
G	____
G#	____
A	____
A#	____
B	____
C	1048

3. Let's try a 4-note combination. Calculate all possible ratios with the notes C, F#, G#, and B. How do you think this will sound?

Einstein

What is the frequency of the highest key on the piano? The lowest key?

Chapter 24
Mathematics and Scuba Diving

Scuba diving is an activity that can be a great deal of fun, but it also has its risks. Dangers such as drowning, running out of air, lung rupture, nitrogen narcosis, and decompression sickness are very real. While these risks cannot be completely eliminated, we can use math to decrease some of the risks associated with scuba diving. In the first part of this chapter we will discuss the underwater air supply, and how our depth affects the amount of time we can spend under water.

We will first talk about the underwater air supply.
M

The word "scuba" is an acronym. It stands for **S**elf **C**ontained **U**nderwater **B**reathing **A**pparatus. This means that you take your air with you when you go scuba diving. The amount of time you can spend with your air underwater, however, can change depending on how deep you go.

So we could both take the same amount of air, but mine would last longer if I don't go as deep as someone else?

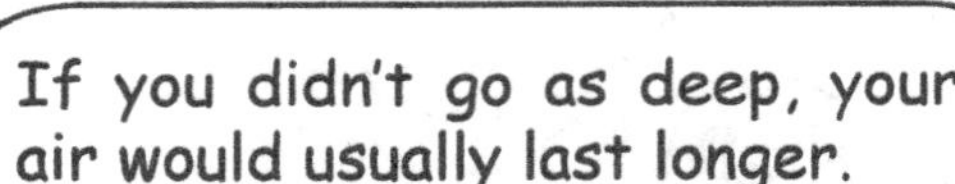

If you didn't go as deep, your air would usually last longer.

Why is that?

The explanation is a little complicated, but I will start by giving you a little information about air pressure.

On land, at sea level, there are about 15 pounds of pressure for every square inch of space. 15 pounds per square inch, or "psi" is an amount of air pressure that is called one "atmosphere". Right now, you have one atmosphere of air pressure pushing against your body. In fact, on each side of your hand right now, there are about 250 pounds of air pushing against your skin! And that is just one of your hands! Just think of how much air is pushing against the rest of your body! The reason we don't feel this pressure is because our bodies are mostly made of water, and liquids cannot be squeezed.

Just think of how much air I'm holding up right now!

Liquids cannot be squeezed, or "compressed," but gases like air can. Try something the next time you are at a pool or in the tub. Take an empty glass and turn it upside down.

The air will be squeezed into a smaller space because of all the water pressing on it from above. At 33 feet, the air will be squeezed into a space half as big as it was at the surface!

My glass is only half full of air, but I didn't let any out! Where did the rest of the air go?

It didn't go anywhere, it was squeezed into a smaller space because of the weight of all the water above us!

What will happen if we take the glass back to the surface?

If you were to take that same glass back to the surface, the air would expand back to its normal size because the pressure decreased back to only one atmosphere, or 15 psi.
The glass is full again!

What will happen if we take it down twice as far as last time to 66 feet?
You might think, if we took our glass down to 66 feet, that all the air would disappear. After all, at 33 feet, the air took up half as much space as it did at the surface, but that's not what happens.

Remember when we talked about air pressure at sea level? Above water, you have one atmosphere of pressure pushing against you. One atmosphere, you remember, is equal to about 15 pounds per square inch. While under water, you only need to go to a depth of 33 feet to double that pressure. So at this depth, we have two atmospheres pushing against us, or 30 psi. For every 33 feet of depth, we add another atmosphere of pressure. At the surface, this glass of air had 1 atmosphere of pressure pushing against it. Since this is the "normal amount", the glass was full. At 33 feet, there are 2 atmospheres of pressure, so it was 1/2 as full. What will happen if we go down to 66 feet and 3 atmospheres of pressure?

The glass is now 1/3 full of air!
0
20
40
60
80

I wonder how we can express this relationship between depth and air volume?

The amount of air in the glass can be expressed as a fraction of the whole. In this case, 1/3. The amount of space the air takes up as a fraction of the whole is the reciprocal of how many atmospheres of pressure are pushing on it.
So if we were to go even further down, to 99 feet, or 4 atmospheres of pressure, the glass would be only 1/4 full of air, and that air would be four times as dense!
0
30
60
90
120

Before we do our next experiment, we need to talk about the air tank that comes underwater with you. It is about 2 feet long and about 7-8 inches wide. When filled, this tank holds about as much air as fits in a telephone booth. All of that air is compressed down to that small size to fit on your back! Inside a filled scuba tank, there are about 3000 pounds of pressure per square inch, or 3000 psi!

Now let's take an empty balloon with us, instead of a glass. We'll go down to 33 feet and fill our balloon with air. What do you think will happen to this balloon if we take it to the surface? Will it get smaller or larger?

Wow! My balloon doubled in size!

There were 2 atmospheres of pressure at 33 feet, now there is only 1, so the balloon got twice as big.
I bet if we filled our empty balloon at 66 feet and brought it to the surface, it would get 3 times as big, or it would pop before we got there!

When you breathe at the surface, you are taking in about a liter of air each time you inhale. If you are underwater with your scuba tank at 33 feet, you are still taking in about a liter of air, but since you are at 30 psi of pressure, or 2 atmospheres, you are taking in twice the amount of air molecules with each breath. The air is twice as dense, therefore, you are pulling air out of your tank twice as fast as you would at the surface.

95
96
97
98
99
100
101
How fast am I pulling air out of my tank now?

You are at 4 atmospheres of pressure, so you are pulling air out of your tank 4 times as fast as you would at the surface.

It is now clear that the deeper you go, the less time you have before your air runs out. Try the questions on the next few pages and remember that if you are going scuba diving, do the math like your life depends on it!!
M

Level 1

1. Luke is swimming at a depth where there are 4 atmospheres of pressure on him. How deep is Luke swimming?

2)How far down would you have to go to make an empty glass 1/6 full?

3) A balloon that had 3 liters of volume at the surface of the water was taken underwater until its volume decreased to 1.5 liters. How deep is the balloon?

Level 2

1) Suppose you took an empty balloon to a depth of 132 feet and filled it with one liter of air. This balloon can only hold 4 liters of air before popping. Will your balloon survive a trip to the surface?

2) Suppose you breathe in a normal 1 liter of air per breath. You are down about 50 feet underwater. Your gear gets caught on a rock, and you can't get loose without taking your tank off. You take a deep breath, remove your tank, and swim quickly to the surface, holding in your air. What will happen to your lungs?

3) Can you think of a way to prevent this from happening?

Level 3

1) If you take an upside down empty glass to a depth of 49.5 feet, what fraction of the glass will be filled with air?

2) How many atmospheres of pressure does a filled scuba tank have inside?

3) How deep would you have to go to have the pressure inside a filled scuba tank be equal to the pressure of the surrounding water?

Einstein level

Steve is swimming at a depth of 33 feet. He is a larger than average person and breathes at a rate of 1.5 liters of air per breath, and breathes once every 5 seconds. Adam is swimming at a depth of 49.5 feet. He is a smaller sized person and breathes in 0.8 liters per breath, and breathes once every 4 seconds. Assuming they stay at those depths, who is using their air up faster?

Chapter 25
Prices Were Really Cheap When My Parents Were Young! *Or Were They?*

You're lucky! I just read that in 1962 a gallon of gas cost only 31 cents.
I agree! I found an old newspaper that cost 10 cents in 1962. I also read that a new home cost only $15,000 in 1962. Prices sure were cheap then!
NEWS 1962

Before you start thinking those prices allowed people living in 1962 to live better, you have to understand a few things.

A dollar in 1962 was worth approximately $6.80 in 2007 dollars.
I'm not sure what you mean by that .

It is like having a time machine and going back to 1962 from the year 2007.

1962 STORE

Oh, I see you have dollars from the year 2007. They look alike, but you will need 6 dollars and 80 cents from the year 2007 to get a 1962 dollar. You see, 2007 dollars are not worth as much as 1962 dollars were.
GUY FROM 1962

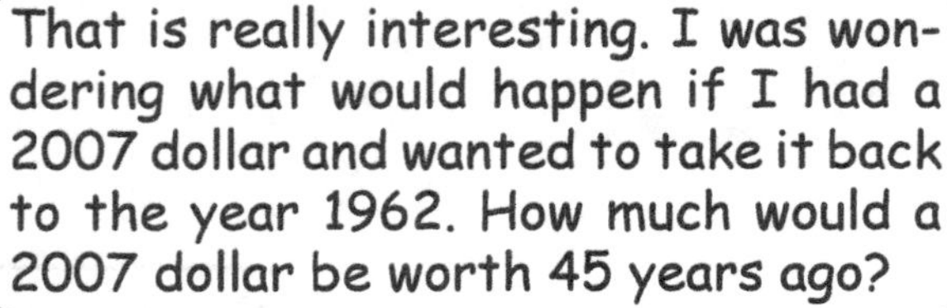
I'm starting to see what is going on. To "translate" prices from 1962 into 2007 dollars, I must multiply by 6.8.
That is really interesting. I was wondering what would happen if I had a 2007 dollar and wanted to take it back to the year 1962. How much would a 2007 dollar be worth 45 years ago?

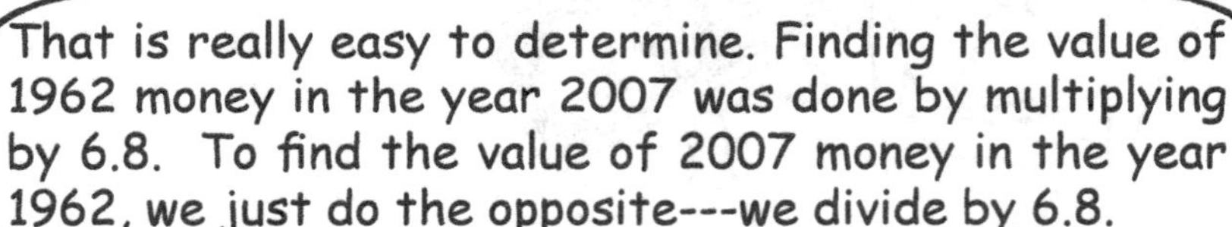
That is really easy to determine. Finding the value of 1962 money in the year 2007 was done by multiplying by 6.8. To find the value of 2007 money in the year 1962, we just do the opposite---we divide by 6.8.

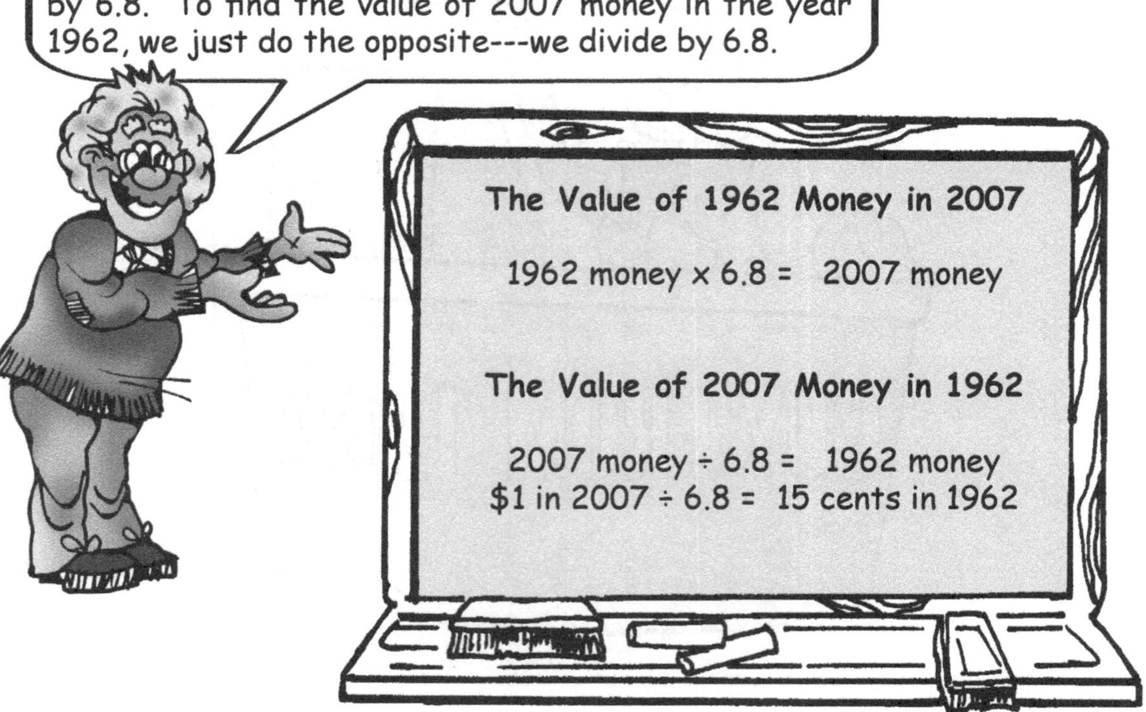
The Value of 1962 Money in 2007
1962 money x 6.8 = 2007 money
The Value of 2007 Money in 1962
2007 money ÷ 6.8 = 1962 money
$1 in 2007 ÷ 6.8 = 15 cents in 1962

Wow!! Today's money sure isn't worth much compared to 1962.

Let's see if that $15,000 house in 1962 is really as inexpensive as you thought it was.

$15,000 in 1962 x 6.8 = $102,000 in 2007 money

So you see, the bargain prices you thought I was paying in 1962 were not as great as you thought.

You can see the value of money in different years by going to this web-site.

http://woodrow.mpls.frb.fed.us/research/data/us/calc/

I can find the cost of things from 1962 in "2007 money" by putting them through the "into the future machine".
x 6.8

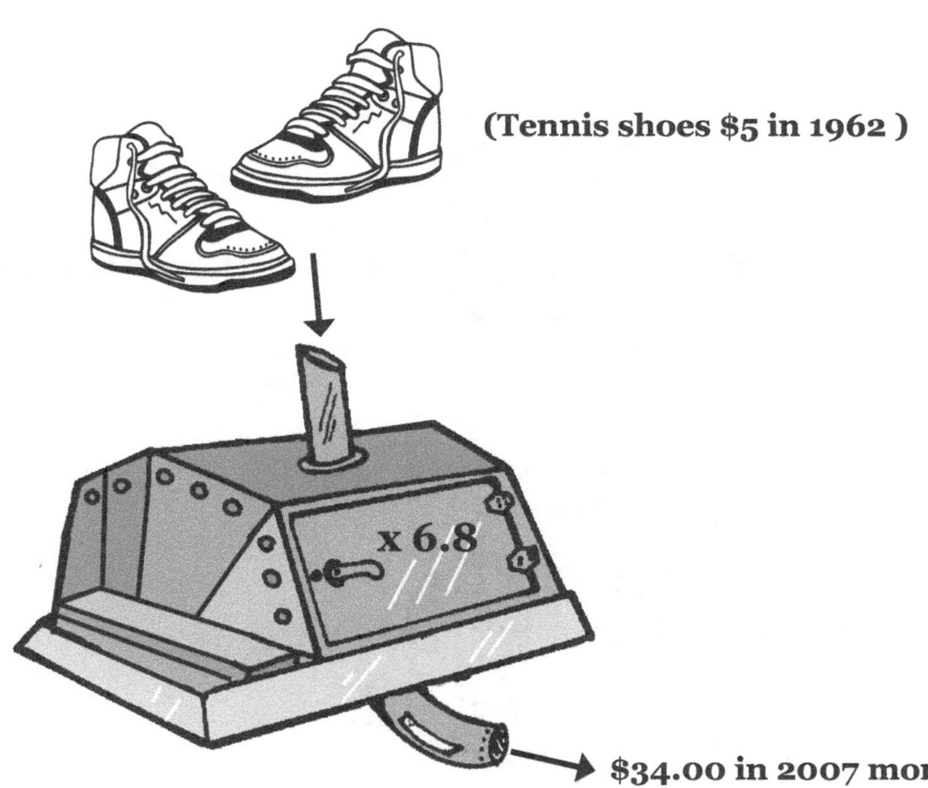
(Tennis shoes $5 in 1962)
x 6.8
$34.00 in 2007 money

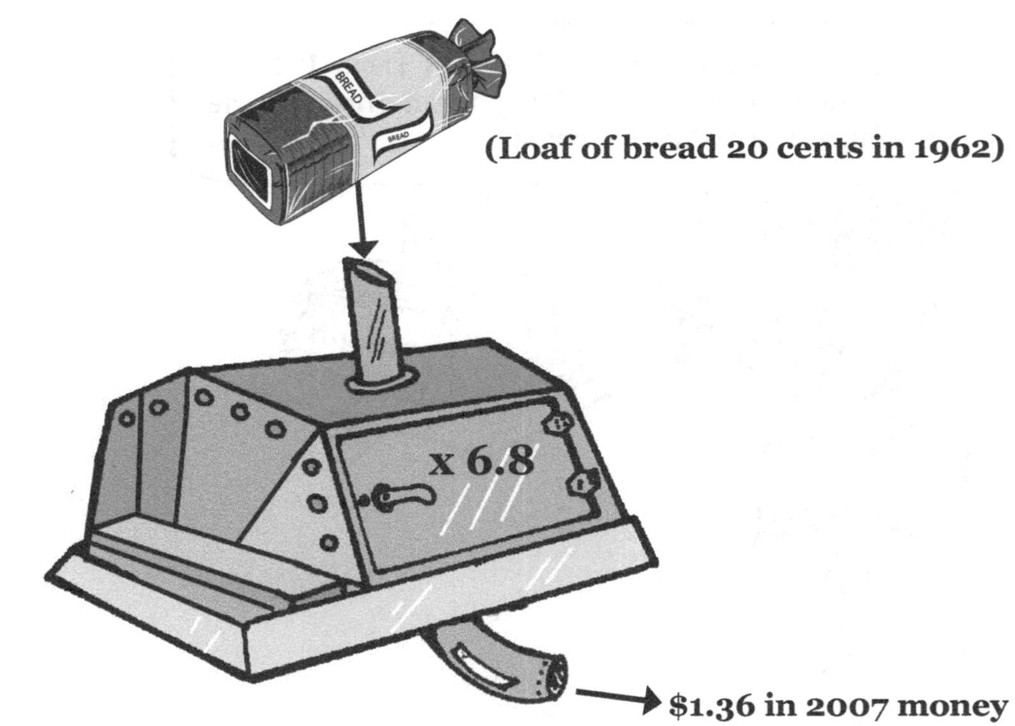
BREAD
BREAD
(Loaf of bread 20 cents in 1962)
x 6.8
$1.36 in 2007 money

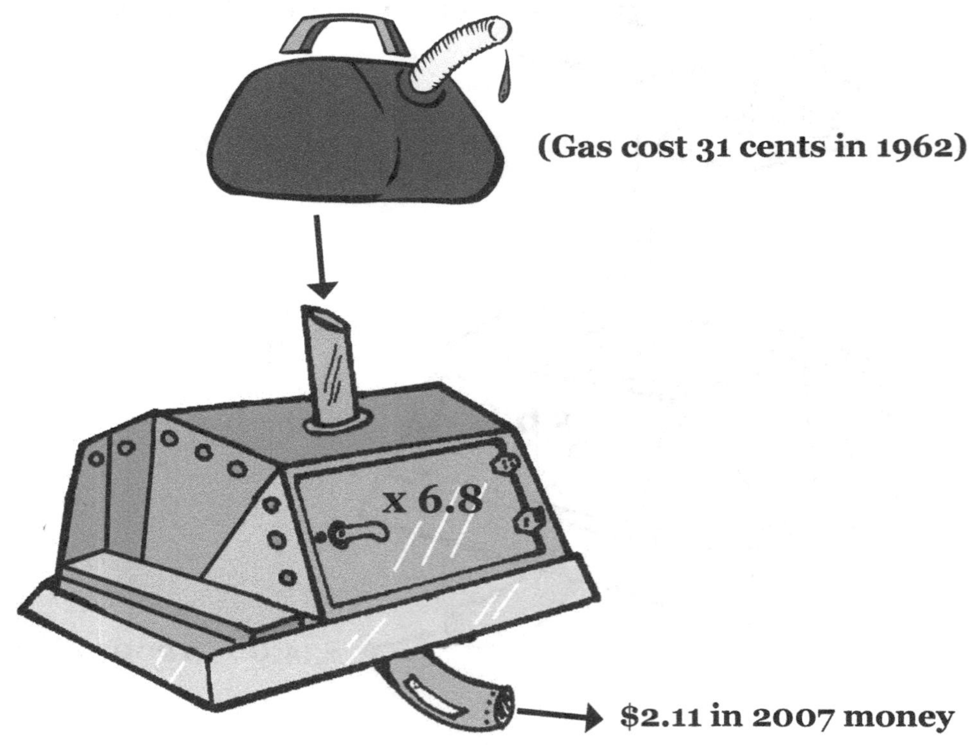
(Gas cost 31 cents in 1962)
x 6.8
$2.11 in 2007 money

To see if the cost of an item was really cheaper in 1962, just put the 1962 price through the "into the future machine" and compare the result to the real price in 2007. I've listed 1962 and 2007 prices in the chart below.

Item	1962 Price	2007 Price
Loaf of bread	$.20	$1.20
Pound of ground beef	$.35	$2.61
Gallon of gas	$.31	$2.75
1st class postage	$.04	$.41
Color television	$400	$200
Newspaper	$.10	$.50
Refrigerator	$500	$1000
Doctor's visit	$5	$60
New home	$15,000	$180,000
New car	$2500	$21,000
Median family income	$6000	$48,000
Minimum wage	$1.25	$5.85

I really want to know if gas was cheaper in 1962. When I put 31 cents through the "Into the Future Machine" $2.11 came out.

Since a gallon of gas is more expensive than $2.11 today, it is **really** more expensive today.

I'll try a color television and see how expensive it would have been to buy one in 1962 with 2007 money.

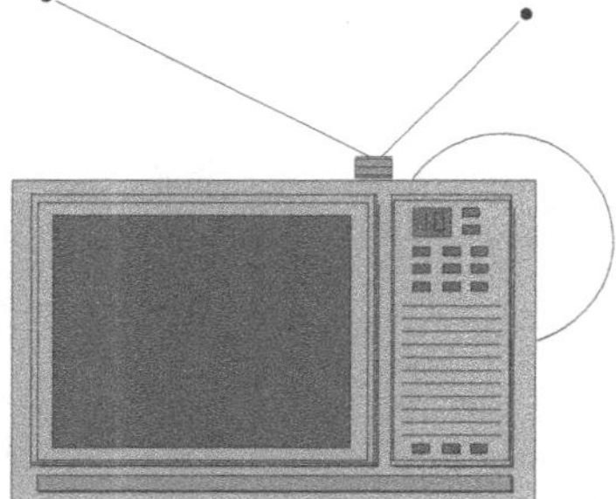

(A television cost $400 in 1962)

$2720 in 2007 money

It seems to me that a better way to determine the real cost of something is to see how many hours of work it takes to buy something.

I found out that it took 260 hours' wages to buy a bicycle in 1872 and only 5-10 hours' wages to buy one today. Even though they cost more in 2007, bicycles really are a lot cheaper now!

An even easier way to compare the amount of labor it took to buy items in different years is to make a ratio of the cost of an item compared to yearly family income. Look at what I did to compare the cost of a new car.

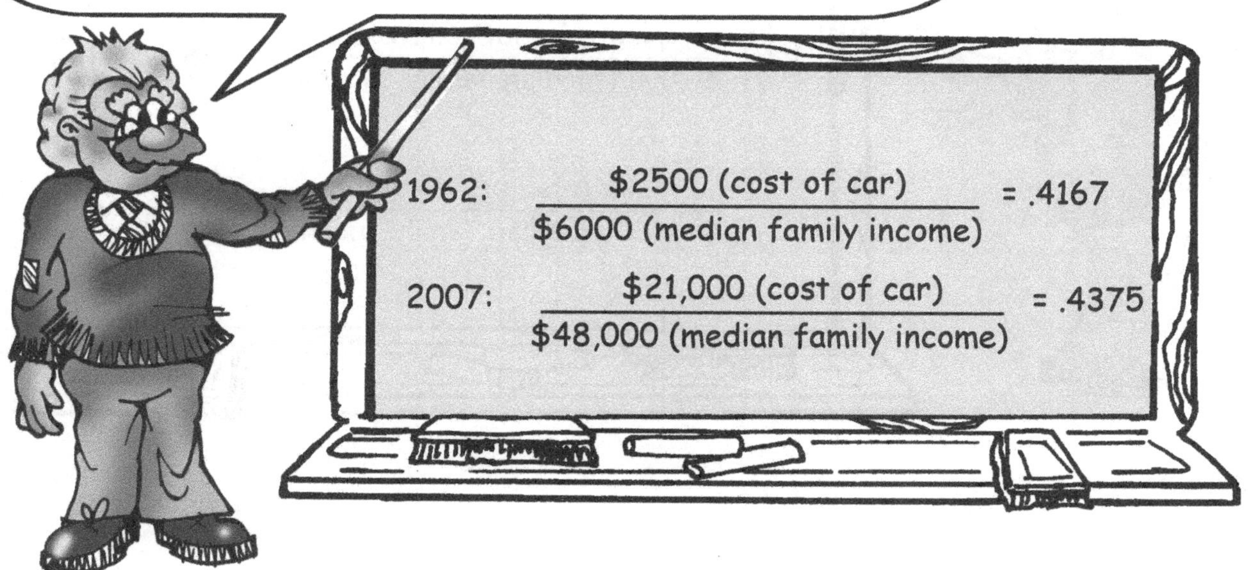

1962: $2500 (cost of car) / $6000 (median family income) = .4167
2007: $21,000 (cost of car) / $48,000 (median family income) = .4375

So it took more family labor to buy a car in 2007.

Another thing we have to keep in mind is that very few women worked outside the home in 1962. The $6000 median family income usually came from one worker.

Look at the difference in the amount of labor it took to buy a color television in 1962 and 2007. This is why you will see many color televisions in a single home today and rarely saw even one in a 1962 home.

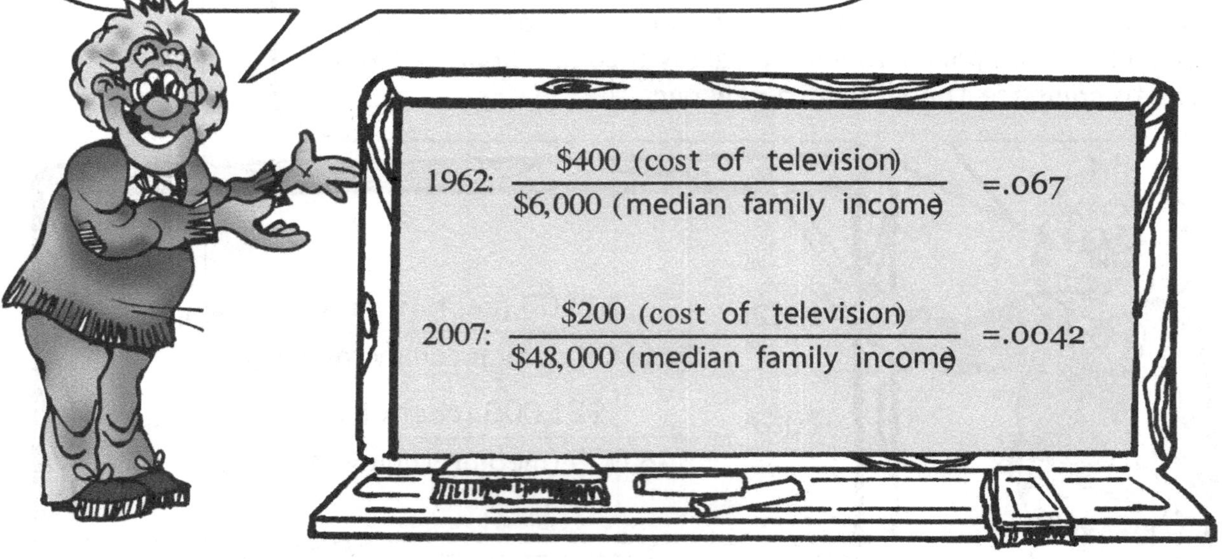

1962: $400 (cost of television) / $6,000 (median family income) =.067
2007: $200 (cost of television) / $48,000 (median family income) =.0042

Wow!! That is almost 16 times the wages in 1962 to buy a television when you compare it to 2007.

Level 1

1) A 1st class stamp cost 4 cents in 1962. What was its cost in "2007 money"?
(Hint: The answer is not 41 cents.)

2) A pound of ground beef cost 35 cents in 1962. What was the cost of this 1962 pound of ground beef in "2007 money"?

3) The minimum hourly wage was $1.25 in 1962. What was the 1962 minimum wage in "2007 money"?

Level 2

1) The cost of a loaf of bread was 20 cents in 1962. The cost for a loaf of bread in 2007 was $1.20. If you are traveling back to 1962, should you buy a loaf of bread in 2007 and bring it with you, or bring "2007 money" with you and buy the loaf in 1962? (Remember, "2007 money" is not worth as much as "1962 money".)

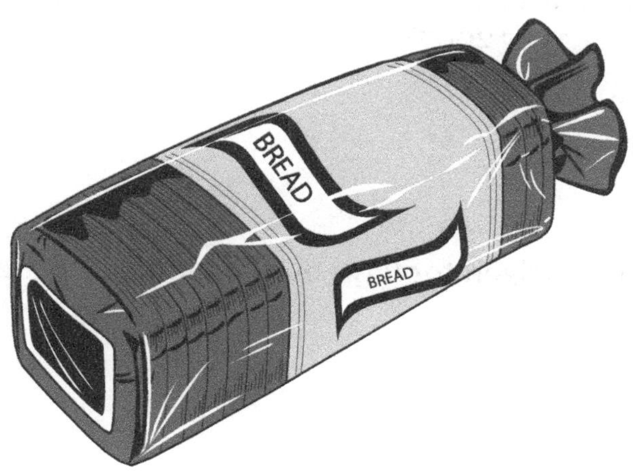

2) The price of a gallon of gas went from 31 cents in 1962 to 36 cents in 1972. Was gas "more expensive" in 1962 or 1972? Why? You will need to go to this web-site:

http://woodrow.mpls.frb.fed.us/research/data/us/calc/

3) By what percent did the median family income increase from 1962 to 2007?

Level 3

1) Did the typical family have more buying power in 1962 or 2007?

2) If the minimum wage increased at the same rate as median family income, what would the minimum wage be in the year 2007?

3) What would the cost of a refrigerator have been in 2007 in "1962 dollars"?

Einstein

If the value of money continues to decrease at the same rate in the next 45 years as it did in the 45 years from 1962 to 2007, what will a "2052 dollar" be worth in "1962 money"?

Answers with Solutions

Chapter 1

Level 1

1) $279.00

27.9% of $1000: .279 x $1000 = $279

2) $60

6% of $1000: .06 x $1000 = $60

3) $60

20% of $300 → .20 x $300 = $60

Level 2

1) About 8 weeks

2 weeks: 1.2 x $300 = $360
4 weeks: 1.2 x $360 = $432
6 weeks: 1.2 x $432 = $518.40
8 weeks: 1.2 x $518.40 = $622.08

2) 12 Years

Start: Any amount, say $1000
Year 1: 1.06 x $1000 = $1060
Year 2: 1.06 x $1060 = $1123.60
Year 3: 1.06 x $1123.60 = $1191.02
Year 4: 1.06 x $1191.02 = $1262.48
Year 5: 1.06 x $1262.48 = $1338.23
Year 6: 1.06 x $1338.23 = $1418.52
Year 7: 1.06 x $1418.52 = $1503.63 (round to $1500)
Year 8: 1.06 x $1500 = $1590
Year 9: 1.06 x $1590 = $1685.40
Year 10: 1.06 x $1685.40 = $1786.52
Year 11: 1.06 x $1786.53 = $1893.72
Year 12: 1.06 x $1893.72 = $2007.34

3) .04997% daily interest rate

18.240% ÷ 365 days in a year = .04997%

Level 3

1) $4000

35% of something = 1400
.35n = 1400
n=$4000

2) August 2007

Start: $2000
2 weeks: 1.18 x 2000 = $2360
4 weeks: 1.18 x $2360 = $2784.80
6 weeks: 1.18 x $2784.80 = $3286.06
8 weeks: 1.18 x $3286.06 = $3877.56
10 weeks: 1.18 x $3877.56 = $4575.52

10 weeks is in the third month of the loan, which is August.

3) Four Months

Start: $1000

1st month: 1.35 x $1000 = $1350 minus payment of $150 = $1200
2nd month: 1.35 x $1200 = $1620 minus payment of $150 = $1470
3rd month: 1.35 x $1470 = $1984.50 minus payment of $150 = $1834.50
4th month: 1.35 x $1834.50 = $2476.58 minus payment of $150 = $2326.58

Einstein

Answer: Approximately 225 Trillion Dollars

(Method 1)

With Exponents: $100 \times (1.2)^{156}$ = 225,047,598,769,261

The amount owed is multiplied by 100% + 20% or 1.2 every two weeks.
There are 156 two-week segments in six years.

(Method 2)

How many weeks until debt doubles (312 weeks in 6 years)

Start $100
2 weeks: $120
4 weeks: $144
6 weeks: $172.80
8 weeks: $207.36

Doubles every 8 weeks (approximately)

(Round to $200)

Week	Money Owed	Week	Money Owed
16	$400	168	$200 million
24	$800	176	$400 million
32	$1600	184	$800 million
40	$3200	192	$1.6 billion
48	$6400	200	$3.2 billion
56	$12,800	208	$6.4 billion
64	$25,600	216	$12.8 billion
72	$51,200 *(round to 50,000)*	224	$ 25.6 billion
80	$100,000	232	$50 billion *(rounded)*
88	$200,000	240	$100 billion
96	$400,000	248	$200 billion
104	$800,000	256	$400 billion
112	$1,600,000	264	$800 billion
120	$3.2 million	272	$1.6 trillion
128	$6.4 million	280	$3.2 trillion
136	$12.8 million	288	$6.4 trillion
144	$25.6 million	296	$12.8 trillion
152	$50 million *(rounded)*	304	$25.6 trillion
160	$100 million	312	$51.2 trillion

This estimate is significantly lower than method one because we rounded. (Rounding $207.36 to $200 dramatically lowers our total.)

Chapter 2

Level 1

1) 62,500 Btu per bushel

7,500,000 Btu per acre
120 bushels of corn per acre

7,500,000 ÷ 120 = 62,500 Btu per bushel of corn

2) 25,000 Btu

Bushel of corn: 62,500 Btu
2.5 gallons of ethanol in a bushel of corn
62,500 ÷ 2.5 = 25,000 Btu for enough corn to make a gallon of ethanol

3) 110,000 Btu

The American Institute of Biological Sciences concluded there is a 10% energy yield in the making of corn-based ethanol.

10% of 100,000 Btu = 10,000 Btu of added energy

Level 2

1) 3.6%

5 billion gallons of ethanol ÷ 140 billion gallons of gasoline and diesel = 3.6%

2) No.

There is only 2/3 the amount of energy in ethanol compared to gasoline.

3) 24.3 billion gallons of ethanol

14% made 3.4 billion gallons of ethanol
Each 1% made 3.4 billion gallons ÷ 14 = .243 billion gallons
If 1% of the corn crop made .243 billion gallons of ethanol, then 100% of the corn crop would make 100 x .243 billion gallons = 24.3 billion gallons of ethanol.

Level 3

1) 240 miles

Ethanol has only 2/3 the energy of gasoline:
80,000 Btu compared to 120,000 Btu.
2/3 of 360 miles = 240 miles

$$\frac{80{,}000 \text{ Btu per gallon}}{120{,}000 \text{ Btu per gallon}}$$

2) Gasoline

Ethanol has 2/3 the energy of gasoline
2/3 of \$3.50 = \$2.33
\$2.33 would be an equivalent cost for ethanol.
\$2.50 ethanol is more expensive than \$3.50 gasoline.

3) 50 cents

$$\frac{1{,}000{,}000 \text{ Btu}}{\$14} = \frac{36{,}000 \text{ Btu for 1 gallon}}{n}$$

Cross-multiply: 1,000,000n = 504,000
Divide both sides by 1,000,000: n = .504 dollars or 50 cents

Einstein

Answer: Corn-based ethanol is not an effective way to lower our use of fossil fuels.

Chapter 3

Level 1

1) 6250 gallons of gas

75,000 miles in 5 years ÷ 12 miles per gallon = 6250 gallons

2) 1875 gallons

75,000 miles in 5 years ÷ 40 miles per gallon = 1875 gallons

3) $3062.50

15,000 ÷ 40 = 375 gallons per year
15,000 ÷ 12 = 1250 gallons per year
1250 gallons – 375 gallons = 875 gallons x $3.50 per gallon = $3062.50

Level 2

1) $1875

Melinda: 15,000 miles ÷ 40 miles per gallon = 375 gallons
375 gallons x $3 per gallon = $1125
Blake: 15,000 miles ÷ 15 miles per gallon = 1000 gallons
1000 gallons x $3 per gallon = $3000
$3000 - $1125 = $1875

2) $4375

Melinda: 375 gallons x $7 = $2625
Blake: 1000 gallons x $7 = $7000
$7000 - $2625 = $4375

3) 359.5 gallons

Jordan: 10,000 miles x 5 years = 50,000 miles ÷ 45 mpg = 1111.1 gallons
LaKisha: 10,000 x 5 years = 50,000 miles ÷ 34 mpg = 1470.6 gallons
1470.6 gallons – 1111.1 gallons = 359.5 gallons

Level 3

1) Automobile 25 mpg • Motorcycle 60 mpg • Jet airplane .146 mpg

Automobile: 500 miles ÷ 20 gallons = 25 mpg
Motorcycle: 180 miles ÷ 3 gallons = 60 mpg
Jet airplane: 8350 miles ÷ 57,285 gallons = .146 mpg

2) Option 1 --- use automobiles

Option 1: 3000 miles ÷ 25 mpg = 120 gallons per car
525 people ÷ 5 people per car = 105 cars
105 cars x 120 gallons = **12,600 gallons**
Option 2: 3000 miles ÷ 60 mpg = 50 gallons of gas per motorcycle
50 gallons x 525 motorcycles = **26,250 gallons**
Option 3: 3000 miles ÷ .146 mpg = **20,548 gallons**

3) $9428

Miles driven each year: 180 miles x 300 days = 54,000 miles
Gallons used at 14 mpg: 54,000 miles ÷ 14 = 3857 gallons
Gallons used at 36 mpg: 54,000 ÷ 36 = 1500 gallons
Cost at 14 mpg: 3857 gallons x $4 per gallon = $15,428
Cost at 36 mpg: 1500 gallons x $4 per gallon = $6000
$15,428 - $6000 = $9428

Einstein

Answer: 7.2 years

Cost of hybrid with tax: $21,960 x 1.07 = $23,497.20
Cost of non-hybrid with tax: $18,390 x 1.07 = $19,677.30
Cost of hybrid with tax credit: $23,497.20 - $2100 = $21,397,20
Extra cost for hybrid: $21,397.20 - $19,677.30 = $1719.90

Gallons of gas used each year:
Hybrid: 12,000 ÷ 50 = 240 gallons
Non-hybrid: 12,000 ÷ 40 = 300 gallons
Savings: 60 gallons x $4 = $240 per year
Extra cost ($1719.90) ÷ savings per year ($240) = 7.2 years

Chapter 4

Level 1

1) 3/4

Four possibilities: BB GG BG GB Three of these have a girl in the pair.
OR
Probability not picking a girl:
1/2 each time 1/2 x 1/2 = 1/4 no girls: So 3/4 has girl or girls

2) 7/8

Eight possibilities: BBB BBG BGB BGG GGG GGB GBG GBB
Seven of these have a girl in them.
Or
Probability of not picking a girl: ½ each time
1/2 x 1/2 x 1/2 = 1/8
If not picking a girl with three picks is 1/8, then picking a girl is 7/8.

3) 1023/1024

It would be too time-consuming to write out all the possibilities, so you must ask "What is the probability of not picking a girl for each of the ten people chosen?"

Probability of not picking a girl: ½ each time.

10 picks:
1/2 x 1/2 x 1/2 x 1/2 x 1/2 x 1/2 x 1/2 x 1/2 x 1/2 x 1/2 = 1/1024 *(No girls chosen)*
1 - 1/1024 = 1023/1024 (Probability at least one girl is chosen)

Level 2

1) 9/400 or approximately 2%

$$\frac{15}{100} \times \frac{15}{100} \quad \text{reduce} \quad \frac{3}{20} \times \frac{3}{20} = \frac{9}{400}$$

9 ÷ 400 = .0225 or 2.25%

2) 27/8000 or 1/3%

$$\frac{3}{20} \times \frac{3}{20} \times \frac{3}{20} = \frac{27}{8000}$$

27 ÷ 8000 = .003375 or .3375%

3) 289/400 or 72.25%

15% are left-handed so 85% are not left-handed $\frac{85}{100} \times \frac{85}{100}$ or $\frac{17}{20} \times \frac{17}{20} = \frac{289}{400}$
289 ÷ 400 = .7225 or 72.25%

Level 3

1) 39%

The probability that a person is left-handed is 15% so the probability that a person is not left-handed is 85%.
For each pick the probability of "not left-handed" is 85% or 17/20
Three people: 17/20 x 17/20 x 17/20 = 4913/8000
Probability that all three are not left-handed (61%)
Probability that there is at least one left-handed person: 100% - 61% = 39%

2) 14.5%

Probability that a person is left-handed: 15%
Probability that a person is left-handed and a girl: 15% x ½ = 7.5%
Probability that a person is not a left-handed girl: 100% - 7.5% = 92.5%
Each pick the probability of not being a left-handed girl:
92.5% or 92.5/100 or 185/200

Two people: Probability of not being a left-handed girl: 185/200 x 185/200
REDUCE 37/40 x 37/40 = 1369/1600 = 85.5%
Probability of two people and neither a left-handed girl is 85.5% so the probability of at least one left-handed girl: 100% - 85.5% = 14.5%

3) 99.6%

Probability that the person would be a left-handed, blue-eyed male:
10% x 8% x 50% = 1/10 x 2/25 x 1/2 = 1/250 or .4%
Probability that the person would not be a left-handed, blue-eyed male:
100% - .4% = 99.6%

Einstein

Answer: 15.6%

Probability of rolling double ones: 1/36
Probability of not rolling double ones for each roll: 35/36
Probability of not rolling double ones for all six rolls:

$$35/36 \times 35/36 \times 35/36 \times 35/36 \times 35/36 \times 35/36 = \frac{1{,}838{,}265{,}625}{2{,}176{,}782{,}336} = 84.4\%$$

Probability of losing: 84.4%
Probability of winning: 100% - 84.4% = 15.6%

Chapter 5

Level 1

1) 27 jumbo jets

5,000,000 deaths each year ÷ 365 days in a year = 13,699 deaths each day from smoking
13,699 deaths each day from smoking ÷ 500 people per plane = 27 jumbo jets

2) $500 each year

$150,000,000,000 ÷ 300,000,000 = $500

3) 36,500,000 children start smoking every year

100,000 children every day x 365 days in a year = 36,500,000 children each year

Level 2

1) 173,611 cigarettes sold every second

60 seconds each minute x 60 minutes in an hour x 24 hours in a day
= 86,400 seconds in a day

15,000,000,000 cigarettes ÷ 86,400 seconds
= 173,611 cigarettes sold every second

2) **480,000,000 adults**

96% of 500,000,000 adults
.96 x 500,000,000 = 480,000,000 adults

3) 213 million adults

20.9% of adults = 44.5 million
20.9% of n = 44,500,000
.209n = 44,500,000 Divide both sides by .209
n = 44,500,000 ÷ .209 = 213,000,000

Level 3

1) 4.2 years

Number of cigarettes smoked in 30 years:
40 per day x 365 days in a year x 30 years = 438,000 cigarettes
438,000 cigarettes x 5 minutes = 2,190,000 minutes of life lost
2,190,000 minutes ÷ 60 = 36,500 hours of life lost
36,500 hours ÷ 24 = 1521 days of life lost
1521 days ÷ 365 = 4.2 years of life lost

2) 47%

Percent of change is found by finding the amount of increase or decrease and then dividing by the original amount.
2900 (1976) – 1545 (2003) = 1355 (Amount of change)
1355 ÷ 2900 = .467 or 47%

3) 24.85 million males smoke

Algebra is very helpful when solving this problem.

Call male smokers: n
Female smokers would then be 44.5 million – n
(This is because there are 44.5 million total smokers and the number of male smokers is n. Total minus male smokers is the number of female smokers.)

$$\frac{23.4\%}{18.5\%} = \frac{n}{44.5 \text{ million} - n}$$

$$\frac{.234}{.185} = \frac{n}{44.5 \text{ million} - n}$$ *Cross-multiply*

.185n = 10,413,000 - .234n *(add .234n to each side)*
.419n = 10,413,000 *(Divide both sides by .419)*
n = 24,850,000 male smokers *(Rounded)*

Einstein

Answer: $6.47 tax on every pack of cigarettes

300,000,000 x 1545 cigarettes per person = 463,500,000,000 cigarettes smoked each year in the United States.

463,500,000,000 cigarettes ÷ 20 in a pack = 23,175,000,000 packs smoked each year

$150,000,000,000 (Cost of smoking related diseases) ÷ 23,175,000,000 packs smoked each year = $6.47 tax per pack

Chapter 6

Level 1

1) 190 chess games

$_{20}P_{2}$

20 students taken 2 at a time: 20 x 19 = 380 permutations

This includes A playing B and B playing A which is really only one game, so we must divide 380 by 2.

380 ÷ 2 = 190 chess games

2) 465 pairs

P
31 2

31 students taken 2 at a time

31 x 30 = 930 permutations

We must divide by 2 to eliminate pairs that are counted twice. (AB and BA)
930 ÷ 2 = 465 pairs.

3) 780 games

P
40 2

40 x 39 = 1560

Divide by 2 to eliminate AB BA situations 1560 ÷ 2 = 780

Level 2

---

1) 3 or 4 matching pairs

P
50 2

50 x 49 = 2450 permutations

Divide by 2 to eliminate AB BA duplicates
2450 ÷ 2 = 1225 pairs

1/365 probability of each pair having matching birthdays. (*Estimate)*

1225 pairs ÷ 365 = 3.4 matching pairs

2) Between 8 and 9 matching pairs

P
30 2

30 x 29 = 870 permutations

Divide by 2 to eliminate AB BA duplicates
870 ÷ 2 = 435 pairs

1/52 probability of each pair matching. (*Estimate)*

435 pairs divided by 52 will give you a good estimate.

435 ÷ 52 = 8.4 pairs

3) $\mathbf{\dfrac{1}{48{,}627{,}125}}$

$$\frac{365}{365} \times \frac{1}{365} \times \frac{1}{365} \times \frac{1}{365} = \frac{1}{48{,}627{,}125}$$

Level 3

1) 161,700 different groups of three

$P_{100\ 3}$

100 people taken 3 at a time

100 x 99 x 98 = 970,200

Eliminate duplicates (Such as ABC ACB BCA BAC CAB CBA)
970,200 ÷ 6 = 161,700

2) Between 13 and 14 matching pairs

$P_{100\ 2}$

100 x 99 = 9900

Divide by 2 to eliminate AB BA duplicates: 9900 ÷ 2 = 4950 pairs

4950 ÷ 365 = 13.5

3) One

$_{100}P_{3}$

100 x 99 x 98 = 970,200 permutations

Eliminate duplicates: 970,200 ÷ 6 = 161,700 groups of three

Probability of three randomly chosen people having matching birthdays:

$$\frac{365}{365} \times \frac{1}{365} \times \frac{1}{365} = \frac{1}{133{,}225}$$

Einstein

Answer: We can predict that there will be one matching birthday that will be Girl/Girl.

$_{16}P_{2}$

16 x 15 = 240 240 ÷ 2 = 120 pairs

31 days in the month of January. Approximately 1 in 31 will match birthdays.

120 ÷ 31 = 4 predicted matches.

Each match will be one of these: Boy/Boy Girl/Girl Boy/Girl Girl/Boy

We expect 4 matches --- only 1 in 4 is predicted to be Girl/Girl
We can predict one match will be Girl/Girl

Chapter 7

Level 1

1) No. The speed limit was 49.68 mph

Kilometers to miles conversion: x .621

80 kilometers x .621 = 49.68 mph

2) Yes. Ryan will be digging 121.92 centimeters deep.

Inches to centimeter conversion: x 2.54

48 inches x 2.54 = 121.92

3) 48,000 kilograms

The aquarium holds 20 x 30 x 80 = 48,000 cubic decimeters of water, which weighs one kilogram per cubic decimeter.

Level 2

1) 299,517 kilometers per second

Kilometers to miles conversion: x .621

Kilometers x .621 = 186,000 miles

Divide both sides by .621:
Kilometers = 186,000 ÷ .621 = 299,517 kilometers per second

2) 22,300 kilograms of water would be equal to 22,300 liters.

Because jet fuel weighs less than water, the flight crew would need more than 22,300 liters to equal 22,300 kilograms. They only had 12,599 liters --- about half of what they needed!

3) 1,000,000 cubic centimeters

The sides of a cubic meter:
Length: 100 centimeters
Width: 100 centimeters
Height: 100 centimeters
Volume: 100 x 100 x 100 = 1,000,000 cubic centimeters

Level 3

1) **$1.06**

Liters to quarts conversion: x 1.057

n liters x 1.057 = 4 quarts

Divide both sides by 1.057

n liters = 4 quarts ÷ 1.057

3.78 liters in 4 quarts (gallon)

3.78 liters in one gallon so 3.78 liters cost $4

One liter cost $4 ÷ 3.78 = $1.06

2) $78.70

How many 1.08's will fit into 85?

85 ÷ 1.08 = $78.70

Ratios:

$$\frac{\text{One US dollar}}{\text{1.08 Canadian}} = \frac{\text{n US dollars}}{\text{85 Canadian dollars}}$$

Cross-multiply: 1.08n = 85

Divide both sides by 1.08: n = 78.70

3) 77,499 liters

$$\frac{\text{8350 miles}}{\text{57,000 gallons}} = \frac{\text{3000 miles}}{\text{n gallons}}$$

Cross-multiply: 8350n = 171,000,000

Divide both sides by 8350: n = 20,479 gallons of jet fuel or 81,916 quarts

Liters to quarts: Liters x 1.057

n x 1.057 = 81,916 quarts

Divide both sides by 1.057: n = 77,499

Einstein

Answer: 17.2 cubic meters

A cubic meter is 39.372 inches x 39.372 inches x 39.372 inches = 61,033 cubic inches

Driveway in inches: 81 x 12 = 972 inches long
15 x 12 = 180 inches wide
½ x 12 = 6 inches thick

Volume of driveway: 972 inches x 180 inches x 6 inches = 1,049,760 cubic inches

1,049,760 cubic inches ÷ 61,033 cubic inches in a cubic meter = 17.2 cubic meters

Chapter 8

Level 1

1) $837

.279 x $3000 = $837

2) $7064.96

.329 x $5316 = $1748.96 additional interest + $5316 = $7064.96

3) Approximately three years

Year 1: .25 x $1000 = $250 additional interest + $1000 = $1250 debt

Year 2: .25 x $1250 = $312.50 additional interest + $1250 = $1562.50 debt

Year 3: .25 x $1562.50 = $390.63 additional interest + $1562.50 = $1953.13 debt

Level 2

1) $7796

Item	Cost New	Rent-to-own
Washer & Dryer	$620	$39 x 78 = $3042
Television 19 inches	$200	$12 x 87 = $1044
Living Room Set	$2100	$85 x 78 = $6630

$6630 + $1044 + $3042 = $10,716 - $2920 (cost new) = $7796

2) $1604

Cost through rent-to-own: $62 x 52 weeks = $3224

Interest on bank loan for one year: 8% of $1500
.08 x $1500 = $120

Total cost with 8% bank loan: $1500 + $120 = $1620

$3224 - $1620 = $1604

3) 2.74%

32.9% ÷ 12 = 2.74%

Level 3

1) $216

Interest rate for one month: 27.9% ÷ 12 = 2.325%

Interest payment for one month: .02325 x $8000 = $186 + $30 late fee = $216

2) An increase of $67.02 to $95.90 each month

Monthly interest rate at 9.9% annual interest: 9.9% ÷ 12 = .825%

Monthly interest payment: .00825 x 3500 = $28.88

Monthly interest rate at 32.9% annual interest: 32.9% ÷ 12 = 2.74 %

Monthly interest payment: .0274 x 3500 = $95.90

$95.90 - $28.88 = $67.02

3) 29.9%

Annual interest charge for $2400: 59.76 x 12 = $717.12

Annual percentage rate: $717.12/$2400 = .2988 or 29.9%

Einstein

Answer: Never - Because his balance will always stay around $1800.

Interest rate for one year: 27.9%

Interest rate for one month: 27.9% ÷ 12 = 2.325%

Month 1:

Loan Amount: $1800.00
Interest Charge: .02325 x $1800 = $41.85
Payment: $50.00
New Amount Owed: $1800.00 + $41.85 - $50 = $1791.85

Month 2:

Loan Amount: $1791.85
Interest Charge: .02325 x $1791.85 = $41.66
Payment: $50.00
New Amount Owed: $1791.85+ $41.66 - $50 = $1783.51

Month 3:

Loan Amount: $1783.51
Interest Charge: .02325 x $1783.51 = $41.47
Payment: $50.00
New Amount Owed: $1783.51 + $41.47 - $50 = $1774.98

We can see that the loan amount is decreasing each month by approximately $8 - $10. The loan amount owed will therefore drop by about $120 in a year.

Because Luke cashes a check for $120 each year, his balance will always increase $120 every year. Because of this, his debt will stay around $1800.

Chapter 9

Level 1

1) Jillian was right because the ad said that apples were ½ cent each.
(.50 cents each is the same as ½ cent.)

2) **B and C are correct**

(A) states that Ruben is selling earthworms for 1/10 of a cent each or 100 for a dime.

3) Their intent was to tax each cigarette 1.5 cents, but they forgot to make it clear that the tax was on EACH cigarette. They passed a law that taxed the tobacco industry a total of 1.5 cents!

Level 2

1) .80 cents does not mean 80 cents and it also does not mean 8 cents.
.80 cents means 8/10 of one cent.

2) 10,000

.01 cents is 1/100 of a cent. It will take 100 → .01 cents to make one cent, so it will take 100 x 100 = 10,000 to make one dollar.

3) .07 cents 2/3 cent .05 dollars $.06

.07 cents = 7/100 of a cent

2/3 cent = 2/3 of a cent or 67/100 of a cent

.05 dollars = 5 cents

$.06 = 6 cents

Level 3

1) $500

.50% = ½ of one percent

1% of $100,000 = $1000

½ of 1% = $500

2) It is impossible to reach a temperature of -480 degrees. Absolute zero (lowest possible temperature) is:

Kelvin: 0°

Fahrenheit: -459.6°

Centigrade: -273°

3) Sara thought that she needed to add the percents to find her discount.

The correct way to determine the discount is to take 50% of \$100 = \$50

Now take the 45% discount: 45% of \$50 = \$22.50 discount

\$50 - \$22.50 = \$27.50

Einstein

Answer: The law should have been written: "Drivers with a blood-alcohol content higher than .18% are guilty of aggravated driving while intoxicated."

If the law remains as written, every driver in New York is guilty of aggravated driving while intoxicated because .18 grams of alcohol occurs naturally in the bloodstream even without drinking a drop of an alcoholic beverage!

Chapter 10

Level 1

1) 479

81	9	1
5	8	2

5 groups of 81 = 405
8 groups of 9 = 72
2 groups of 1 = 2

405 + 72 + 2 = 479

2) 820

729	81	9	1
1	1	1	1

1 group of 729 = 729
1 group of 81 = 81
1 group of 9 = 9

1 group of 1 = 1

729 + 81 + 9 + 1 = 820

3) 252

Each column is found by multiplying by 5..

125	25	5	1
2	0	0	2

2 groups of 125 = 250
0 groups of 25 = 0
0 groups of 5 = 0
2 groups of 1 = 2

250 + 2 = 252

Level 2

1) 1138

How many 729's are in 845? 845 ÷ 729 = 1 group of 729 with 116 left over.

How many 81's are in 116? 116 ÷ 81 = 1 group of 81 with 35 left over.

How many 9's are in 35? 35 ÷ 9 = 3 groups of 9 with 8 left over.

How many groups of 1 are in 8? 8

729	81	9	1
1	1	3	8

2) 11

How many groups of 9 are in 10? 10 ÷ 9 = 1 with 1 left over.

How many groups of 1 are in 1? 1

6561	729	81	9	1
			1	1

3) 1100100

100 ÷ 64 = 1 group of 64 with 36 left over.

36 ÷ 32 = 1 group of 32 with 4 left over.

No groups of 16 in 4.

No groups of 8 in 4.

1 group of 4 in 4 with 0 left over.

Each column is found by multiplying by 2.

128	64	32	16	8	4	2	1
	1	1	0	0	1	0	0

Level 3

1) 8 4 2 1 . 1/2 1/4 1/8

2) $2\frac{19}{25}$

Columns for base 5:

25	5	1	.	1/5	1/25
		2		3	4

This means:

2 groups of 1 = 2

3 groups of 1/5 = 3/5

4 groups of 1/25 = 4/25

3) The base 10 number .9999 approaches one without reaching it.
In base 2, .11111 approaches one without reaching it.

$$\frac{1}{2} + \frac{1}{4} + \frac{1}{8} + \frac{1}{16} + \frac{1}{32} + \frac{1}{64}$$

Einstein

Answer: $117 \frac{33}{125}$

1000	100	10	1	.	1/10	1/100	1/1000

Base 10 has these columns.

125	25	5	1	.	1/5	1/25	1/125
	4	3	2		1	1	3

Base 5 has these columns.

4 groups of 25 = 100
3 groups of 5 = 15
2 groups of 1 = 2
1 group of 1/5 = 1/5
1 group of 1/25 = 1/25
3 groups of 1/125 = 3/125

100 + 15 + 2 + 1/5 + 1/25 + 3/125 =

117 + $\frac{1}{5}$ $\frac{25}{125}$

$\frac{1}{25}$ $\frac{5}{125}$

$\frac{3}{125}$ $\frac{3}{125}$

$\frac{33}{125}$

Chapter 11

Level 1

1)

-Write down a 2-digit number	n
-Add 100 to the number	n + 100
-Multiply by 10	10n + 1000
-Subtract 40	10n + 960
-Divide by 10	n + 96
-Subtract the number you picked	96
-You are left with 96!	96

2)

n	Pick a number
n + 50	Add 50
5n + 250	Multiply by 5
5n + 100	Subtract 150
n + 20	Divide by 5
20	Subtract number you picked. You are left with 20.

3)

-Pick a number from 1 to 9 and enter it into your calculator	n
-Multiply by 18,518.5	18,518.5n
-Now multiply by 6	111,111n

-You will now have a row of the number you picked on your calculator!

Whatever number you picked will be multiplied by 111,111. This will make many copies of your number.

Example: If n = 8 then 111,111n will be 888,888

Level 2

1)

-Pick a 2—digit number	n
-Add 102	n + 102
-Multiply by 2	2n + 204
-Add 96	2n + 300
-Divide by 2	n + 150
-Subtract 149	n + 1
-Subtract your original number	1
-Divide by 9	1/9
-You are left with .11111	1/9 = .111111

2)

-Pick a number	n
-Multiply by 2	2n
-Add 100	2n + 100
-Multiply by 8	16n + 800
-Subtract 400	16n + 400
-Divide by 16	n + 25
-Subtract the number you picked	25
-You ended up with 25	25

3)

-Pick a 3-digit number	n
-Add 100	n + 100
-Multiply by 7	7n + 700
-Subtract 28	7n + 672
-Divide by 7	n + 96
-Add 159	n + 255
-Subtract your original number	255

-Change the digits in the remaining number into letters.
(A = 1   B = 2   C = 3   D = 4 and so on)   2=B 5 = E 5 = E

-You now have spelled out BEE.

Level 3

1)

-Pick two 3-digit numbers and add them	a + b
-Add 850	a + b + 850
-Multiply by 3	3a + 3b + 2550
-Subtract 1440	3a + 3b + 1110
-Divide by 3	a + b + 370
-Subtract the sum of the two number you picked	370

-You are left with 370

2) $$\frac{n}{525{,}600}$$

n minutes old

n/60 hours old because there are 60 minutes in an hour.

n/1440 days old because there are 1440 minutes in a day.

n/525,600 years old because there are 525,600 minutes in a year.

3) 991

Smallest number: n
Next odd: n + 2
Next odd: n + 4
Next odd: n + 6
Next odd: n + 8
Next odd: n + 10
Next odd: n + 12
Next odd: n + 14
Next odd: n + 16
Largest number: n + 18

Add all ten numbers: $10n + 90 = 10{,}000$

Subtract 90 from both sides: $10n = 9910$

Divide both sides by 10: $n = 991$

Einstein

Answer: 20 years old

Language of algebra:

Albert Einstein: n
Marie Curie: 1.5n
Franklin Roosevelt: .75n
Sir Alexander Fleming: .75n + 1

Add all ages: $n + 1.5n + .75n + (.75n + 1) = 81$

Collect n's: $4n + 1 = 81$

Subtract 1 from both sides: $4n = 80$

$n = 20$

Chapter 12

Level 1

Length of a football field in yards	10^{2}
Number of millimeters in a meter	10^{3}
Number of kilograms in 22 pounds	10^{1}
Millimeters in a kilometer	10^{6}
Number of stars in the universe	10^{22}
Number of moons orbiting the Earth	10^{0}

Level 2

If you weighed 70 pounds on Earth, how many pounds would you weigh on a neutron star?	10^{13}
Number of molecules in a little more than a cup of water.	10^{25}
If you weighed 37 pounds on Earth, how many pounds would you weigh on the sun?	10^{3}
If your weight on Earth is 150 pounds, how many pounds would you weigh on Pluto?	10^{1}
How many cubic millimeters in a cubic meter?	10^{9}
The weight of a grain of sand on Earth is 1/1,000,000 of an ounce. How many pounds does a grain of sand weigh on a neutron star?	10^{4}

Level 3

1) 10^{38}

$10^{18} \times 10^{20} = 10^{38}$

2) 10,000 stars for each grain of sand

Dropping from 10^{20} to 10^{18} is 100 times smaller.

Therefore there must be 100 x 100 stars per grain of sand = 10,000.

3) 10 trillion or 10^{13}

Needed zeros: 10^{100}

Zeros in the universe: 10^{87}

10^{100} divided by 10^{87} equals (10,000,000,000,000)

Einstein

Answer: Between 6 and 7 million TONS of TNT

Magnitude 1: 6 ounces of TNT or 6/16 (.375) pounds or .375 ÷ 2000 = .0001875 tons

Magnitude 2: .0001875 tons x 32 = .006 tons of TNT

Magnitude 3: .006 tons x 32 = .192 tons of TNT

Magnitude 4: .192 tons x 32 = 6.144 tons of TNT

Magnitude 5: 6.144 tons x 32 = 196.608 tons of TNT

Magnitude 6: 196.608 tons x 32 = 6291.456 tons of TNT

Magnitude 7: 6291.456 tons x 32 = 201,326.592 tons of TNT

Magnitude 8: 201,326.592 x 32 = 6 to 7 million tons of TNT

Chapter 13

Level 1

1) One person

99.9% x 1000 = 999 get accurate results

2) 200 people

80% reliability means 80% x 1000 = 800 will get accurate results.

3) Person A would have a 1 in 11 chance of having the disease, but Person B would have a much higher chance of having the disease because he had symptoms of the disease. (He wasn't randomly chosen to take the test.)

Level 2

1) 1 in 2

In a group of 100 people, we can predict that one person will have the disease and one will test positive, but not have the disease. Two test positive, but only one will have the disease.

2) 1 in 6

If we selected 100 people at random, we could predict that there would be one case of the disease. If these 100 people were tested for the disease, five healthy individuals would test positive. (Test is 95% accurate.) There will be six positive tests and only one who really has the disease.

3) 5 out of 7

In a group of 100 people we can predict there will be five illegal drug users and also 2 people who will test positive, but do not use illegal drugs. Seven positive tests, five of the tests are accurate. 5/7 probability a positive test means the person uses illegal drugs.

Level 3

1) 10,980 people will test positive

1% of the population have the disease: 1% of 1,000,000 = 10,000

10,000 have the disease and 99.9% of those will test positive: .999 x 10,000 = 9,990

99% of population do not have Disease X: 99% of 1,000,000 = 990,000

.1% of healthy population test positive: .1% x 990,000 (.001 x 990,000) = 990

990 healthy test positive plus 9990 sick test positive = 10,980

2) 989,020 people will test negative

If 10,980 test positive, then 1,000,000 – 10,980 = 989,020 will test negative.

3) 1000 people will be given incorrect results

99.9% will be given correct results: 99.9% of 1,000,000 = 999,000

1,000,000 – 999,000 = 1000 incorrect results

990 false positive plus 10 false negatives

Einstein

Answer: 50%

Every 10,000 tests there will be one case of the disease.

If 10,000 people were tested, 99.99% of the negative tests would be accurate.

99.99% or .9999 x 10,000 tests = 9999 accurate negative tests and therefore one incorrect positive test.

Every 10,000 tests there will be one case of the disease and one false positive.

If an individual tests positive, there is a 1 in 2 probability that he has the disease.

Chapter 14

Level 1

1) 1/6

The first die rolled is on its way to being a match no matter what is rolled. A six, five, four, three, two, or a one are all okay.
The second die now must match the first die. It has a 1 in 6 chance of doing so.

1/1	x	1/6	= 1/6
first roll		second roll	

2) 1/36

The probability that the first roll will be a six is 1 in 6.

The probability that the second roll will also be a six is 1 in 6.

1/6	x	1/6	= 1/36
first roll		second roll	

3) 1/8

Each child born has a 1 in 2 chance of being a boy.

½	x	½	x	½	=	1/8
first child		second child		third child		

Level 2

1) Monica's thinking is incorrect

Monica is correct when she says that there is a 1/32 probability of flipping five heads in a row, but each flip has a 1 in 2 probability of being heads.

What is the probability of flipping five heads in a row? Answer: 1/32

What is the probability of flipping five heads in a row after the first four are heads? Answer: ½

2) 1/1000

You have a 1/10 chance of picking each number correctly.

1/10	x	1/10	x	1/10	= 1/1000
first number		second number		third number	

3) 1/1296

Roll one of the dice: Always successful because any number is okay. (6/6 success probability)

Second die: 1/6 probability of matching first roll

Third die: 1/6 probability of matching

Fourth die: 1/6 probability of matching

Fifth die: 1/6 probability of matching

$$\frac{6}{6} \text{ x } \frac{1}{6} \text{ x } \frac{1}{6} \text{ x } \frac{1}{6} \text{ x } \frac{1}{6} = \frac{1}{1296}$$

Level 3

1) $\frac{1}{10{,}939{,}383}$

You must match the first five balls drawn before the last "hot ball" is picked. The probability that the first ball picked will match any of your five numbers is 5/39. If you get a match, then the probability that the second pick will match any of your four remaining balls is 4/38 because there are 38 ping-pong balls left in the box.

Third ping-pong ball pick: 3/37

Fourth ping-pong ball pick: 2/36

Fifth ping-pong ball pick: 1/35

Now there is a 1/19 probability that your "hot ball" pick will be correct.

Probability of winning the lottery:

$$\frac{5}{39} \text{ x } \frac{4}{38} \text{ x } \frac{3}{37} \text{ x } \frac{2}{36} \text{ x } \frac{1}{35} \text{ x } \frac{1}{19}$$

Reduce:

$$\frac{1}{13} \text{ x } \frac{1}{19} \text{ x } \frac{1}{37} \text{ x } \frac{1}{9} \text{ x } \frac{1}{7} \text{ x } \frac{1}{19} = \frac{1}{10{,}939{,}383}$$

2) 1/146,107,962

The probability that the first ping-pong ball picked will be one of the player's five is 5/55.

The probability that the second ping-pong ball will match is 4/54 because the player has four numbers left and there are 54 ping-pong balls left in the box.

Third pick: 3/53

Fourth pick: 2/52

Fifth pick: 1/51

The chance that the Powerball is correct is 1/42.

Probability of winning:

$$\frac{5}{55} \times \frac{4}{54} \times \frac{3}{53} \times \frac{2}{52} \times \frac{1}{51} \times \frac{1}{42}$$

Reduced

$$\frac{1}{11} \times \frac{1}{54} \times \frac{1}{53} \times \frac{1}{13} \times \frac{1}{17} \times \frac{1}{21} = \frac{1}{146{,}107{,}962}$$

3) $\frac{1}{649{,}740}$

There are four tens, four jacks, four queens, four kings, and four aces in a deck of cards. The first card dealt, therefore, has a 20/52 probability of being a "successful" card.

After the first pick, there are only four "good" cards left because you are committed to one suit. (If you select the jack of clubs on your first pick, the only cards that will get you to a royal flush are the 10 of clubs, queen of clubs, king of clubs, and the ace of clubs.

Probability of winning:

$$\frac{20}{52} \times \frac{4}{51} \times \frac{3}{50} \times \frac{2}{49} \times \frac{1}{48}$$

Reduced

$$\frac{1}{13} \times \frac{1}{17} \times \frac{1}{5} \times \frac{1}{49} \times \frac{1}{12} = \frac{1}{649{,}740}$$

Einstein

Answer: ¼

When you learn that your friend has three children, then you know the children must be in one of eight possible combinations.

BOY BOY BOY
BOY BOY GIRL
BOY GIRL GIRL
BOY GIRL BOY
GIRL GIRL GIRL
GIRL GIRL BOY
GIRL BOY GIRL
GIRL BOY BOY

When your friend says that at least two of her children are boys, then the only combinations possible for her children are:

BOY BOY BOY
BOY BOY GIRL
BOY GIRL BOY
GIRL BOY BOY

Only one of these four combinations has the remaining child as a boy. Answer: 1 in 4

Chapter 15

Level 1

1) $770

$3500 x 22%   .22 x $3500 = $770

2) $1320

$72,000 ÷ 12 = $6000 monthly income

$6000 x 22%   .22 x $6000 = $1320

3) No. She should have limited her monthly payment to $462 per month.

22% of $2100   .22 x $2100 = $462
April's monthly payment: $55 + $220 + $1050 + $100 = $1425

Level 2

1) $1100

½% of $220,000 .005 x $220,000 = $1100

1% of $220,000 is $2200 so half of one percent is $2200 ÷ 2 = $1100

2) 34%

Gross monthly salary: $63,000 ÷ 12 = $5250

House payment: $1800

Percentage: $1800 ÷ $5250 = .34 or 34%

3) $1050 monthly charge for interest

An "interest only" loan means that you do not pay principal, only the interest. Because you pay only interest, the amount you owe on the loan never goes down.

9% annual interest: 9% ÷ 12 = ¾% interest each month

¾% of $140,000 = .0075 x $140,000 = $1050 interest each month

Level 3

1) $101,550

Interest charge per year: 5.75% x $100,000 .0575 x $100,000 = $5750

$100,000 + $5750 interest = $105,750 owed at the end of one year if no payments are made.

Amount Ruben paid: \$4200

Ruben did not even pay the interest he owed on the loan for the year.

Ruben will owe \$105,750 - \$4200 = \$101,550

2) \$119,000

\$51,000 ÷ 12 = \$4250 monthly gross income

What Daniel can afford: 22% of \$4250 .22 x 4250 = \$935 monthly payment limit

\$60 + \$180 + \$100 = \$340 cost for insurance, taxes and principal

\$935 - \$340 = \$595 left for monthly interest payment

Interest rate each month: 6% ÷ 12 = ½% each month

½% of some loan amount = \$595 (highest allowed monthly interest payment)

.005 x n = \$595 n = \$119,000

3) \$40,000 - \$50,000

Weekly pay: \$11.50 x \$40 = \$460

Yearly pay: \$460 x 52 weeks = \$23,920

Monthly pay: \$23,920 ÷ 12 = \$1993.33

22% of \$1993.33 .22 x \$1993.33 = \$438.53
(Maximum monthly house payment)

\$100 + \$50 + \$75 (property tax + insurance + principal)= \$225

\$438.53 - \$225 = \$213.53 left to pay interest each month on a loan.

6% yearly interest: 6% ÷ 12 = ½% monthly interest (.005)

½% of loan amount = 213.53

.005n = \$213.53

n = \$42,706

Einstein

Answer: 4.5% loan payments were 22% of Martha's salary
9.5% loan payments were 35% of Martha's salary

4.5% loan:

Martha's monthly salary: $38,400 ÷ 12 = $3200

Yearly interest with 4.5% loan: .045 x $102,400 = $4608

Monthly interest with 4.5% loan: $4608 ÷ 12 = $384

Property tax: 2.8 $\frac{1}{8}$ % x $102,400 = $2,880

Monthly property tax payment: $2880 ÷ 12 = $240

Total house payment 4.5% loan:
$384 (interest) + $240 (property tax) + $80 (insurance) = $704

Percentage: $704 ÷ $3200 = .22 or 22%

9.5% loan:

Martha's monthly salary: $38,400 ÷ 12 = $3200

Yearly interest with 9.5% loan: .095 x $102,400 = $9728

Monthly interest with 9.5% loan: $9728 ÷ 12 = $810.67

Total house payment 9.5% loan:
$810.67 (interest) + $240 (property tax) + $80 (insurance) = $1130.67

Percentage: $1130.65 ÷ $3200 = .35 or 35%

Chapter 16

Level 1

1) $1600

Annual interest: 8% of $240,000 .08 x $240,000 = $19,200

Monthly interest: $19,200 ÷ 12 = $1600

2) 2/3%

Monthly interest: 8% ÷ 12 = 2/3%

3) 9%

$25,200 ÷ $280,000 = .09 or 9%

Level 2

1) $187.50

Steve's annual interest: 5.75% x $180,000 .0575 x $180,000 = $10,350

Steve's monthly interest: $10,350 ÷ 12 = $862.50

Jasmine's annual interest: 7% of $180,000 .07 x $180,000 = $12,600

Jasmine's monthly interest: $12,600 ÷ 12 = $1050

$1050 - $862.50 = $187.50

2) Savings of $750 each month

Annual interest 6.75%: 6.75% of $240,000 .0675 x $240,000 = $16,200

Monthly interest: $16,200 ÷ 12 = $1350

Annual interest 3.5%: 3.5% of $240,000 .035 x $240,000 = $8400

Monthly interest: $8400 ÷ 12 = $700

Monthly payments 6.75% fixed-rate loan: $1350 + $100 principal = $1450

Monthly payment 3.5% interest-only loan: $700

$1450 - $700 = $750

3) $2150

Annual interest 10.75%: 10.75% x $240,000 = $25,800
Monthly interest: $25,800 ÷ 12 = $2150

Level 3

1) This is a negative amortization loan - You will owe $312,000 at the end of the first year.

Annual interest 7.5%: 7.5% x $300,000 .075 x $300,000 = $22,500

Annual amount paid on loan with monthly payments of $875: 12 x $875 = $10,500

Amount added to loan: $22,500 (interest) - $10,500 (payments) = $12,000

Balance after one year: $312,000

2) $523,024

Annual interest owed: 8.2% of $500,000 .082 x $500,000 = $41,000

Annual amount paid on loan: 12 x $1498 = $17,976

Amount added to loan: $41,000 (interest) - $17,976 (payments) = $23,024

$500,000 + $23,024 = $523,024

3) $4046.88

Annual interest at 9.25%: 9.25% of $525,000 .0925 x $525,000 = $48,562.50
Monthly payment at 9.25% interest: $48,562.50 ÷ 12 = $4046.88

Einstein

Answer: $447,000

First year

Annual interest at 7.25%: 7.25% of $400,000 .0725 x $400,000 = $29,000

Annual amount paid on loan first three years: 12 x $1200 = $14,400

Amount added to loan first year: $29,000 (interest) - $14,400 (payments) = $14,600

Amount owed at end of year one: $400,000 + $14,600

Second year

Annual interest at 7.25%: 7.25% of $414,600 .0725 x $414,600 = $30,058.50

Annual amount paid on loan first three years: 12 x $1200 = $14,400

Amount added to loan first year: $30,058.50 (interest) - $14,400 (payments) = $15,658.50

Amount owed at end of year two: $414,600 + $15,658.50 = $430,258.50

Third year

Annual interest at 7.25%: 7.25% of $430,258.50 .0725 x $430,258.50= $31,193.74

Annual amount paid on loan first three years: 12 x $1200 = $14,400

Amount added to loan first year: $31,193.74 (interest) - $14,400 (payments) = $16,793.74

Amount owed at end of year two: $430,258.50+ $16,793.74 = $447,052.24

Chapter 17

Level 1

1) 4th place

Teenage driver: 67 deaths per 100,000

This would place it between pilots and structural metal workers.

2) There are far more truck drivers than fishermen.

3) 7 times more likely to die on the job.

Roofer: 30.2 deaths per 100,000 roofers per year

Average job: 4.3 deaths per 100,000 workers per year

30.2 ÷ 4.3 = 7

Level 2

1) There are far more drivers in the 35-44 age category and they travel more miles per driver than teenagers travel.

There are 40,394,000 drivers in the 35-44 age category and only 9,396,000 in the under 20 category.

2) 4 times as likely

Texas teenage driver fatalities: 83 deaths per 100,000 drivers per year

On-duty deaths for police officers: 20.4 deaths per 100,000 police officers per year

83 ÷ 20.4 = 4

3) 53.6 deaths per 100,000 drivers

Current rate: 67 deaths per 100,000

20% of 67: .2 x 67 = 13.4

67 – 13.4 = 53.6

Level 3

1) 1/992

Pilot fatality rate:

$$\frac{100.8}{100{,}000} = \frac{1}{n}$$

Cross-multiply: 100.8n = 100,000

Divide both sides by 100.8

n = 992

2) 1/787

Fatality rate for The District of Columbia:

$$\frac{127}{100{,}000} = \frac{1}{n}$$

Cross-multiply: 127n = 100,000

Divide both sides by 127: n = 787

3) 85,890 timber cutters did not die

We first need to find the number of timber cutters.

Rate: 122.1 died for every 100,000 timber cutters

Actual number who died: 105

$$\frac{122.1 \text{ died}}{100{,}000 \text{ timber cutters}} = \frac{105 \text{ died}}{n \text{ timber cutters}}$$

Cross-multiply: 1221.n = 10,500,000

Divide both sides by 122.1: n = 85,995 timber cutters
105 died = 85,890 did not die

Einstein

Answer: Six fatalities

North Carolina has a death rate of 104 per 100,000 drivers who are 16-20 years of age.

Each year 1500 students drive at Jackie's high school.

$$\frac{104}{100{,}000} = \frac{n}{1500}$$

Cross-multiply: 100,000n = 156,000

Divide both sides by 100,000: n = 1.56

Statistics tell us we can predict there will be 1.5 fatalities each year.
Four years: 1.5 x 4 = 6 fatalities

Chapter 18

1) It would be approximately one mile in height

1/16 or .0625 inches x 1,000,000 = 62,500 inches

62,500 inches ÷ 12 = 5208 feet

One mile is 5280 feet

2) -40 degrees

Conversion formula: $F = 1.8C + 32$

If Centigrade and Fahrenheit are the same, then $C = 1.8C + 32$

Get C's on only one side by subtracting C from both sides: $0 = .8C + 32$

Subtract 32 from both sides: $.8C = -32$

Divide both sides by .8: $C = -40$

3) 1,000,000

Volume of the sun:
3.4×10^{17} *cubic miles*

Volume of the earth:
2.7×10^{11} *cubic miles*

Volume of the sun ÷ Volume of the earth

$$\frac{3.4 \times 10^{17} \text{ cubic miles}}{2.7 \times 10^{11} \text{ cubic miles}} = 1{,}000{,}000 \text{ (approximately)}$$

4) Weight of the Empire State Building on Earth

Weight of an African Elephant on Earth: 6500 Kilograms

Weight of the Empire State Building on Earth: 332,000,000 kilograms

Weight of a person on Earth: 100 kilograms

Weight of a bowling ball on Earth: 7 kilograms

Weight of a penny on Earth: 2.5 grams

Weight of a penny on a neutron star: 350,000,000 kilograms

5) 100,000 years

6) 7000 degrees/15,000,000 degrees

7) A googol times larger

$$\frac{10^{100}}{10^{10}} = 10^{100}$$

Googol has 100 zeros or 10^{100}

8) 1,000,000,000,000

10^6 is equal to 1,000,000

10^{-6} is equal to .000001

1,000,000 ÷ .000001= 1,000,000,000,000

Einstein

Answer: $\frac{1}{11{,}784{,}960{,}000}$ **Seconds**

Light travels 186,000 miles in one second

186,000 miles per second x 5280 feet per mile = 982,080,000 feet per second

982,080,000 feet per second x 12 inches in a foot = 11,784,960,000 inches per second

$$\frac{11{,}784{,}960{,}000 \text{ inches}}{\text{one second}} = \frac{\text{one inch}}{n \text{ seconds}}$$

Cross-multiply: $11{,}784{,}960{,}000n = 1$

Divide both sides by 11,784,960,000: $n = \dfrac{1}{11{,}784{,}960{,}000}$

Chapter 19

Level 1

1) Unfair

It is not mentioned that over 99% of the people who voted for Hoover also died. (Selective statistics)

2) A significant number of people die in a bed because that is where they go when they are sick. The bed did not cause the deaths.

(Cause/correlation confusion)

3) The contest involved only Brian and Matthew.

1st place: Matthew

2nd place: Brian

Brian did come in 2nd place and Matthew was the winner, but also next to last.

Level 2

1) To make a judgment about how dangerous each job is, Jay must know not only the number of deaths, but also the number of workers in each occupation.

In this case, the dangers of timber cutting are far higher than truck driving because of the number of workers employed in each occupation.

Timber cutter: 86,000 employed
Death rate: 122 deaths per 100,000

Truck driver: 3.1 million employed
Death rate: 28 deaths per 100,000

2) Yes

3) It is really not proper to say that the Chevy Astro is a safer vehicle based on these statistics alone. They are both large vehicles; but the most significant factor when comparing the two vehicles is usually who is driving each one.

In this case, Chevy Astros are often driven by couples with children. (Typically a very safe group of drivers.)

Level 3

1) No

Even though statistics clearly show the benefits of helmet requirements for motorcyclists, this statistic does not.

Before the helmet law was repealed, there were very few "unhelmeted deaths" because helmets were required by law and therefore, very few motorcyclists were not wearing helmets. If thousands of motorcyclists now are driving without helmets, there will be a jump in "unhelmeted deaths" whether helmets are an effective safety feature or not. (They clearly are effective.)

"On July 1, 2000, Florida's universal helmet law was weakened to exempt riders 21 and older who have at least $10,000 of medical insurance coverage. A study found that the motorcyclist death rate in Florida increased by about 25 percent after the state weakened its helmet law. The death rate rose from 31 fatalities per 1,000 crash involvements before the law change (1998-99) to 39 fatalities per 1,000 crash involvements after (2001-2002). An estimated 117 deaths could have been prevented during 2001-02 if the law had not been changed."

"An evaluation of the Florida law change by NHTSA found a similar effect; motorcyclist deaths per 10,000 motorcycle registrations increased 21 percent during the two years after the law was changed compared with the two years before."

2) The graph is not fair because it makes it appear that eating oats leads to a dramatic drop in cholesterol. The drop is only 4%!

3) Comparing a 4% drop in cholesterol to a 4% increase in taxes is not a fair comparison. (You could even call it ridiculous.) You might as well ask if having 4% of the population of New York City over to your house would have a significant impact on your life; or raising your body temperature by 4% is significant! Of course both of these would have a dramatic impact on your life, but it does not speak to whether a 4% drop in cholesterol is significant.

In the experiment with Crestor, the placebo dropped cholesterol 7%. If taking nothing (placebo) drops cholesterol 7%, how meaningful is a 4% drop?

Einstein

Answer: Both medicines are equally effective.

Medicine A: .4% to .3% is a 25% drop

Change divided by original determines percent of change.

Change: 1/10 of 1%
Original: 4/10 of 1%

Medicine B: 25% drop

Chapter 20

Level 1

1) $600

4% of $15,000 .04 x $15,000 = $600

2) $256,000

Remember, you can find the approximate doubling time in years by dividing the interest rate into 72.

72 ÷ 12 = 6 Money will double every 6 years.

Age 18: $1000

Age 24: $2000

Age 30: $4000

Age 36: $8000

Age 42: $16,000

Age 48: $32,000

Age 54: $64,000

Age 60: $128,000

Age 66: $256,000

3) $2,048,000

Remember, you can find the approximate doubling time in years by dividing the interest rate into 72.

72 ÷ 12 = 6 Money will double every 6 years.

Birth: $1000

Age 6: $2000

Age 12: $4000

Age 18: $8000

Age 24: $16,000

Age 30: $32,000

Age 36: $64,000

Age 42: $128,000

Age 48: $256,000

Age 54: $512,000

Age 60: $1,024,000

Answer Age 66: $2,048,000

Level 2

1) $146

Yearly interest: 5% of $5000 .05 x $5000 = $250

Monthly interest: $250 ÷ 12 = $20.83

7 months interest: $20.83 x 7 = $145.83

2) $4033

Yearly interest: 11% of $40,000 .11 x $40,000 = $4400

Monthly interest: $4400 ÷ 12 = $366.67

11 months interest: $366.67 x 11 = $4033.33

3) $119,101.60

Value after one year: 1.06 x $100,000 = $106,000

Value after two years: 1.06 x $106,000 = $112,360

Value after three years: 1.06 x $112,360 = $119,101.60

Level 3

1) $5076

Mitt: 10,000 x $(1.015)^{10}$ = $11,605
Rudy: 10,000 x $(1.0525)^{10}$ = $16,681
$16,681 - $11,605 = $5,076

2) $284,865

Hillary: 100,000 x $(1.06)^{20}$ = $320,714
Dennis: 100,000 x $(.95)^{20}$ = $35,849

(Dennis has 95% of his money each year. $100,000 x .95 x .95 x .95 etc.)

$320,714 - $35,849 = $284,865

3) $368,934,881,474,191,030

Birthday 2^0 pennies = 1 penny
1st Birthday 2^1 pennies = 2 pennies
2nd Birthday 2^2 pennies = 4 pennies
3rd Birthday 2^3 pennies = 8 pennies
4th Birthday 2^4 pennies = 16 pennies
65th birthday: 2^{65} =
36,893,488,147,419,103,000 pennies or $368,934,881,474,191,030

Einstein

Answer: Yes $101,000

Birth: $3000 Multiplied by 1.06 ⟶ 18 times

First birthday: $3000 Multiplied by 1.06 ⟶ 17 times

Second birthday: $3000 Multiplied by 1.06 ⟶ 16 times

Third birthday: $3000 Multiplied by 1.06 ⟶ 15 times

And so on until $3000 is added on the child's 18th birthday.

Add all amounts = $101,000 rounded

Chapter 21

Level 1

1) 216

Each die has six possible outcomes.

Three dice: 6 x 6 x 6 = 216

2) 1/216

There are 216 possible outcomes when three dice are rolled. Only one is 6-6-6.

3) 3/8 or 37.5%

A and C must each be 3/8

Level 2

1) Section A: 8 dolls
Section B: 4 dolls
Section C: 2 dolls
Section D: 1 doll
Section E: 1 doll

The probability the spinner will land on each area:

Section A: 1/2
Section B: 1/4
Section C: 1/8
Section D: 1/16
Section E: 1/16

The number of dolls placed in each section should correspond to the probability of the spinner landing on that section.

Section A: ½ of 16 = 8
Section B: ¼ of 16 = 4
Section C: ⅛ of 16 = 2

Section D: 1/16 of 16 = 1
Section E: 1/16 of 16 = 1

2) 1/65,536

The probability of landing on section A is ½ for each spin.

16 spins:

$$\frac{1}{2} \times \frac{1}{2} \times \frac{1}{2} \times \frac{1}{2} \times \frac{1}{2} \times \frac{1}{2} \times \frac{1}{2} \times \frac{1}{2} \times \frac{1}{2} \times \frac{1}{2} \times \frac{1}{2} \times \frac{1}{2} \times \frac{1}{2} \times \frac{1}{2} \times \frac{1}{2} \times \frac{1}{2} = \frac{1}{65{,}536}$$

3) Section A: 2 **Section B: 1** **Section C: 1**

Section A: ½ of 4 = 2
Section B: ¼ of 4 = 1
Section C: ⅛ of 4 = 1/2
Section D: 1⁄16 of 4 = 1/4
Section E: 1⁄16 of 4 = 1/4

Level 3

1) Three more 7's than 6's

There are 36 possible outcomes when two dice are rolled.

Six or 1/6 of those outcomes add up to "7":

1-6 6-1 3-4 4-3 2-5 5-2

Five or 5/36 of those outcomes add up to "6":

3-3 1-5 5-1 4-2 2-4

With 100 rolls, "7" is "expected" 1/6 of 100 = 16.67 times
With 100 rolls, "6" is "expected" 5/36 of 100 = 13.9 times

16.67 – 13.9 = 3 (approximately)

2) 14,976 outcomes

Rolling two dice: 36 outcomes

Pick a card: 52 outcomes

Flip a coin: 2 outcomes

Spinner: 4 outcomes

36 x 52 x 2 x 4 = 14,976 possible outcomes

3) 1/70 or 1.4%

1st pick: 4 of the 8 cards are aces---probability of picking an ace is ½.

If you are successful, then you pick again.

2nd pick: 3 of the remaining 7 cards are aces---probability of picking an ace is 3/7.

If you are successful, then you pick again.

3rd pick: 2 of the remaining 6 cards are aces----probability of picking an ace is 1/3.

If you are successful, then you pick again.

4th pick: One of the remaining 5 cards is an ace----probability of picking an ace is 1/5.

Probability of all four aces being picked:

$$\frac{1}{2} \times \frac{3}{7} \times \frac{2}{6} \times \frac{1}{5} = \frac{1}{70}$$

Einstein

Answer: Challenge A has a higher probability of winning.

Challenge A: 51.77% probability of winning
Challenge B: 49.14% probability of winning

At first glance, it may appear as though both challenges have an equal opportunity of succeeding:

Challenge A: 4 tries with 6 outcomes = 2/3

Challenge B: 24 tries with 36 outcomes = 2/3

This is not correct!!

Challenge A probability of losing each roll: 5/6

Challenge A probability of losing 4 rolls: $\frac{5}{6} \times \frac{5}{6} \times \frac{5}{6} \times \frac{5}{6} = \frac{625}{1296}$

Challenge A probability of winning: $1 - \frac{625}{1296} = 51.77\%$

Challenge B probability of losing each roll: 35/36

Challenge B probability of losing with 24 rolls: $\left(\frac{35}{36}\right)^{24} = 50.86\%$

Challenge B probability of winning: 1 −50.84%= 49.14%

Chapter 22

Level 1

1) 81 feet

When the angle is 45°, both legs of the triangle are the same.

2) 60 feet

Special ratio for 31° is: $\frac{.60}{1}$

$$\frac{\text{Tree Height (call } n\text{)}}{\text{Side next to angle (100 feet)}} = \frac{.60}{1}$$

Cross-multiply: $n = 60$ feet

3) 162 feet

Special ratio for 61° is: $\frac{1.80}{1}$

$$\frac{\text{Tree Height (call } n\text{)}}{\text{Side next to angle (90 feet)}} = \frac{1.80}{1}$$

Cross-multiply: $n = 162$ feet

Level 2

1) 37°

$$\frac{\text{Tree Height (60 feet)}}{\text{Side next to angle (80 feet)}} = \frac{60}{80} = .75$$

.75 is the special ratio for 37°.

2) 71°

$$\frac{\text{Tree Height (232 feet)}}{\text{Side next to angle (80 feet)}} = \frac{232}{80} = 2.9$$

2.9 is the special ratio for 71°.

3) 45° or 46°

$$\frac{\text{Tree Height (100 feet)}}{\text{Side next to angle (98 feet)}} = \frac{100}{98} = 1.02$$

1.02 is the ratio for an angle between 45° and 46°. It is a little closer to 46°.

Level 3

1) 31.75 feet

Ratio (tangent) for 50° is 1.19

$$\frac{\text{Opposite side of angle (house)}}{\text{Side next to angle (25 feet)}} = \frac{1.19}{1}$$

Cross-multiply: house = 1.19 x 25 = 29.75 feet

Add two feet because ladder is two feet below top of house. 31.75 feet

2) No, it is at 7°

8 inches is 2/3 of a foot or .67

$$\frac{5}{41.67} = .12$$

.12 is the tangent of 7°

3) 2100 feet

Tangent of 30° is .58
Distance to center of tunnel: 5280 ÷ 2 = 2640 feet

2640 feet + 1000 feet = 3640 feet

$$\frac{\text{Height of Mountain (n)}}{\text{Side next to angle (3640 feet)}} = \frac{.58}{1}$$

Cross-multiply: n = 2100 feet

Einstein

Answer: River is 256.5 feet wide

Special angle for 9° or the tangent of 9° is .16

$$\frac{\text{Height of Tree (42 feet)}}{\text{Side next to angle (n)}} = \frac{.16}{1}$$

Cross-multiply: .16n = 42 feet

Divide both sides by .16: n = 262.5 - 6 feet = 256.5

Chapter 23

Level 1

1) Yes, this is an elegant ratio of 3/2, or 1.5
The musical term for this ratio is a "perfect fifth".

2) Yes, this is an elegant ratio of 4/3, or 1.33. The musical term for this ratio is a "perfect fourth".

3) No, this is one of the worst combinations of notes. The ratio is about 1.42, or 71/50 - not elegant at all. The musical term for this ratio is called a "tritone".

Level 2

1) C and E, C# and F, D and F#, E and G#, F and A, F# and A#, G and B, G# and C.

The musical term for this ratio is called a "Major third," and most people believe it sounds good.

2) Low C and high B, or low C# and high C.

The musical term for this ratio is called a "major 7th". This is a ratio of almost 2/1, which is called an "octave" in musical terms.

3) It does sound good.

The ratio between low C and G is 3/2, or a "perfect fifth". The ratio between G and high C is 4/3, or a "perfect fourth". The ratio between low C and high C is, as we know, 2/1, or a "perfect octave". All possible ratios are clean and elegant, so we can predict that the notes will sound good together.

Level 3

1) 1048

Each higher note of the same name, or octave, is double the frequency of the lower one. Remember, an octave's ratio is 2/1. The even higher C would have a frequency of 2096.

2)

Note	Frequency in Hertz
C	262
C#	278
D	294
D#	312
E	330
F	350
F#	371
G	393
G#	416
A	441
A#	467

B	495	
C	524	answers
C#	____	**(556)**
D	____	**(588)**
D#	____	**(624)**
E	____	**(660)**
F	____	**(700)**
F#	____	**(742)**
G	____	**(786)**
G#	____	**(832)**
A	____	**(882)**
A#	____	**(934)**
B	____	**(990)**
C	1048	

3) C and F# - about 71/50. C and G# - about 79/50. C and B - about 47/25. F# and G# - about 28/25. G# and B - about 6/5.

With all of these ugly and complicated ratios, these notes sound awful together.

Einstein

Answer: About 4192 Hz, and about 27.6 Hertz

The lowest A on the piano is 4 octaves below our A at 441 Hz. So we take 441, and divide by 2 four times to get about 27.6 Hertz.

The highest C on the piano is 4 octaves above middle C, which is 262 Hz. So we double it 4 times to get 4192 Hz.

Chapter 24

Level 1

1) 99 feet

Each 33 feet of depth adds an atmosphere. 33 feet = 2 atmospheres
66 feet = 3 atmospheres
99 feet = 4 atmospheres

2) 165 feet

33 feet down is 2 atmospheres, 66 is 3, and so on.

3) 33 feet

The volume of air at the surface decreases by half at a depth where there are two atmospheres of pressure. There are two atmospheres of pressure at 33 feet.

Level 2

1) No

132 feet down is 5 atmospheres, so a balloon filled with one liter of air at that depth would swell to 5 liters at the surface - too much for this balloon.

2) If you hold in your air as you rush for the surface, the amount of air in your filled lungs will increase in volume by a factor of about 2.5. Your lungs will probably rupture.

3) Scuba divers are taught that if they need to drop their gear and swim to the surface, they need to take a deep breath and exhale slowly as they ascend. This way, they can let the air out slowly as they move toward the surface. This will keep their lungs from rupturing.

Level 3

1) 2/5 of the glass

Remember that the amount of space the air takes up as a fraction of the whole is the reciprocal of how many atmospheres of pressure are pushing on it. There are 2.5 atmospheres in this problem. The reciprocal of 2.5 (5/2) is 2/5.

2) There is the equivalent of about 200 atmospheres inside a filled scuba tank.
(3000 psi divided by 15 psi (one atmosphere) equals 200.)

3) You would have to go down 6,567 feet - more than a mile underwater. (You don't multiply 200 by 33, you multiply 199 by 33. 33 feet down is two atmospheres, not one. Therefore, you have to subtract one atmosphere before multiplying.)

Einstein

Answer: Steve is using more air at 36 surface liters per minute while Adam is using 30 surface liters per minute.

Steve, at 2 atmospheres, is using the equivalent of 3 surface liters per breath. (1.5 liters x 2 atmospheres). Since he breathes every 5 seconds, he is breathing 12 times per minute. At 3 surface liters per breath, he is using 36 surface liters of air per minute. (3 surface liters per breath x 12 breaths per minute)

Adam, at 2.5 atmospheres, is using the equivalent of 2 surface liters per breath (.8 liters x 2.5 atmospheres). Since he breathes every 4 seconds, he is breathing 15 times per minute. At 2 surface liters per breath, he is using 30 surface liters of air per minute. (2 surface liters per breath x 15 breaths per minute)

Chapter 25

Level 1

1) 27.2 cents

4 cents x 6.8 = 27.2 cents

2) $2.38

35 cents x 6.8 = $2.38

3) $8.50

$1.25 x 6.8 = $8.50

Level 2

1) Bring "2007 money" with you

$1.20 ÷ 6.8 = $.18

2) 1962

1962 cost of gas was 31 cents.
1972 cost of gas (36 cents) is equal to 43 cents in 1962 money.
For the price of gas to be equal in both years, the cost in 1972 would have been 43 cents.

3) 700%

Percent of increase or decrease is change divided by original.
Increase of $42,000 divided by $6000 = 7 or 700%

Level 3

1) 2007

The 1962 median family income was $6000. This income, in 2007 dollars, is equal to $6000 x 6.8 = $40,800.

The median family income in 2007 was $48,000

2) $10.00

Median family income increased from $6000 to $48,000. This is an increase of $48,000 ÷ $6000 = 8 times larger

$1.25 x 8 = $10

3) $147.06

To change 1962 dollars into 2007 dollars we multiply by 6.8. To change 2007 dollars into 1962 dollars we need to divide by 6.8. $1000 divided by 6.8 = $147.06

Einstein

Answer: 2 cents

It took 45 years for 1962 money to become 6.8 times as valuable as 2007 money. If money loses value at the same rate, in 45 more years, 2007 money will be 6.8 times more valuable than 2052 money. A 2052 dollar would be equal to 1.00 ÷ 6.8 = 14.7 cents in 2007 money.

14.7 cents in 2007 would be worth 14.7 ÷ 6.8 = 2 cents in 1962 money.